CRITICAL RE

‖‖‖‖‖‖‖‖‖‖‖‖‖‖‖‖
T0028497

Terry Eagleton is Distinguished Visiting Professor of English Literature at Lancaster University, and the author of more than fifty books in the fields of literary theory, postmodernism, politics, ideology and religion.

Further praise for *Critical Revolutionaries*:

'A presentation of key critics who taught us that reading is both a technical skill and a vital human concern. Essential for those who want to understand why we still need literature in the days of Twitter and Instagram.'

Professor Maria Elisa Cevasco, University of São Paulo

'Terry Eagleton's probes into English literature are conducted with tremendous fluency, humour, and the knowledgeable experience of a skilled diagnostician . . . Richly informed writing.'

Sean Sheehan, *PopMatters*

'Eagleton offers a stimulating introduction to those approaching the criticism of T.S. Eliot, I.A. Richards, William Empson, F.R. Leavis and Raymond Williams for the first time, while making a forceful contribution to the critical tradition being constructed and analysed.'

Professor Daniel G. Williams, Swansea University

CRITICAL REVOLUTIONARIES

FIVE CRITICS WHO CHANGED THE WAY WE READ

TERRY EAGLETON

YALE UNIVERSITY PRESS
NEW HAVEN AND LONDON

For information about this and other Yale University Press publications, please contact:
U.S. Office: sales.press@yale.edu   yalebooks.com
Europe Office: sales@yaleup.co.uk   yalebooks.co.uk

Set in Adobe Garamond Pro by IDSUK (DataConnection) Ltd
Printed in Great Britain by Clays Ltd, Elcograf S.p.A

Library of Congress Control Number: 2023931878

ISBN 978-0-300-26448-7 (hbk)
ISBN 978-0-300-27044-0 (pbk)

A catalogue record for this book is available from the British Library.

10 9 8 7 6 5 4 3 2 1

For Tony Pinkney

CONTENTS

INTRODUCTION

The conviction underlying this book is that a vital tradition of literary criticism is in danger of being neglected. This is so to some extent even in academia, as well as in the wider literary world. If not many students of literature today are likely to be familiar with the work of, say, I.A. Richards or Raymond Williams, the same may well be true of some of their teachers. Yet the five critics discussed in this book rank among the most original and influential of modern times, which is why I have chosen them.

They also represent a specific intellectual formation, one of the most remarkable in twentieth-century Britain. All but one of them taught at the University of Cambridge. The exception is T.S. Eliot, yet Eliot had close connections with Cambridge, not least through his friend I.A. Richards, and as an informal consultant was a powerful influence on the shaping of English studies there. These men were part of what has been hailed as a critical revolution, one that transformed the academic study of literature and lent it a fresh centrality in

1

Britain and beyond. Ironically, however, what one might call Cambridge English was never the orthodox creed of the Cambridge English Faculty. On the contrary, it was always a marginal, minority affair, though its combativeness and evangelical sense of mission lent it at times a presence disproportionate to its size. Despite this, the careers of Richards, Empson, Leavis and Williams were made possible in part by a radical reform of the Cambridge English course as far back as 1917, sidelining Anglo-Saxon and philology for a course of study that was overwhelmingly modern, critical and literary (rather than linguistic) in orientation.

The new Cambridge course was entitled 'English Literature, Life and Thought' – the last two terms a couple of absurdly large abstractions, yet indicative of the fact that literature was to be studied in its social and intellectual context. There was also a cosmopolitan dimension to the course: the Tragedy paper in the final examinations encompassed such dramatists as Sophocles and Racine as well as Shakespeare, while the English Moralists paper included such honorary Englishmen as Plato, St Paul and Augustine, along with a host of other non-indigenous thinkers.

That the critical revolution should have its source in Cambridge, a university with a strong scientific pedigree and a record of openness to innovation, was not entirely accidental. There were other factors at work as well. Like British society in general, the culture of the university had been deeply shaken by the First World War, which seemed to herald a break with the past and the onset of a new era. There were ex-servicemen among the student body, while middle-class students on state or university scholarships were making their presence felt in an institution which had traditionally been dominated by the private schools and the upper classes. Only one of the critics portrayed in this book, William Empson, enjoyed such a privileged upbringing, as the son of a Yorkshire squire and a former pupil of Winchester College. The genteel amateurism of an older generation of upper-class literary scholars was under challenge from a new, rigorously analytical approach to literary works, of which I.A. Richards's method of 'practical criticism' was exemplary. This involved taking anonymous passages of prose or poetry, submitting them to tenaciously detailed scrutiny and passing judgement on their quality. Value was no longer simply a matter of taste; instead, it had to be vigorously argued for. There was a paper devoted to this practice in the final English exams, which included what was known as 'dating', or assigning an approximate date to a set of anonymous literary passages. Students today might be surprised to learn that dating several times in quick succession was once compulsory for Cambridge English students.

Traditional literary scholarship had been largely insulated from society at large, whereas younger critics like Richards, F.R. Leavis and his partner Q.D. Leavis, who stemmed from less sheltered backgrounds, were more alive to the general culture, as well as more troubled by the place of literary studies within it. Leavis, the son of a shopkeeper, had lived through the trauma of the First World War. In a period of social and political turbulence in the wake of that conflict, English could either take the pressure of social change or consign itself to irrelevance. Opening it up also involved setting it in the context of other academic disciplines, which some of these pioneers knew at first hand. Richards came over to English from Mental and Moral Sciences, F.R. Leavis from History and William Empson from Mathematics. Q.D. Leavis took a keen interest in psychology and anthropology. Eliot wrote his doctoral thesis on philosophy, not literature. Several decades later, Raymond Williams was to move from literary criticism to cultural studies, a subject which he helped to invent.

The early years of the reformed English Faculty coincided with the heyday of literary modernism, and something of the boldness and bravura of that experiment was part of its ethos. The Cambridge of Richards and Leavis, for example, was also that of Malcolm Lowry, whose novel *Under the Volcano* is a late masterpiece of English modernism. The fact that world-class literature was being produced in English at the time seemed to conspire with the Faculty's focus on the present day, while the august figure of T.S. Eliot acted as a link between modernism and criticism. The two currents had a number of other features in common: both were tough-minded, impersonal, quick to detect sham emotion, conceptually ambitious and sensitively attuned to language. They also shared a certain elitism, as we shall see later in the case of criticism. Modernism was the product of a historical crisis, and so was the new critical work being undertaken at Cambridge. At its centre was the belief that the close reading of literary texts was a profoundly moral activity which cut to the heart of modern civilisation. To define and evaluate qualities of language was to define and evaluate the quality of a whole way of life. As I.A. Richards put it, 'A decline in our sensitiveness and discrimination with words must be followed soon by a decline in the quality of our living also'.[1] One could take this remark as the motto of Cambridge English. To focus attentively on the words on the page may sound like an attempt to exclude larger concerns, but larger concerns are already implicit in it.

There is a problem with this argument. To what extent is verbal capability bound up with moral sensitivity? If the two are really as interwoven as Richards seems to suggest, does this imply that men and women who lack linguistic dexterity are insensitive and imperceptive in their everyday dealings? Are only the eloquent able to feel courage and compassion? Obviously not. It is not true that those who can produce coruscating commentaries on Rudyard Kipling or Angela Carter are invariably more subtle and discerning in daily life than the mass of humanity. In fact, the opposite has sometimes been claimed – that those who are deeply versed in the humanities may be displacing forms of feeling and attention which might more usefully be deployed in everyday affairs. 'Education sometimes cohabits with such barbarity, such cynicism, that you are filled with disgust', remarks the narrator of Fyodor Dostoevsky's *The House of the Dead*. Conversely, those whose vocabulary is less than Shakespearian in scope may be far more morally admirable than the silver-tongued.

To imagine a language, the Cambridge philosopher Ludwig Wittgenstein writes, is to imagine a form of life. English studies dealt with qualities of language, and thus had a direct bearing on matters such as broadcasting, advertising, political propaganda, bureaucratic jargon and the nature of public discourse. As such, it offered an alternative to what it saw as opposing errors. One could tread the formalist path and treat literature as though it were an autonomous object, attending to its verbal strategies and devices; or one could take a broader view of the work, seeing it as an exploration of the human condition or a commentary on civilisation. By taking the moral temperature of that civilisation in the language of the literary work, it was possible to move beyond both of these limited approaches. The critic needed to be vigilant to what was called 'the words on the page', renouncing the aesthetic waffle of an earlier age for a rigorously detailed analysis of tone, pace, pitch, mood, rhythm, grammar, syntax, texture and the like. What for other subjects was a taken-for-granted medium of inquiry was for criticism an object of inquiry in itself. Yet in the act of examining the words, the critic was also exploring the moral and historical context in which those words were rooted. Only by a delicate attentiveness to the words on the page could one grasp them as symptoms of the sickness or vitality of the civilisation from which they sprang.

By and large, Cambridge English represented a reaction to what seemed the impoverishment of both life and language in a commercial, utilitarian civilisation increasingly under the sway of film, radio, the popular press, advertising and popular fiction. Modernism, likewise, felt itself confronted by a drastic depletion of linguistic resources. Literary criticism was a way of diagnosing these social ills, but it could also pose a solution of sorts. Its task was to investigate the workings of a different form of discourse altogether, one which freed language from the purely instrumental ends to which a crass technological society had harnessed it. This discourse was known as literature, and it pointed to a different form of living – one in which language, persons, values and relationships could be treated as ends in themselves.

It followed that the literary critic bore responsibilities as grave as those of the priest, prophet or politician. He or she was no mere academic, but a monitor of the spiritual health of the modern age. Criticism had a vital moral and social function to perform, and it was precisely because of this that its textual analyses needed to be as scrupulous as they were. In this sense, the two distinctive keynotes of Cambridge English – practical criticism and a concern for the social and intellectual context of literature – were aspects of a single project. Far from being an evasion of social responsibility, unpacking a metaphor or registering a shift of tone were actually exercises of it. Whether this was an absurd piece of self-aggrandisement, or a cogent justification of literary studies to those in thrall to science and technology, was a matter of heated dispute. It was not, one might note, a project particularly congenial to William Empson, who had no inclination to see the words on the page as symptoms of a way of life in urgent need of repair. Yet as the closest reader of all, he was a true member of the tribe.

Richards in particular saw the need to professionalise a subject which seemed to lack all intellectual discipline. As we shall see, he even tried to place English studies on a scientific basis. Impressionistic prattle was to be banished from the seminar room. Yet the strength of the new criticism lay in coupling technical expertise with a deep vein of moral humanism, the latter at its most evident in the work of Leavis. Cambridge English could thus draw on its tough new professionalism to counter the genteel amateurism of the old guard, while at the same time decrying fusty literary scholarship from the standpoint of a humane concern with the general culture. Tightly focused when faced with a literary work, yet prepared to pronounce on the moral quality of a whole culture, it promised to reap the best of both worlds.

Most literary critics, like most academics, hail from the middle class; but of the five figures discussed in this book, only one, I.A. Richards, fits this description. Even he began life as an outsider to English metropolitan culture, having grown up in the industrial north of England as the son of a man whose family hailed from the Gower peninsula in Wales. Eliot, who came from Missouri, was in American terms more upper-class than middle-class. William Empson hailed from the English gentry. F.R. Leavis was the lower-middle-class son of a provincial shopkeeper, while Raymond Williams grew up in Wales as the child of a railway worker. These were not socially typical intellectuals, a fact which is surely relevant to their eagerness to innovate, and (in the case of all but Eliot) their disdain for orthodoxy. Three of them (Eliot, Richards and Empson) also took a keen interest in Eastern thought, which was among other things a sign of their critical stance towards Western civilisation.

It is also relevant to the link between Cambridge English and the literature of the period that all of these figures except one were creative writers. Eliot and Empson were major poets, Richards was a mediocre one, while Raymond Williams published several novels and wrote drama for television. Writing fiction was at least as important to him as literary criticism, and in the latter part of his career rather more so. In fact, he once described himself as 'a writer who also happened to be a professor'.[2] Only Leavis stuck to criticism, though even he considered writing a novel.[3] One might add that all of these men except for the rather cerebral Empson had an intensely physical sense of writing – of its involvement with breathing, the visceral regions, the nervous system and so on – which among other things may be a mark of critics who are writers themselves.

They were also public intellectuals rather than cloistered academics, though this applies rather less to Empson. At the same time, though Empson was somewhat less of a public figure than the others, he could hardly be described as cloistered. All of them had an ambiguous relationship to academia. Eliot, though much lauded in that sphere, was never part of it himself. Instead, he moved from being a hard-pressed freelance journalist, while also working as a teacher and a banker, into what was then the rather more relaxed milieu of publishing. Richards was a reluctant don who soon launched out into more ambitious terrain; Empson enjoyed scandalising the traditional scholarly mind with his racy prose and iconoclastic judgements; Leavis, as we shall see, specifically targeted the academic as the enemy; and Raymond Williams, who spent the first part of his teaching career in adult education, felt a deep alienation from Cambridge when he returned as a lecturer to the university where he had been a student. Of the five, only Leavis spent the whole of his career teaching in an English university.

The relation between speech and writing in the style of each of these authors is worth a passing comment. Empson writes nonchalantly, in conversational, even garrulous style, while Eliot occasionally writes as though he is preaching in a particularly resonant cathedral. Richards's brisk, rather bloodless prose is quite distinct from the speaking voice; but the rhythms of that voice, with its pattern of emphasis and irregular stops and starts, sound through the tortuous syntax of F.R. Leavis, a writer who is constantly interrupting himself by inserting queries, sub-clauses, parentheses, recursions, afterthoughts and qualifications into his sentences. Like Empson, Leavis seems deliberately to avoid the formality of academic prose. Raymond Williams's abstract, ponderous style of writing might appear far removed from the living voice, but as those who knew him can testify, he spoke in much the same way as he wrote. Leavis writes as though he were speaking, while Williams spoke as though he were writing.

As the reader is about to discover, this book is not an act of homage to a pantheon of heroes. In fact, it is sometimes so critical of these figures that the reader might well wonder whether they are worthy of the stature assigned to them. The only way to find out is to read them. If I may end this Introduction on a personal note: I myself never met Eliot, but I knew a few people who did, some of whom recounted how he would hold forth at inconvenient length not about Dante or Baudelaire but about the various routes taken by London buses, of which he seemed to have a voluminous knowledge. I gazed with awe as a student on the slender figure of Richards at a Cambridge garden party, and sat in an English Faculty meeting in which Leavis denounced the idea of introducing a paper on the novel into the syllabus on the grounds that it took a term to read *Anna Karenina*. Before that, I had attended some of his lectures, though he was just on the point of retirement and his voice was weak, fading at times to an unintelligible drone in which his nasal Cambridge accent was still dimly audible. From time to time, however, the odd derogatory term would surface from his mumblings, like a jabbing finger: 'BBC', '*New Statesman*', 'C.P. Snow', 'British Council' and the like. At these carefully calculated cues, the well-drilled Leavisite devotees in the front rows of the lecture theatre would send up a chorus of scoffing and snorting with Pavlovian predictability, while the rest of us would simply stare at our shoes and wait for it to stop. Empson had long since taken his leave of Cambridge, but some years later I was to hear him lecture in his extraordinarily contorted upper-class accent without once falling off the stage, a mishap to which he was particularly prone. Raymond Williams was my teacher, friend and political comrade. In this book, then, I look back across 60 years to a critical milieu which helped to form me, and to the later history of which I hope to have made some small contribution.

TE

1

T.S. ELIOT

For much of the twentieth century, the most revered, influential figure in English literary criticism was unquestionably T.S. Eliot. He was poet, critic, dramatist, essayist, editor, reviewer, publisher and public intellectual; and although he had rivals in some of these fields and superiors in others, none of them could match his authority as a whole. In an age when it was customary to add a title (Dr, Mrs, Mr and so on) to the names of people still living, Eliot was often referred to not as 'Mr T.S. Eliot' but simply as 'Mr Eliot', as though nobody could be dim-witted enough to be in doubt about which particular Eliot was intended. (At that time, the courtesy of a title could occasionally be extended to the dead: one of my teachers at Cambridge used to refer to the author of *Pride and Prejudice* as 'Miss Austen', though he did not insist on 'Mr Chaucer'.) Eliot's consecration as high priest of English letters was all the more remarkable given the outrage which had greeted his early work as a poet. In the words of one of his first champions, F.R. Leavis, he had been regarded as a 'literary Bolshevik', audaciously avant-garde and bafflingly opaque; yet by the early 1930s he was being hailed as the pre-eminent literary mind of his generation. His publicly proclaimed conversion to royalism, conservatism and Anglo-Catholicism in 1927 no doubt played some part in this shift of status. The more attracted he was to incense, the more his own reputation was wreathed in its fumes.

Like many of the leading writers and intellectuals of twentieth-century England, Thomas Stearns Eliot, as we have seen, was not in fact English. He was born in 1888 in St Louis, Missouri, the son of a family so patrician that they refused to use the term 'OK', and could trace their residence in America back over two hundred years. The Eliots were prominent among the intellectual aristocracy of the city, though Eliot's own father was a businessman. His grandfather had founded the local university, and championed an ideal of public service by which his grandson was to be deeply influenced. We shall see that the theme of self-surrender – of sacrificing one's own paltry ego to some higher cause – runs steadily throughout his work. The current of Christianity associated with the St Louis elite was Unitarianism, a moderate, high-brow form of religious faith at odds with the crude evangelical passions of the Puritan middle classes.

Yet the civilised, socially responsible class to which the Eliots belonged was being gradually displaced in the city by industrial and commercial forces, as a philistine middle class rose to power. The cultural leadership of the Eliots and their colleagues was in steep decline, as St Louis became flagrantly boss-ridden and corrupt. The Eliot who will later speak sourly of the 'dictatorship of finance' found himself an internal émigré in the place where he grew up, and would shortly become an exile in reality. (The poet whom he came to revere more than any other, Dante, grew up in the wealthy burgher class of Florence but rebelled against the city's increasingly powerful plutocracy and was finally driven into exile.) During Eliot's childhood, then, the ground was being laid for the clash between alternative forms of value which would mark his later thought: a trust in tradition versus a brash faith in progress, a belief in the corporate rather than the individualist, culture versus utility, order against anarchy, the surrender of the self against the unconstrained expression of it. Part of what he reacted against in his native country was too overpowering a sense of identity: the Puritan, self-fashioning, autonomous ego which underpinned the nation's industrial capitalism. In fact, it is not too much to claim that such individualism, in which the self acknowledges no fidelity to a larger social or spiritual order, is Eliot's adversary from start to finish. Human beings cannot thrive, he maintains, without giving allegiance to something outside themselves. Those who feel no such loyalty to particular institutions might end up, like some Romantic poets, identifying instead with the cosmos; but 'a man does not join himself with the Universe so long as he has anything else to join himself with' (SE, p. 131).[1]

After studying at Harvard, Eliot abandoned his homeland for Paris and Oxford, and was persuaded to stay on in England by his friend, mentor and compatriot Ezra Pound. Like a number of other expatriate writers (Wilde, Conrad, Henry James, V.S. Naipaul, Tom Stoppard), he compensated for his status as an outsider by seeking to outdo the English Establishment at its own game. He worked in a London bank and later for the distinguished publishing house of

Faber & Faber, and had connections with the Bloomsbury Group. In 1927, he sealed his loyalty to his adopted country by converting to the Church of England and professed himself a classicist in literature, a royalist in politics and an Anglo-Catholic in religion. The divine right of kings was in his eyes a 'noble faith'. Truly to flourish, he maintained, meant being rooted in a single spot. 'To be human', he remarked, 'is to belong to a particular region of the earth' (OPP, p. 251). That the local and regional take priority over the national and international is a familiar article of conservative faith. 'On the whole', this refugee from St Louis to London shamelessly announced, 'it would appear to be for the best that the great majority of human beings should go on living in the place in which they were born' (NDC, p. 52).

Yet if he was something of a parody of a pukka Englishman, like Wilde and James, he nonetheless continued to feel like a foreigner in the English capital. Indeed, the former was partly a consequence of the latter. He remained to some extent a spirit 'unappeased and peregrine' (i.e. wandering), as he puts it in 'Little Gidding'; and one reason for the hostility to Jews in his early writings, over and above the casual, pervasive anti-Semitism of the time, may be because he saw in the stereotypical Jewish outcast and wanderer a monstrous image of himself. He once used the pseudonym 'Metoikos', which is Greek for 'resident alien'. It is related to the word *métèques*, used of Jews by the French right-wing thinker Charles Maurras, whose work influenced Eliot considerably.

There was, however, some benefit to be reaped from living on the margins of Europe on a small island which was formally

European but, like the United States, ethnically Anglo-Saxon. His compatriot Henry James, Eliot wrote, no doubt with himself in mind as well, was a European in the way that only a non-European could be. He meant, presumably, that the outsider is more likely to be conscious of the spirit and culture of a place as a whole than those brought up within it, who tend to take it for granted and to lack an overall view of it. So there were advantages to not being a native European, as well as not having grown up in provincial Britain. Eliot may have been a pin-striped London publisher: he was jocularly known as 'The Pope of Russell Square', which was where his publishing house, Faber & Faber, was located; but like many leading modernist artists he was nothing if not cosmopolitan, roaming freely in *The Waste Land* across a whole span of civilisations, appropriating chunks of them in order to cobble together a synthesis which suited his own spiritual needs. He was an unstable compound of bourgeois stuffiness and literary saboteur, moving between genteel Mayfair and bohemian Soho.

Eliot put to good use the instability of selfhood which his spiritual and then literal exile had brought him. It meant that he could 'decentre' himself all the more readily into literary tradition, the Anglican Church, a corporate culture, the resources of a collective mythology and what he liked to call the European mind. Like his friend James Joyce, he discovered that those who are strangers at home are able to belong more or less anywhere. As with many a modernist, his art was nourished by the fact that he was at once inside and outside the civilisation in which he settled. Perhaps a certain sexual ambiguity in his early years (he circulated some of his gay pornographic verse among a coterie of friends) reinforced this duality. In some ways, the alien can see more than the native: Eliot comments of Rudyard Kipling, who spent part of his early life in India, that his experience of another country gave him an understanding of England that the English themselves would do well to heed. To *choose* a cultural allegiance, as Eliot did, signifies a deeper commitment than that of the average insider; yet at the same time the insiders have the edge over you, since – having the culture and tradition in their blood – they do not need to make a conscious issue out of it.

This matters particularly in England, where blood is traditionally considered to be thicker than intellect and custom more cherished than consciousness. The insider's problem is parochialism, while the outsider risks too rootless a lifestyle. Eliot resolves this dilemma by insisting that only by inhabiting a particular region of European culture can you gain access to the whole. Besides, émigré writers are able to mine the resources of a specific culture and heritage; but because they are also part-outsiders, they are released from the constraints of that form of life and are freer to wander, subvert and experiment. Joyce maintained that the source of his revolutionary art lay in the fact that he was not English, and something similar can be said of his champion T.S. Eliot.

For most moderately enlightened readers today, Eliot's social views range from the objectionable to the obnoxious. In *The Idea of a Christian Society* (1939) and *Notes Towards the Definition of Culture* (1948), he portrays his ideal social order, which seems more rural than urban. There will be a culture of values and beliefs shared in common; but though society will thus constitute an organic unity, it will also be strictly stratified. There will be a governing elite, consisting of the traditional English rural class along with an intellectual coterie of men not entirely unlike Eliot himself. Elizabethan drama, he believes, is the product of such a common culture, distinguished as it is by 'a fundamental homogeneity of race, of sense of humour and sense of right and wrong' which includes dramatists and audiences alike (UPUC, p. 52). Like all authentic theatre, it is 'an organ for the expression of the consciousness of a people' (OPP, p. 307) – a people Eliot assumes to form a unity.

The task of the elite is to protect and disseminate the (largely Christian) values of the society as a whole. It is a vital undertaking, since if Christianity were to founder the whole of Western civilisation would collapse along with it. Yet since the mass of men and women are in Eliot's view incapable of what might properly be called thinking, their participation in the culture will be less conscious than that of their superiors. Instead, it will take the form of custom and tradition, myth and sentiment, ritual observances and spontaneous habits of feeling. All individuals will share in the same form of life, but they will share in it in different ways and at different levels of consciousness. The organic and the hierarchical can thus be reconciled. If the former is an alternative to liberal individualism, the latter is a bulwark against Bolshevism. Like the poet W.B. Yeats, with whom he was acquainted, Eliot is shrewd enough to perceive that elites must be rooted in the common life if they are to flourish. Otherwise their privileged status may prove their downfall. Their mission is to elaborate at a conscious level the values which for most people are a matter of habitual behaviour. The knowledge of the minority must be founded on the wisdom of the folk.

In this way, the two main senses of the term 'culture' – artistic and intellectual activity on the one hand, and the way of life of a whole people on the other – may be conveniently coupled. We shall see later that Eliot regards a poem in much the same way. It has a layer of conscious meaning, rather as a common culture has a minority whose task is to define and diffuse its values; but beneath this, and constantly animated by it, lies what one might call the poetic unconscious, that vast reservoir of forces and images which eludes all conscious articulation. The same may be said of Eliot's ideal theatre audience, which is likely to contain a small minority of patrons who understand what is spiritually afoot in his plays, a middle stratum of reasonably intelligent types who can glimpse something of their deeper meaning, and a mass of philistine ground-lings (bankers, politicians, accountants and so on) who haven't a clue what is going on but who, like the Women of Canterbury in Eliot's *Murder in the Cathedral*, may nevertheless respond to the meaning of the drama at some subliminal level. (The title *Murder in the Cathedral*, incidentally, may well be one of its author's impish jokes, as theatregoers flock to what promises to be an Agatha Christie-type whodunnit only to be confronted with an intellectu-ally exacting drama notably short on action. A good many of Eliot's theatre audiences probably failed to realise that what they were hearing was couched in verse, an oversight which one imagines would not have troubled him in the least.)

The ideal, then, is a common but stratified culture; yet the social reality is very different. Like many of his fellow modernists, Eliot had little but contempt for most aspects of actual civilisation, with its godless materialism, worship of the machine, cult of utility, spiritual vacancy and bogus humanitarianism. In this, he is at one with F.R. Leavis, as we shall see later; but whereas Leavis's religion is in effect the philosophy of D.H. Lawrence, Eliot's is staunchly Anglo-Catholic. The love of man and woman, he remarks witheringly, is either made reasonable by a higher (i.e. divine) love, or else it is simply the coupling of animals. 'If you remove from the word "human" all that the belief in the supernatural has given to man', he warns, 'you can view him finally as no more than an extremely clever, adaptable and mischievous little animal' (SE, p. 485). He praises Machiavelli, of all rebarbative thinkers, for his low estimate of humanity, as well as for his promotion of order over liberty (FLA, pp. 46, 50). It is Eliot's conviction that the number of individuals in any generation capable of intellectual effort is very small. Indeed, he seems to derive a well-nigh erotic frisson from the phrase 'only a very few'. He would no doubt have been deeply rattled had the minuscule readership of his journal the *Criterion* shot up by 10 thousand overnight.

Most men and women, like the Hollow Men of Eliot's poem of that title, are too spiritually shallow even to be damned, which means that 'the possibility of damnation is so immense a relief in a world of electoral reform, plebiscites, sex reform and dress reform' (SE, p. 429). In a faithless age, the idea of hell is to his mind a considerable source of comfort. Writing in the age of Auschwitz, he declares in the spirit of

Charles Baudelaire that it is better to do evil than to do nothing. Evil people, as opposed to the merely immoral, are at least acquainted with higher spiritual realities, in however negative a fashion. Humanism overlooks what for Eliot is perhaps the most fundamental of all Christian dogmas: original sin. Humans are wretched creatures, and humility is consequently the greatest of Christian virtues. (For the Christian orthodoxy which Eliot is supposed to uphold, the greatest virtue is in fact charity, of which the other virtues are so many versions.) The Romantic faith in the potential infinitude of humanity is a dangerous illusion. So is the ideal of progress so zealously promulgated by the middle classes. Eliot's poetry is full of journeys either not undertaken, abandoned or ending in disenchantment. It would seem that history neither improves nor deteriorates. 'I do not mean that our times are particularly corrupt', he writes; 'all times are corrupt' (SE, p. 387). Yet it is clear elsewhere in his work that the modern era represents a drastic falling-off from the age of belief which preceded it. Like many a conservative thinker, Eliot equivocates between the view that things are getting steadily worse and the claim that they have been pretty appalling from the outset.

One must ensure that ordinary men and women do not receive too much education. The number of those in universities should be cut by a third. It is preferable for a small number of people to be highly cultivated, and for the rest to make do with some rudimentary learning, rather than that everyone should receive an inferior education. All education must ultimately take a religious form, and it may prove necessary to revive the monastic orders in order to preserve classical learning from the barbarism which lurks beyond the cloister.

The whole of modern literature, including a certain 'Mrs Woolf', is tainted by the secular spirit. We must read according to Christian standards, a belief that modern literature disastrously rejects. Literary censorship, either of the communist or Roman Catholic kind, is in principle to be favoured. That a Catholic should feel a certain solidarity with communism is not surprising. Eliot reveals a grudging admiration for Marxism, a creed he politically detests, precisely because it is as much an orthodoxy as Anglo-Catholicism.

This is one reason why he published a range of left-wing writers in his periodical the *Criterion*. In general, however, he has little admiration for diversity, and regards a liberal pluralist society which encourages contending viewpoints as less creditable than a culture which holds its beliefs in common. The struggle against liberalism, he declares, is the struggle to renew our sense of tradition and 'establish a vital connection between the individual and the race' (ASG, p. 48). It is, to do him justice, the human race, not simply the white-skinned sector of it, that he has in mind. Liberalism involves tolerance, while Eliot considers that 'the virtue of tolerance is greatly overestimated, and I have no objection to being called a bigot myself' (EAM, p. 129). He is presumably hoping to infuriate his antagonists, though he may also be speaking the truth.

One problem with running a conservative political journal is that conservatives of Eliot's stripe do not really regard their own beliefs as political. On the contrary, they see them as springing from certain unchanging principles which are not to be compromised by the vulgar realm of political utility. The *Criterion* was thus embarrassed from the outset by seeking to address an urgent political crisis in the 1920s and

1930s while apparently having little faith in politics. Rising above all strident partisanship, it sought to strike a dispassionate note. A literary review, Eliot insists, must avoid all social, political or theological bias. It is not clear how this Arnoldian disinterestedness is to be attained, short of drawing one's contributors from the ranks of the seraphim. Nor does it reflect the reality of Eliot's editorship of his journal, where he is often enough to be found nudge-winking a reviewer into assuming a certain attitude.[2] It is true that the publication took a relatively non-partisan line on the Spanish Civil War, an issue on which Eliot commends the kind of even-handedness recommended by Arjuna, hero of the *Bhagavad Gita*. A refusal to condemn Spanish fascism, however, is hardly to his credit, and he displayed no such impartiality when it came to the battle against communism. He was also less than dispassionate about another Iberian fascist dictator, the Portuguese General Salazar, whom he blandly describes as 'a Christian at the head of a Christian country'.[3] Salazar's regime, he remarks, is to be praised as enlightened.

There is an oracular, supercilious tone to much of Eliot's prose. It suggests an hauteur curiously at odds with the self-doubting protagonist of 'The Love Song of J. Alfred Prufrock'. Nor does it fit well with his early philosophical conviction that all knowledge springs from a specific standpoint, and that no valid judgement is more than approximately true. One might claim that *The Waste Land*, despite its climate of futility and fragmentation, has a similar if rather less resonant aura of authority about it. On what Olympian peak must the poet himself be standing to be capable of seeing so widely and deeply in a shattered world? And why is it that this standpoint cannot be included within the piece itself, but acts rather as its frame? Is the synoptic form of the poem at odds with its fragmented content? Eliot's lordly tone may be distasteful to a modern reader, but later in his career it began to strike him as objectionable as well. 'The occasional note of arrogance, of vehemence, of cocksureness or rudeness' in his earlier writings was, he confesses in a splendid phrase, 'the braggadocio of the mild-mannered man safely entrenched behind his typewriter' (TCC, p. 14), which is to say a stylistic compensation for personal insecurity. He also criticises the protagonist of his play *The Family Reunion* as an insufferable prig, and compares him unfavourably with the minor character of the chauffeur. Perhaps a new, more fulfilling, marriage helped to soothe his acerbic temper.

Even so, the majestic self-assurance of the early Eliot, or perhaps of his critical persona, is remarkable. He is a past master of the suavely malicious put-down. The critic George Saintsbury is 'an erudite and genial man with an insatiable appetite for the second-rate' (TCC, p. 12). 'Akenside [the eighteenth-century poet] never says anything worth saying, but what is not worth saying he says well' (OPP, p. 199). Some of Byron's verses 'are not too good for the school magazine' (OPP, p. 227). William Hazlitt, one of the greatest critics in the English literary canon, is dismissed as 'undistinguished', a judgement doubtless influenced by the fact that he was an ardent political radical. Horace is 'somewhat plebeian' in comparison with Virgil (OPP, p. 63). D.H. Lawrence is provincial, snobbish, ill-educated and has 'an incapacity for what we ordinarily call thinking' (ASG, p. 58). If Eliot can be caustic, however, he also enjoys a spot of roguish teasing. Writing on nineteenth-century

English poetry, he asks in typically mischievous spirit, 'What about Mrs Browning's *Aurora Leigh*, which I have never read, or that long poem by George Eliot of which I don't remember the name?' (OPP, p. 42). No doubt it is significant that both these works are by women. What may look at first glance like a humble confession of ignorance is probably a calculated put-down. It is sometimes hard to know how serious Eliot is intending to be, as when he dismisses literature as 'a form of superior amusement' (SW, p. viii).

The finest of all English political philosophers, Thomas Hobbes, is disdainfully dismissed as 'one of those extraordinary little upstarts whom the chaotic motions of the Renaissance tossed into an eminence which they hardly deserve and have never lost' (SE, p. 355). It is not inconceivable that this snapshot of Hobbes as a freakish lower-class parvenu in the world of polite letters may be related to Eliot's visceral aversion to his materialist philosophy. The lower classes of Eliot's own time 'ride ten to a compartment to a football match in Swansea, listening to the inner voice, which breathes the eternal message of vanity, fear, and lust' (SE, p. 27). Words like 'television' are ugly either because of their 'foreignness or ill-breeding', though Eliot fails to make it clear to which of these contemptible categories the word 'television' belongs. There are vacuous generalisations which fail to make much sense, such as 'I believe the Chinese mind is very much nearer to the Anglo-Saxon than it is to the Indian' (ASG, p. 41). There is also a good deal of faux ignorance and sham humility, as Eliot feigns not to understand some statement whose meaning is blindingly obvious, or coyly regrets that his mind is too ponderous to grasp certain abstractions which he repudiates in any case. 'I have no general theory of my own' (SE, p. 143), he declares. Others have theories; Eliot himself has beliefs, doctrines and convictions. Throughout his criticism, there is the shadowy sense of a poseur – of an author who may be less convinced of his own imperious proclamations than he sounds, who has a strategic eye to the effect of his rhetoric on an audience, and who can cobble together a persona to suit the occasion.

Rather less innocuous are some of his observations on culture and tradition. Lecturing at the University of Virginia in 1933, he informs his audience that the culture of the American South has been less industrialised and 'less invaded by foreign races' (ASG, p. 16), and is all the more robust for it. The population of the region is attractively homogeneous; there is no mention of the African-Americans whose enslaved ancestors laid the material foundations of the region he is gracing with his presence. If two or more cultures coexist, both become 'adulterate'. As if this were not disreputable enough, Eliot throws in what is perhaps his most odious observation of all, when he adds that 'reasons of race and religion combine to make any large number of free-thinking Jews undesirable' (ASG, p. 20). He made no comment on the Holocaust.

By this point, the enlightened reader may well be wondering whether anything of value can be salvaged from this full-blooded reactionary. The answer is surely affirmative. For one thing, Eliot's elitism, anti-Semitism, class prejudice, demeaning estimate of humanity and indiscriminate distaste for modern civilisation are the stock in trade of the so-called *Kulturkritik* tradition which he inherits.[4] Many an eminent twentieth-century intellectual held views of this kind, and so did a sizeable proportion of the Western population of the time. This doesn't excuse their attitudes, but it helps to explain them. For another thing, such attitudes put Eliot at loggerheads with the liberal-capitalist ideology of his age. He is, in short, a radical of the right, like a large number of his fellow modernists. He believes in the importance of communal bonds, as much liberal ideology does not; he also rejects capitalism's greed, selfish individualism and pursuit of material self-interest. 'The organisation of society on the principle of private profit', he writes, 'as well as public destruction, is leading both to the deformation of humanity by unregulated industrialism, and so to the exhaustion of natural resources . . . a good deal of our material progress is a progress for which succeeding generations may have to pay dearly' (ICS, pp. 61–2). There is nothing here with which an ecologically minded socialist would disagree. His first published review, of a handful of books on India, is strongly anti-imperialist. He is hostile to a social order which exalts the solitary ego, and which jettisons the past as dead and done with. For his part, Eliot understands that the past is what we are mostly made of, and that to nullify it in the name of progress is to annihilate much that is precious. It is thus that he can write that by abandoning tradition, we loosen our grip on the present.

Radicals of the left may reject the inheritance to which Eliot pays homage, but this is not to suggest that they are opposed to tradition as such. It is rather that they embrace alternative lineages – that of the Levellers, Diggers, Jacobins, Chartists, Suffragettes, for example. 'We Marxists have always lived in tradition', observes Leon Trotsky in his *Literature and Revolution*. 'A society is poor indeed if it has nothing to live by but its own immediate and contemporary experience', writes Raymond Williams in *Culture and Society 1780–1950*.[5] The idea of tradition is by no means benighted in itself. It encompasses both the monarchy and the freedom to press for its abolition. If Trooping the Colour is traditional, so is the right to strike. In the modern age, Eliot protests, there is a provincialism not of space but of time, for which history is merely the chronicle of human devices which have served their turn and have now been scrapped – a viewpoint for which 'the world is the property solely of the living, a property in which the dead hold no shares' (OPP, p. 72). The Marxist Walter Benjamin would have heartily agreed, along with critics of the conversion of history into a readily consumable commodity known as 'heritage'. Eliot goes on to speak of 'our continued veneration for our ancestors' (OPP, p. 245); but in practice, as we shall see, his approach to the past is a good deal more innovative and iconoclastic than such piety would suggest. 'Veneration' is not quite the word for his scathing assessment of Milton or most eighteenth-century verse.

Nor does Eliot accept the arid rationalism which underpins the modern order, with its indifference to kinship, affection, the body and the unconscious. Confronted with the creed that men and women are wholly self-determining, he insists instead on their finitude and fragility, an awareness of which belongs to the virtue of humility. Human beings are dependent on each other, as well as on some larger whole. For Eliot, as for D.H. Lawrence, we do not belong to ourselves. The idea that we can 'possess' our selves like a piece of property is a bourgeois fantasy. The attachment to a specific place which Eliot admires may have sinister overtones of blood and soil, but it also serves in our own time as a rebuke to global capitalism – to the jet-setting CEOs who feel at home only in an airport VIP lounge. A belief in social order need not be authoritarian; it may rather be an alternative to the anarchy of the marketplace. It may also be preferable to a liberal civilisation in which everyone may believe more or less what they want – but only because convictions don't matter much in any case, and because the idea of human solidarity has withered at the root.

In this sense, Eliot is as much a critic of the social orthodoxies of his day as, say, George Orwell or George Bernard Shaw. It is just that his critique is launched from the right rather than the left. It is true that the case smacks of self-contradiction, since in practice Eliot was a loyal servant of the very capitalism which fragments community, junks tradition and has scant regard for spirituality. The alternative in his eyes would be communism; and when he wonders aloud how he would choose between communism or fascism, he plumps for the latter. He regarded the Russian Revolution as the most momentous event of the First World War, and viewed the conflict between the Soviet Union and 'Latin' civilisation as a spiritual war between Asia and Europe. Yeats believed much the same. In fact, the battle against Bolshevism is high on the *Criterion*'s agenda.

Yet Eliot was by no means a fascist, even though his first wife became a Blackshirt or member of the British Union of Fascists. There are, to be sure, affinities between fascist ideology and Eliot's brand of conservatism, which is not to be equated with the tenets of today's Conservative Party. Both are elitist creeds; both are ready to sacrifice freedom to order, reject liberal democracy and economic individualism and exalt myth or custom over rational analysis. Yet conservatives like Eliot believe in the church, tradition, the monarchy, a decentralised society and a paternalist aristocracy, none of which is in the least congenial to fascism. Nor is the idea of social hierarchy, since fascism knows only one social distinction, that between the Leader and the people. Fascism regards itself as a revolutionary creed, whereas conservatism of course does not. Like all brands of nationalism, fascism is a thoroughly modern invention, despite its invocation of Nordic gods and ancient heroes. Conservatism has a lengthier pedigree.

Both brands of politics have a high regard for rural society; but whereas the Nazis spoke in demonic terms of blood and soil, the conservative thinks rather more angelically of village fetes and Morris dancers. The conservative is devoted to the family, the local community and civil society, while the fascist pays allegiance only to Leader, race and nation. Fascist societies glorify violence and are usually on a permanent military footing, which is not the case with conservative ones. They are run by a brutally authoritarian state, whereas Eliot's type of politics favours regionalism rather than centralism. In fact, it was fascism which helped to wind up the *Criterion* on the eve of the Second World War. It had become clear that the cultural equivalent of the Holy Roman Empire which the journal hoped to see re-established was yielding in Continental Europe to an altogether more sinister form of imperial power. The classical 'European mind', Eliot laments in the final edition of the journal, has disappeared from view, even though it was never clear how a periodical whose circulation probably never topped eight hundred was going to put it back on its feet.

Eliot is certainly an elitist, but we have seen already that elitism need not exclude a concern for the common people. This unabashed reactionary may have wanted to shut an alarmingly high number of students out of universities, but he also taught for some years in adult education, a largely left-wing project at the time. As far as moral values go, the number of those who can discriminate between good and evil is in Eliot's view very small; but he also holds that the company of those hungry for some kind of spiritual experience is very large. He speaks in an essay on Kipling, chronicler of life in India, of 'people of lower cultures', yet maintains that Kipling enriched the English language to the benefit of all, whether philosophers or railway porters. There must, he insists, be lines of communication between the poet and a wider public; and for poetry to work, the two must share a common background. Poetry, for this most mandarin of intellectuals, must be rooted in common speech and a common sensibility. It represents the most refined point of consciousness, and most intricate sensibility, of a whole community, not simply of an individual author. One needs a small vanguard of writers who are in advance of their time, but a vanguard is not to be confused with a coterie. A vanguard is in the service of a larger body marching behind it, which is hardly true of a coterie or clique. The changes it effects in language and sensibility, Eliot maintains, will eventually work their way through to the public as a whole

– even, indirectly, to those who don't read poetry at all. This, at root, is the social function of poetry.

There are times when Eliot presses this case to the point of absurdity. He remarks in *On Poetry and Poets* that if Norwegians stopped writing poetry, which is to say ceased to perfect and enrich their own language and feelings, the consequences of this would eventually be felt by everyone on the planet. It would eventually affect even those who could not name a single poet, let alone a Norwegian one. If a nation fails to breed eminent writers, its language and sensibility will deteriorate to the detriment of the species as a whole. That the sensibility of Glaswegians would grow coarser because Norwegian poets they have never heard of had given up writing is not the most plausible of propositions. Rather more persuasively, Eliot maintains that when language is in a healthy state, 'the great poet will have something to say to all his fellow countrymen at every level of education' (OPP, p. 9). In articulating the emotions of others, the writer also modifies them, rendering them more self-conscious and making his readers more finely aware of what they spontaneously feel. The poet 'discovers new variations of sensibility which can be appropriated by others' (OPP, p. 9). The perfect classic is one which will find a response 'among all classes and conditions of men' (OPP, p. 69). Its music is already latent in everyday speech. 'The poetry of a people', Eliot remarks, 'takes its life from the people's speech and in turn gives life to it; and represents its highest point of consciousness, its greatest power and its most delicate sensibility' (UPUC, p. 15).

There is, then, a reciprocity between poet and populace, which is not the case with the coterie or cabal. The poet in Eliot's view wants to give pleasure to as large and diverse a mass of people as possible; and in seeking such popularity he or she aspires to the role of the music-hall comedian. Eliot took a keen interest in this brand of popular culture, and wrote an admiring essay on the legendary music-hall performer Marie Lloyd. The Elizabethan dramatists, he remarks, took a form of popular entertainment and plucked some matchless art from it, and music hall offers the modern writer a similar opportunity. A great many people, he insists, are able to reap some gratification from poetry. He also suggests in his mock-humble, archly provocative style that he himself would like an audience for his work which could neither read nor write. In quite what sense they would constitute an audience is left unclear. Maybe what he had in mind was his declaiming his verse to them, though anyone who has heard a recording of Eliot reading *The Waste Land* would be unlikely to rank this as among his more inspired achievements. It is not, however, as fatuous an idea as it may seem. We shall see later that Eliot regarded poetic communication as a largely unconscious affair, which is one reason why he is so blasé about the conscious meaning of a poem. It follows that you do not need to be well educated to appreciate his work. In fact, your erudition might even constitute an obstacle to your enjoyment of it. Even so, words can only communicate unconsciously if you can read them in the first place.

In this sense, Eliot is less hidebound by his conservatism than one might expect. Nor is his attitude to tradition at all traditional. On the contrary, his reconstruction of the concept is one of his most renowned critical innovations, and the essay in which it is to be found, 'Tradition and the Individual Talent', one of the most celebrated critical statements of the twentieth century. For such a youthful author, it is an astonishingly bold, authoritative piece of argument. It proposes what one might call a modernist notion of tradition, one which has broken with a linear, one-thing-after-another conception of literary history. The idea of tradition must be rescued from the middle-class delusion of progress, upward evolution and perpetual improvement; and if literature is a convenient means of challenging this self-satisfied ideology, it is partly because there is indeed no simple upward trek from Horace to Margaret Atwood. In Eliot's view, tradition is a two-way street. It works backwards as well as forwards, since the present alters the past just as much as the past gives birth to the present. The historical sense involves a perception not only of the pastness of the past, but of its presentness. As so often with modernism, we are speaking of a form of spatialised time, so that a poet writes 'with a feeling that the whole of the literature of Europe from Homer and within it the whole of the literature of his own country has a simultaneous existence and composes a simultaneous order' (SE, p. 14).

When a new piece of writing enters the literary canon, it retrospectively changes the relations between previous works, allowing us to view them in a new light. One may talk of the influence of Keats on Tennyson, but what, Eliot might ask, of the influence of Tennyson on Keats? He writes:

> The existing [literary] monuments form an ideal order among
> themselves, which is modified by the introduction of the new
> (the really new) work of art among them. The existing order is

complete before the new work arrives; for order to persist after
the supervention of novelty, the *whole* existing order must be, if
ever so slightly, altered; and so the relations, proportions, values
of each work of art toward the whole are readjusted; and this is
conformity between the old and the new. (SE, p. 15)

An example of this backward transformation can be found in F.R.
Leavis's *New Bearings in English Poetry*, in which Eliot's own revolution in the writing of poetry allows Leavis to reassess Gerard Manley
Hopkins as a proto-modernist rather than a somewhat freakish late
Victorian. It is worth adding that Eliot's poetic practice combines
the old and the new rather as his idea of tradition does. By being
faithful to a certain hallowed moment of the past (roughly speaking,
the period from Marlowe to Marvell), his work is able to disrupt the
conventions of the present. One can read 'Tradition and the
Individual Talent' as among other things an attempt to reclaim its
author's avant-garde literary practice for a conservative poetics.
What looks aberrant is in fact loyal to the legacy of the past, when
viewed from a long way off.

The works of the past constitute a complete, coherent order;
there is no concession that the literary canon might be marked by
conflict and dissonance. Nothing is ever lacking from it; and though
its internal relations are altered each time it offers houseroom to a
new work, it then proceeds to unfold unperturbedly as an organic
whole. In this sense, the tradition perpetuates itself by means of
change, not in spite of it. Though it is in continual flux, it 'abandons
nothing en route' (SE, p. 16) – though en route to what is a question

worth posing, since Eliot's tradition, unlike the socialist movement or the Victorian vision of material progress, lacks any distinctive goal. It can never be wrong-footed by some outlandish new literary creation, since it simply reorganises itself in order to accommodate it. Innovation is co-opted rather than rebuffed. You cannot really break with tradition, because this itself will turn out to be a move within it. It is a self-adjusting, self-unifying organism with its own autonomous life, and in this sense resembles an enormous work of art extended in time and space. Rather as Hegel's World Spirit works secretly in and through individuals who fondly imagine themselves to be self-determining, so the tradition uses writers as a cunning way of reproducing itself. They are the humble instruments of a mighty power whose depths they can never fathom, rather like religious believers in their relation to God. In fact, the idea of tradition is one of the modern period's many surrogates for the Almighty, a less secular version of whom Eliot will come to embrace some years after completing his 'Tradition' essay.

A way of writing, Eliot observes in *To Criticize the Critic*, can come to feel stale and shop-soiled, no longer responsive to contemporary modes of feeling, thought and speech, in which case a poetic revolution may prove essential. Such an upheaval is greeted at first with affront and disdain, but finally comes to be seen as vitalising rather than destructive, lending a fresh lease of life to the heritage it appears to undercut. Its legitimacy will finally be acknowledged, rather like that of property stolen many centuries ago. There are times when you need to deviate in order to stay in line. One test of a work's value, Eliot claims, is that it 'fits in' with what has gone before.

Conformity is the decisive criterion. But how exactly does 'Prufrock' do that, however sophisticated one's sense of what counts as fitting in? Eliot commends Samuel Johnson's belief that innovation must remain within the bounds of propriety, but this may be one instance of a mismatch between his theory and his practice. 'Proper' is the last word one would use of his early poetry.

There is another problem as well. The entry of a newcomer into the tradition ensures that the past is kept alive; but if it does so by altering the values, proportions and relations of existing works, then this view of literary history opens the door to relativism. Eliot is rightly opposed to treating works of art in isolation; instead, they draw their significance from their place in a larger formation (tradition), and can be truly judged only by mutual comparison. (This view may stem in part from his study of the late nineteenth-century philosopher F.H. Bradley, for whom the reality of an object lies in its relations with others.) Yet this suggests that no individual poem or novel can possess an inherent, unalterable value, as a certain classical viewpoint would seek to maintain. And this classical viewpoint is one which Eliot also seems to endorse, while at the same time insisting that no poetic reputation ever remains exactly the same. There are ripples and readjustments throughout the canon, as its occupants, rather like the passengers on a crowded subway train, shuffle around a little in order to make room for new arrivals. Might there, then, be an innovation which retrospectively reduced Homer or Shakespeare to minor status? Or is it to guard against this possibility that the relations and proportions are changed by the newcomer only 'ever so slightly'?

It would seem that Eliot tries to combine a classical sense of tradition, for which certain literary works are timelessly valuable, with a more relational or historicist view of them. And this is not an entirely coherent standpoint. There is fixity but also flux, as there is for Eliot in an individual poem, which tends to involve a continuous 'unperceived evasion of monotony' by constantly varying its sounds and rhythms (TCC, p. 185). So-called free verse, for example, continually evokes but skilfully eludes the beat of a regular metre. The iambic pentameter plays off the irregular rhythms of the speaking voice against a regular metrical scheme. We also learn to our surprise that the tradition 'does not at all flow invariably through the most distinguished reputations' (SE, p. 16). So it is not just a galaxy of illustrious works. It is a matter of value, but not in the sense that it is made up of authors who are generally agreed to be of the highest rank. That would include Milton, Blake, Shelley and Tennyson, who in Eliot's eyes do not belong to the tradition at all. We shall see later that this is because he means by the tradition a particular *kind* of literary writing, whether or not the writers who exemplify it are generally considered the most prestigious.

Thus, for Eliot as for Leavis, John Donne (a minor figure for some critics at the time) is part of the tradition, but John Milton is not. Donne writes in a way which is deemed compatible with a specific use of the English language, while Milton's poetic style represents a mortal threat to it. So the tradition comprises not the whole range of one's literary ancestors but a particular, partisan selection of them – partisan, because roughly speaking these are the precursors who will help Eliot and others to write their own poetry in the present. This is another way in which the supposedly timeless is relative to a specific standpoint. As Raymond Williams comments, 'the traditional culture of a society will always tend to correspond to its *contemporary* system of interests and values, for it is not an absolute body of work but a continual selection and interpretation'.[6] Tradition thus has a pragmatic value. It is fashioned in accordance with the needs of the contemporary, which is hardly what a 'traditionalist' defender of it would claim. As a young poet, Eliot himself could find no foothold in the stale late-Romantic poeticising of his day, and was thus forced to look back over the head of this well-groomed verse to a more resourceful past. Yet the authority with which he invests the tradition is not quite at one with a view of it as a convenient artifice. Besides, are there not conflicting heritages, or writers who belong to more than one literary legacy at the same time? Eliot's conservative sense of the past as forming an organic whole forbids him from confronting such possibilities, even if his conservatism has its radical aspects as well. It involves carrying out something of a demolition-and-salvage job on English literature, which one critic, no doubt with Eliot's national origins in mind, rather more bluntly describes as 'the most ambitious feat of cultural imperialism the [twentieth] century seems likely to produce'.[7]

Those writers who do not inherit what Eliot calls 'the accumulated wisdom of time' (SE, p. 29) must trade on their own resources, and these in his view are bound to be scantier than those of the tradition. Such authors are 'heretics' – men and women who are unconstrained by orthodoxy, in the sense of a taken-for-granted set of beliefs shared spontaneously in common, and therefore fall victim to the cranky, fanciful, extravagant and eccentric. D.H. Lawrence, who in Eliot's judgement lacks a richly sustaining culture, has no guidance except the 'inner light', and is spiritually sick. Even so, Eliot protests in the teeth of conventional prejudice that no writer was less of a sensualist. It is Lawrence's deviation from the main current, not his scandalous explorations of sexuality, which thrusts him into the outer darkness. (It will be left to F.R. Leavis to point out that the provincial, lower-middle-class culture from which Lawrence sprang was a good deal more fruitful than the loftily contemptuous Eliot will allow.) James Joyce, by contrast, is in Eliot's eyes the most orthodox of all contemporary authors. The fact that he is an avant-garde atheist whose work was banned as pornographic is less important than the fact that he draws on a stable structure of ideas derived from Aristotle and Aquinas. No doubt Eliot quietly relished the shock effect of ranking the author of Molly Bloom's steamy soliloquy alongside such classical worthies as Dante. Joyce's compatriot W.B. Yeats, whose lack of orthodox beliefs leads him astray into the swamps of 'folklore, occultism, mythology and symbolism, crystal-gazing and hermetic writings' (ASG, p. 45), receives no such accolade, even though in general Eliot has a high opinion of his work.

William Blake's writing 'has the unpleasantness of great poetry' (SE, p. 128); but as the work of a Dissenter it, too, falls outside an orthodox frame of reference and is forced to invent a quaint, homespun philosophy of its own. Blake is patronisingly compared to a man fashioning an ingenious piece of home-made furniture. The fact that he cannot rely on an established set of doctrines to do the work of belief for him means that he is too preoccupied with ideas. He, too, is afflicted in Eliot's view by a certain meagreness of culture, a charge which is no truer of him than it is of Lawrence. It is simply that Eliot cannot recognise either provincial nonconformism or metropolitan radicalism as genuine cultures. He finds a similar paucity of cultivation, linked once again to religious Dissent, in the work of John Milton, in whose Puritan mythology he discerns a certain thinness, and whose celestial and infernal regions in *Paradise Lost* he describes in an agreeable flourish as 'large but insufficiently furnished apartments filled by heavy conversation' (SE, p. 321). Thomas Hardy is another author bereft of any objective system of beliefs. No doubt he is also too Godless, plebeian and socially progressive for Eliot's taste.

Eliot's desire to belong – to a church, tradition or social Establishment – is in part a result of his émigré status. It is not surprising that one should find such zeal for tradition in a disinherited poet who stems from a nation not remarkable for its reverence for the past. Tradition is among other things Eliot's revenge on the philistines of St Louis. Yet the immigrant artist, as we have seen, is also less likely to be constrained by a cultural heritage than those reared within it, and thus more ready to subject it to a scissors-and-paste job. In Eliot's critical essays, minor Jacobean dramatists are upgraded, the eighteenth century damned with faint praise and whole squadrons of Romantic and Victorian poets sent packing. Even Shakespeare is the target of some astringent judgements. There is also something rather un-English about this Anglophile's sheer intellectual ambitiousness

– about the way he can speak in such grandly generalising terms of the 'European mind', or of European literature as forming an organic totality. Perhaps you need to come at the place from the outside to grasp Europe in this all-inclusive way. It is also typical of an outsider to idealise it so much. The claim that European literature constitutes an organic unity is surely as much a delusion as Eliot's insistence that one must read all of Shakespeare's plays in order to understand any one of them. He even suggests that *world* literature constitutes a unity, as improbable a case as claiming that the stars are meticulously arranged to spell out some momentous statement. In any case, the belief that unity is always a positive value is one of the more question-able assumptions of literary criticism, as well as one of the most enduring.

Tradition, then, turns out to be for the most part a matter of interpretation. It is a construct as much as a given; indeed, in the thought of F.H. Bradley, the line between the two is notably blurred. Poets must surrender their petty personalities to this sovereign power, allowing it to speak through them; yet in doing so, there is a sense in which they are sacrificing themselves to their own creation, rather like those who immolate themselves before idols carved by their own hands. The notion of self-sacrifice also lies at the root of another of Eliot's renowned doctrines, the idea of impersonality. Roughly speaking, while the Romantic poet wants to express the self, Eliot wants to extinguish it. In this, he is at one with many of his fellow modernists. Poetry is not a matter of 'personality' but a question of escaping from it. To write is a matter of constant self-surrender. An author is no more than a 'finely perfected medium in which special, or very varied, feelings are at liberty to enter into new combinations' (SE, p. 18). The more perfect the artist, the greater distinction there will be between 'the man who suffers and the mind which creates' (SE, p. 18). The difference between art, and the personal events or sentiments it may record, is absolute. Experiences which are vital to the author may play no part in their poetry, and what is important in the poetry may be of negligible significance in their life. The Victorian critic Matthew Arnold, Eliot comments, mistakenly focuses on the feelings of the poet rather than the feelings of the poem itself. Emotion for Eliot is to be found *in* the words of a poem, precisely configured there, rather than lurking somewhere behind them in the artist's heart or mind.

The literary work is thus in no sense a 'reflection' of the mind that contrives it. Some writers may have crude or simple emotions in real life but subtly nuanced ones in their art. Or their feelings may be too obscure and elusive for them to grasp at all fully. Eliot does not assume *à la* Descartes that we are transparent to ourselves. What matters is not to experience profound or original emotions but the intensity of the artistic process itself. Originality is for Eliot an over-rated Romantic value, and whether there are any emotions as yet undiscovered is surely doubtful. By the time an experience has crystallised into a poem, it may differ so much from the author's initial state of mind as to be scarcely recognisable to him. Indeed, Eliot presses this case even further, claiming that what a poem communicates does not exist outside the act of communication itself. It is as though the experience is constituted in the process of conveying it. Like those charismatic types moved to prophecy by the Holy Spirit,

poets do not know what they have to say until they overhear themselves saying it.

The contrast with Romanticism could not be clearer. The poet for
Eliot is not in the business of self-expression. Besides, Romantic poets
are typically *agents* – active subjects who recreate the world by the
power of their imagination. There is little place for such agency in
Eliot's aesthetics, and no room for the creative imagination. Given the
pious exaltation of this modest faculty in literary circles, this is an
oversight to be welcomed. The Eliotic poet, by contrast with the
strenuously self-making Romantic, is strikingly passive – 'a receptacle
for seizing and storing up numberless feelings, phrases, images, which
remain there until all the particles which can unite to form a new
compound are present together' (SE, p. 19). In a much cited passage
from his path-breaking essay on the Metaphysical poets, Eliot speaks
of the poet's mind as constituting new wholes out of experiences
(falling in love, reading Spinoza, hearing the sound of the typewriter,
smelling the dinner cooking) which for non-poetic minds are quite
distinct. It is this capacity to fuse a range of diffuse sensations into a
complex whole which distinguishes the poet, not the nature or value
of the sensations themselves. Since this process nowhere engages
conscious choice, there may be some unconscious significance in
Eliot's choice of the name Spinoza here, a philosopher renowned for
his implacable determinism. The poet's mind is like a catalyst in a
chemical experiment: in fusing certain gases to form a compound, it
remains neutral, inert and unaltered in itself.

There is a politics behind this poetics. Between the Romantics
and the modernists lies a historic change in the whole notion of

subjectivity. The Romantics lived through an age of industrial and political revolution, which called for free, self-determining individuals who could forge their own history; by the early twentieth century, with its faceless bureaucracies and anonymous corporations, these men and women have become the passive subjects of a more impersonal civilisation. Yet in poetry, if not in society as a whole, it is an impersonality of which Eliot approves. It is an antidote to the Romantic fantasy that at the nub of the world lies a self which is potentially boundless in scope – a daydream typical of the United States on which Eliot turned his back, with its 'I can be anything I want to be' delusions of grandeur. As a conservative Christian, he regards human beings as limited, defective creatures, who can thrive only if they are rigorously disciplined. Order must be elevated over freedom, which is to say conservatism over liberalism. Rootedness is preferable to restless enterprise. Humility is a cure for the hubris of the modern self. Tradition, orthodoxy and convention must curb a wayward individualism which can see no further than its own selfish interests.

It is this individualism which Eliot has constantly in his sights, whether he calls it liberalism, Protestantism, Romanticism, Whiggery, humanism, freethinking, moral relativism, the cult of personality or the 'inner voice' of the solitary individual conscience. 'What is disastrous', he declares in *After Strange Gods*, 'is that the writer should deliberately give rein to his "individuality", that he should even cultivate his difference from others; and that his readers should cherish the author of genius, not in spite of his deviations from the inherited wisdom of the race, but because of them' (ASG, p. 33). One should

45

note, however, that *After Strange Gods* is one of the most hard-line of all his critical writings, full of dyspeptic remarks like 'a spirit of excessive tolerance is to be deprecated' (ASG, p. 20) and (in what sounds more like a tone of regret than relief) 'social classes, as distinct from economic classes, hardly exist today' (ASG, p. 19). One commentator, hardly noted for his radicalism, describes the book as 'half-demented',[8] while Eliot himself remarked to William Empson that he was 'very sick in soul' when he wrote it.

We have seen already that as an émigré in Europe, in flight among other things from American Puritanism's too robust sense of self, Eliot was sceptical of the unified ego in its search to subjugate the world. In the form of the middle-class industrial magnate, it was part of what was ousting his own more leisured social class. The 'characters' of his early poems are less individuals than zones of consciousness, collections of disparate experiences looking for an identity to attach themselves to. It is not surprising that as one of the few English-language poets to master the technicalities of philosophy, Eliot should have been so captivated by the thought of F.H. Bradley, whose starting-point is not the self but what he calls Immediate Experience or Feeling. For Bradley, it is only by a process of abstracting from this immediacy that we arrive at the concept of the self, along with the idea of a not-self or external object. Consciousness is bound up with its various objects, which means that it shifts and fluctuates as they do. The human subject is by no means a solid substance. One might have expected that Eliot's conversion to Christianity would have brought him to acknowledge the reality of the self, which is, after all, what is corrupted by sin and redeemed by divine grace; yet selfhood in the post-conversion *Four Quartets* would still seem remarkably unstable, just as it is in the pre-conversion *The Waste Land*. And the doctrine of the Incarnation seems not to have made Eliot any more favourably disposed to the life of the flesh.

Eliot's theory of poetic impersonality involves severing the work from its producer. What a poem means is as much what it signifies for its readers as for the writer; and over the course of time the poet becomes simply one more reader of his or her own work, perhaps forgetting or reinventing its original sense. No writer can exert absolute command over the reception of their poems or novels. There is no question of proprietorship at stake here. A reader's interpretation may be quite as valid as the author's own, or may actually improve on it. There is never only one possible reading of a literary text, and to explicate it is not to deliver an account of what the author was consciously or unconsciously trying to say. When Eliot remarks, no doubt in a characteristic piece of mischief making, that *The Waste Land* is nothing but a piece of rhythmical grousing, it is perfectly open to a reader to tell him that this is nonsense. Perhaps it is a sly invitation for the reader to do so. When an actor during the rehearsal of one of his plays gave a line of verse an inflection which seemed to alter its meaning entirely, Eliot himself, ensconced in the stalls, remarked that this might well be what the line meant. Nor, however, is the poem reducible to the reader's experience of it, a case exemplified in Eliot's view by the work of I.A. Richards. The significance of a poem cannot lie simply in certain fortuitous states of mind which it happens to evoke in the reader; instead, there must be a necessary relation between the work and the reader's response to it. The poem is a quasi-objective entity, rather like meaning itself, which is neither purely subjective (I cannot just decide that 'meat pie' means 'Member of Parliament') nor objective in the sense that a taxi cab is.

Like his view of tradition, Eliot's view of impersonality is not entirely coherent. We feel in a great poet, he claims, 'one significant, consistent, and developing personality' (SE, p. 203) – though by 'personality' he can sometimes mean the distinctive flavour or pattern of sensibility of a literary work. Shakespeare's characters, he maintains, act out certain conflicts in the poet's soul, a claim curiously at odds with the idea of the work as independent of its author. He sometimes speaks of one's sense of the presence of an author in his or her work, or suggests that we need more biographical information about a writer. At other times, however, as in the case of Dante, he complains that biographical information impairs his enjoyment of the poetry. Eliot's concept of impersonality does not mean that the poem is a self-contained object, as it does for the American New Criticism. If it stands free of both its author and its reader, it is nevertheless anchored in a specific historical context. Art and everyday life are interwoven: one's taste in poetry, Eliot insists, cannot be divorced from the rest of one's passions and interests, and the evolution of both poetry and criticism is shaped by elements which infiltrate them from outside. One cannot draw a clear line between the moral, social, religious and aesthetic. The critic must take account of history, philosophy, theology, economics and psychology, even if Eliot himself rarely engages in such inquiries.

Both the form and content of literary works are bound up with their specific time and place.

This is not in his view to license a sociological criticism. Conservatives have commonly found sociology distasteful, and in Eliot's day a literary criticism which took it seriously would probably stem from the Marxist camp. Nor, he insists, should one overlook the eternal, imperishable elements in art. Even so, he speaks like any Marxist of Renaissance art as being shaped to its roots by the rise of a new social class, and claims that the function of poetry alters along with changes in society. So does the nature of wit, a faculty illustrated at its finest for Eliot by the work of the seventeenth-century poet Andrew Marvell. A comment of his on the peculiar quality of Marvell's verse – 'a tough reasonableness beneath the slight lyric grace' (SE, p. 293) – has justly entered the collective literary consciousness. Wit he describes as a combination of levity and seriousness, the product of a mind rich in generations of experience. It is true that his historical approach to literature is alarmingly broad-brush: the so-called dissociation of sensibility, a doctrine we shall be looking at later, 'has something to do with the Civil War' (OPP, p. 173), a proposition which would be unlikely to swing one a place to read history at Harvard. Literature's fall from grace coincides with a conflict in which, in Eliot's opinion, the wrong side won. His historical commentary consists largely in a series of grandiose generalities, whereas his critical observations are for the most part delicate and precise. Witness, for example, his remark that 'Marlowe gets into blank verse the melody of Spenser, and he gets a new driving power by reinforcing the sentence period against the line period'

(SE, p. 76). This is the comment of a master craftsman, not simply of an academic critic.

'Any radical change in poetic form', Eliot writes, 'is likely to be the symptom of some very much deeper change in society and the individual' (UPUC, p. 75). Poetic form is not simply 'aesthetic' but social and historical through and through. Raymond Williams, as we shall see later, argues just the same. Conventions in art reflect common agreements in society. Only in a close-knit, homogeneous society, Eliot claims, will you find the development of intricate formal patterns, as a common set of values gives rise to certain parallels and symmetries. A literary form like the Shakespearian sonnet embodies a definitive way of thinking and feeling, and forms of thought and feeling are anchored in the social conditions of their time. A different metre represents a different mode of thought. Form and content are mutually determining.

It is an odd feature of Eliot's criticism that though as a classicist he advocates impersonality, he consistently places feeling at the centre of a poem, in the manner of the Romanticism of which he is so distrustful. 'What every poet starts from', he declares, 'is his own emotions' (SE, p. 137). It is hard to see how this is true of the *Iliad* or Pope's *Essay on Man*. Not all literature can be modelled on the lyric. It is just as doubtful that (as Eliot argues) Shakespeare's artistic evolution is based on his degree of emotional maturity at any given time, which supposedly determines his choice of theme, dramatic form and poetic technique. If the two cases (impersonality and the central role of feeling) can be reconciled, it is largely because the task of the poet is to impersonalise his or her emotions rather than lend them direct expression. 'The emotion of art', Eliot informs us, 'is impersonal' (SE, p. 22). Once the poet has found the appropriate words for his or her state of feeling, that emotional condition disappears, to be replaced by the poem itself. The poet is preoccupied with 'the struggle to transmute his personal and private agonies into something rich and strange, something universal and impersonal' (SE, p. 137). (One wonders why it is agony the poet starts from, rather than, say, rancour or exuberance.) There is a hint of what Freud would call 'sublimation' here, as one's everyday tribulations are raised to a loftier level, and what is distressing in life becomes delectable in art. There is also a sense of the poem as a kind of therapy, or alternatively as a way of coping with one's feelings by evading them. Sublimation for Freud is a form of repression.

The philosopher Bradley also views states of consciousness as impersonal. (It is, incidentally, typical of the cordial climate of Oxford University that though Eliot worked on Bradley, who was then still alive, at the philosopher's own small college, the two men never actually met. But this may be partly because Bradley was a nocturnal animal.) In Bradley's view, the subjective and objective are aspects of a single reality, with a notably fluid frontier between them. We can identify states of feelings only by reference to the objects with which they are bound up; and if this is so, then there is a sense in which our emotions and experiences are 'in' the world rather than simply in us. Conversely, objects are reducible to the relations between different states of consciousness. It is on this idea that Eliot draws for another of his celebrated doctrines, the so-called objective correlative. In an essay on *Hamlet* he writes:

The only way of expressing emotion in the form of art is by finding an 'objective correlative'; in other words, a set of objects, a situation, a chain of events which shall be the formula of that *particular* emotion; such that when the external facts, which must terminate in sensory experience, are given, the emotion is immediately evoked. (SE, p. 145)

Emotion finds its way into poetry only indirectly, crystallised in a set of external situations which act as code or shorthand for inner ones. Perhaps this is because spontaneous lyrical effusions would strike hard-boiled modern readers as embarrassingly naive, rather as a poem which explicitly tried to teach them something might seem objectionable. But it is also because poetry for Eliot, being an escape from personality, is necessarily a flight from feeling, not an outpouring of it. This is one reason why the concept of sincerity has little place in his criticism. There is also something rather English about the idea that one does not wear one's emotions on one's sleeve, and Eliot was English in almost everything except the fact that he was American.

Object and emotion are fused together in poetry, as they are in the work of Bradley. Yet for Bradley the relation between subject and object is an 'internal' or necessary one, whereas there is something slightly strange about Eliot's use of the phrase '*which shall be* the formula of that particular emotion'. One might take it to suggest a somewhat arbitrary connection between subject and object – one which the poet legislates into existence, as though forging a special contract between himself and the reader. Yet it would be curious to say 'whenever you come across water imagery, think of envy'. There is a necessary rather than contingent link between most of our states of feeling and our 'external' speech or behaviour, so that (for example) we learn the concept of pain by becoming familiar with how people in pain typically speak and behave. If there were no such necessary relations – if everyone who was in a blind panic behaved quite differently from everyone else in the same state – it would be hard for small children to learn the language of feeling.

Eliot finds *Hamlet* an artistic failure because the hero's state of mind lacks an adequate objective correlative, which is a fancy way of saying that his spiritual torment seems to have no sufficient cause. His emotion is in excess of the facts as they appear. This, to be sure, is not an unusual situation: 'The intense feeling, ecstatic or terrible, without an object or exceeding its object, is something which every person of sensibility has known' (SE, p. 146). In fact, for Sigmund Freud the name of this condition is desire, which is always in excess of any specific goal. Melancholy, Freud comments, is mourning without an object. One might even call this surplus subjectivity itself. It is not clear, however, why one cannot turn this situation to poetic advantage, rather than censure it as a literary defect. 'The Love Song of J. Alfred Prufrock', in which the speaker's feelings appear to lack a determinate cause or object, resisting all attempts to formulate them, might be thought a peculiarly fine example of it.

In general, however, Eliot prefers his subjects and objects to coalesce into seamless chunks of experience. For all his admiration for Baudelaire's work, he finds that 'the content of feeling (in it) is constantly bursting the receptacle' (SE, p. 424), so that the mismatch between subject and object becomes a fissure between content and form. Subjective emotion or experience represents the content of a work, while form is the poet's way of crafting an impersonal object out of it. By contrast, F.H. Bradley's prose style is praised for being perfectly matched to the content of his thought, so that the philosopher's own writing is an example of what it argues for. In the prose of the early-modern cleric Lancelot Andrewes, the emotions are in Eliot's view wholly contained in and explained by the subjects on which the author meditates. Another aspect of this unity of form and content is that sound and sense in poetry must pull together, as in Eliot's view they conspicuously fail to do in Milton's *Paradise Lost*. In truly accomplished poetry, the music is inseparable from the meaning, whereas in the grand Miltonic style the two seem to move at different levels.

'It may be, as I have read', Eliot writes in *On Poetry and Poets*, 'that there is a dramatic element in much of my early work' (OPP, p. 98). It is typical of his non-proprietorial stance to his own verse that he should pick up this fact from the critics, or at least that he should pretend to. (Once more, there is probably some puckish humour afoot here.) Critics can tell you what your poems are about, or what qualities they reveal. One reason why Eliot is so airily agnostic about what a poem means, including those he has written himself, is that he does not regard meaning as fundamental to poetry. He is, he confesses, devoted to a good deal of poetry which he doesn't fully understand, or which at first reading he didn't grasp at all. He was, for example, enchanted by reading Dante in the original even before he could understand Italian. Poetry can communicate before it is comprehended. Meaning in a poem, he declares in a wonderfully apposite image, is like the piece of meat the burglar throws to the house dog to keep it quiet while he goes about his stealthy business. The dog here is the reader and the burglar the poet; and the latter's task is to distract readers with some readily consumable meaning while he proceeds to raid their unconscious.

It is ironic that Eliot is often regarded as an 'intellectual' poet, no doubt because so many of his poems are difficult to decipher. But obscurity and intellectualism are not the same thing. Dylan Thomas is obscure, but his work is hardly packed with profound ideas. Despite Eliot's formidable erudition as a critic (he seems to have read everything in literature and philosophy, including certain Sanskrit texts in the original), it would not be entirely unfair to call him an anti-intellectual poet. He certainly holds that all the most important processes in poetry work at a level far deeper than reasoning. In fact, his suspicion of everyday rationality is one link between his avant-garde practice and his conservative opinions. The avant garde are out to challenge received forms of reason, sometimes by the use of nonsense, disorder, outrage and absurdity. Conservatives naturally repudiate all such wild experiment; but they, too, are suspicious of rational analysis, which they associate with the bloodless, blue-printing political left. Against this, he commends the virtues of custom, affection, loyalty, intuition and whatever has withstood the test of time. It is thus that the author of *The Waste Land*, a poem which shocked some conventional readers to the core, is also the pontifical right-winger of 'Tradition and the Individual Talent', an essay published three years earlier, and the Anglo-Catholic Tory is an enthusiast of perhaps the most audacious novel ever published in

English, James Joyce's *Finnegans Wake* – 'a monstrous masterpiece', as he describes it (OPP, p. 120).

The poet, Eliot remarks, must have a feeling for syllable and rhythm which penetrates far below conscious levels of thought and feeling, sinking to 'the most primitive and forgotten, returning to the origin and bringing something back' (UPUC, p. 118). Poets must find words for the inarticulate, ranging beyond the frontiers of everyday consciousness in order to return from this uncharted territory and report on what they have discovered there. In doing so, they unite 'the old and obliterated and the trite, the current, and the new and surprising, the most ancient and the most civilised mentality' (UPUC, p. 119). Poetry may help to break up stale modes of perception, making us see the modern world afresh; but in doing so it also dredges up 'the deeper, unnamed feelings which form the substratum of our being, to which we rarely penetrate; for our lives are mostly a conscious evasion of ourselves, and an evasion of the visible and sensible world' (UPUC, p. 155). The innovative techniques of a poem like *The Waste Land* – pastiche, fractured imagery, colloquial speech, recondite allusions, snatches of mythology, typographical experiment and the like – are at the cutting edge of the poetry of the time; but one of the ironies of the work is that these avant-garde devices are pressed into the service of the archaic and atavistic. By shattering our customary false consciousness, the poem is supposed to delve below daily experience to put us in touch with our most primordial feelings, which run back to the origins of humanity. In a familiar modernist move, the very new and the very old are looped together. There is a secret compact between them, and it is from their complicity or collision that the most fertile art flows.

Poets, in Eliot's view, must be both the most primitive and sophisticated of creatures. If they are more alive to the present than others, it is largely by virtue of being the bearers of a living past. There is a parallel here with Eliot's concept of tradition, in which the past still lurks as a shaping force within the present. It is this primitive bedrock of our being to which Freud and his disciples give the name of the unconscious – a region which is both antique and unchanging, like the mythological archetypes which secretly inform *The Waste Land*. For Freud, the unconscious is a stranger to temporality, rather as for Eliot the most fundamental emotions remain constant from Homer to Housman. In this way, one of the most scandalous, ground-breaking projects of Eliot's time – psychoanalysis – can be yoked to a conservative view of humanity as essentially unchangeable.

The unconscious, with its attendant myths and symbols, can also be used to underpin Eliot's aversion to individualism. True self-hood lies far deeper than individual personality. It has its roots in a submerged domain of collective images and impersonal emotions. The individual, not least the individual author, is of relatively trifling significance. He or she is merely the tip of an iceberg whose depths are unsearchable. We are dealing here with an early version of what would later be known as the 'death of the author' theory, or at least with the author's drastic diminishment. The poet, Eliot remarks in a passage of unusual emotional intensity, is haunted by a demon, an obscure impulse which has no face or name, and poetry is an exorcism of this 'acute discomfort' (OPP, p. 107). It is a darker version of the Romantic idea of inspiration. When authors have finally arranged their words in an appropriate form, they can purge themselves of this demonic urge and in doing so rid themselves of the poem altogether, handing it over to their readers so that they can relax after their labours. It sounds more like a peculiarly painful childbirth than a piece of imaginative creation. Poetry is something to get out of your system. And whatever its mysterious source, it is certainly not the individual mind.

Poets cannot predict when these obscure upsurges will occur: they must simply devote themselves to the task of perfecting their craft in anticipation of such spiritual seizures. There is, then, a good deal of conscious labour involved in the poetic process, but it is not what is most essential to it. It is rather that the poem forces itself into the poet's consciousness like a blind, implacable force of Nature; and when it has taken root inside them, something has occurred that cannot be explained by anything that went before. In a typically astute comment on Ben Jonson, Eliot remarks that the polished veneer of his verse means that 'unconscious does not respond to unconscious' in the transaction between poem and reader. 'No swarm of inarticulate feelings is aroused' (SE, p. 148) – which is to say that Jonson's otherwise admirable work, which Eliot finely characterises as an art of the surface rather than as simply superficial, lacks 'a network of tentacular roots reaching down to the deepest terrors and desires' (SE, p. 155). The most powerful poetry in Eliot's view sets up an enormous echo chamber of resonances and allusions, all of which will infiltrate the reader's unconscious in a way quite beyond the poet's control. Perhaps the most magnificent example of this process in Eliot's own work is

'Gerontion'. If modern *reality* is spiritually bankrupt, one can compensate for this to some extent with a richness of *experience*, and much of this is a subliminal affair. It is no wonder, then, that Eliot is so casual about conscious understanding – about, for example, the scholarly business of tracking down allusions and explicating difficult passages. The Notes to *The Waste Land* purport to do just this, but it is now generally accepted that they are there mostly to fill in a few blank pages. Conscious meaning is not the issue – indeed, readers may well be understanding a poem at some unconscious level whether they know it or not. It is welcome news to the student who timorously opens Pound's *Cantos* or the poems of Paul Celan.

The idea of poetic impersonality is closely related to Eliot's self-declared classicism. Classicism is in general less subject-centred than Romanticism. The classic in Eliot's view is not in the first place the work of an individual genius. It is rather a piece of literary art which is resonant of a specific civilisation – one whose language gives voice to a particular culture and history at the peak of its maturity. The unique genius which produces it is not that of an individual author but the spirit of a particular age and a particular people. Virgil's greatness springs from his place in the history of the Roman Empire, as well as in the evolution of the Latin language. The classical work brings a national language to a point of perfection, and its ability to do so, ironically, is what makes its appeal so universal. If works of this kind transcend their historical moment, they do so by belonging to it so intimately. Eliot speaks of reading the ancient Greek poet

Sappho and feeling the 'spark which can leap across those 2,500 years' (OPP, p. 131). A classical age is one of stability, shared belief, common standards and subtle shades of feeling. The world in Virgil's view is characterised by order, equipoise and civility, and so must be the poetry which portrays it. The closest English literature comes to a classical period is the eighteenth century, not least in the poetry of Alexander Pope; but the range of feeling of the age is too constricted for Eliot's taste, lacking the amplitude and versatility of the genuine classic. The period suggests a certain feebleness of spirit, and Eliot is notably lukewarm about even its most exemplary literary art.

There is, however, a problem here. A classical civilisation represents Eliot's social and cultural ideal, and the classical author who moulds his mind most deeply is Dante. Yet though he produces a stunning pastiche of Dante's verse in a passage in *Four Quartets*, the influence is strictly limited when it comes to the composition of his own work. There are two reasons why this is so. If the classical work thrives on shared values and standards, the liberal pluralism which Eliot finds so displeasing in modern society means that there can be precious little of this. Poets can no longer assume that they and their readers share the same sensibility. There is no longer a community of meaning and belief. At the same time, if a classic is to capture the spirit of an entire civilisation, it must be in touch with its common life and language. Poetic discourse should not be identical with daily speech, but it should display the finest virtues of prose, which brings it close to the everyday. But to stay faithful to the common life and language of early twentieth-century Europe involves registering a sterility and spiritual devastation which is nearer to Baudelaire than to Dante. It is thus that Eliot announces that the modern poet must see not only the beauty and the glory but also the boredom and the horror of human existence.

For Eliot to be loyal to one criterion of a classic, then, is to flout certain others: order, balance, harmony, nobility and the like. It means producing a poetry marked by spiritual disorder, sordid imagery, broken rhythms, banal snatches of speech and barren inner landscapes. It was from Baudelaire, Eliot tells us, that he learned that the poet's business was to make poetry out of the unpoetical. Order and harmony can be hinted at only obliquely, either by dim allusion, ironic juxtaposition or (as in *The Waste Land*) through a mythological subtext which intimates the possibility of regeneration. Baudelaire, Eliot remarks, draws some of his most striking imagery from the common life, but at the same time makes that life gesture to something more than itself. It is a familiar strategy in his own early poetry. By presenting a situation in all its squalor, you can suggest the need to transcend it without having to spell out an alternative, which might demand a verse with too obvious designs on the reader. It is not until *Four Quartets* that this negative form of transcendence becomes explicitly thematised. If poetry must cling to the unregenerate nature of the present, it is partly because its language must be wedded to everyday experience, and partly because literary works which propose an abstract ideal will fail to engage sceptical modern readers. Instead, their language must infiltrate their reader's nervous system, sensory organs and unconscious terrors and desires, all of which a remote ideal is unlikely to accomplish. We shall be looking more closely at this aspect of Eliot's poetics later.

The classical, then, is more to be admired than imitated. More relevant to the modern age is a period which in Eliot's view is distinctly unclassical, that of the Elizabethans and Jacobeans. There is, he claims, no framework of order to this civilisation, as there is in his opinion to the world of Sophocles and Racine. On the contrary, it strikes him as an era of anarchy, dissolution and decay – of a wayward, extravagant individualism which refuses to brook constraint. There is a kind of 'artistic greediness' abroad – a desire to explore every conceivable form and bizarre effect, which in time will culminate in the unbridled egoism of modern Europe. 'The age of Shakespeare', Eliot comments, 'moved in a steady current, with back eddies certainly, towards anarchy and chaos' (SE, p. 54). It is an era of muddled scepticism and clashing faiths, along with a confusion over what counts as a literary convention. Even Shakespeare indulges in strained and mixed figures of speech, displaying 'a tortured perverse ingenuity of images' (SE, p. 74). Samuel Johnson thought much the same. His is too prodigal and undisciplined a genius for Eliot's taste, in contrast to the neo-classical Racine, whose work he highly esteems.

Yet it is just these aspects of the early-modern period which Eliot can bring to bear on his own tumultuous times; and literary history must be rewritten to highlight this affinity. In the language of Walter Benjamin, a state of emergency in the present evokes a moment of the past, and the two form a 'constellation' across the centuries. The 'anarchism' of the Renaissance is also the unleashing of a wealth of complex feeling and exhilarating new modes of language, so that, to adopt a phrase of Karl Marx, history progresses by its bad side. For Marxism, early capitalism is 'progressive' as well as exploitative because it releases new forms of creative energy, which brings Eliot's case incongruously close to a theory of history he abhors. 'If new influences had not entered', he remarks, 'old orders decayed, would the language not have left some of its greatest resources unexplored?' (SE, p. 91). It is this fertile legacy that authors like Eliot himself will inherit some centuries later. The loss of social and cosmic order may be a spiritual disaster, but it also represents an inestimable gain for language and sensibility, which break through traditional constraints to become more subtle, diverse, volatile and exploratory. The textures of poetry grow finer and their images more richly compacted. It is a language close to the bone yet fast-moving, packed with perception but intellectually agile. The late sixteenth and early seventeenth centuries bear witness to 'a progressive refinement in the perception of the variations of feeling, and a progressive elaboration of the means of expressing these variations' (SW, p. 67). That this stretch of time is also the matrix of much of what Eliot detests – materialism, democracy, individualism, secularisation – is an instance of the cunning of history, which takes with one hand what it gives with the other.

Eliot was a seminal influence on F.R. Leavis, who as we shall see later locates the so-called organic society in the seventeenth century; so it is tempting to assume that Eliot is the source of this Leavisite doctrine. But this is the opposite of the truth. Eliot's social and religious ideal is to be found in the world of Dante, writing in a period which (so we are told) manifests a unified sensibility more strikingly than any other age. But it is precisely because that world is imploding in early seventeenth-century England that the latter era represents Eliot's *literary* high ground, since the erosion of the traditional, along with the turbulent emergence of the modern, re-energises both language and sensibility more thoroughly than anything we have witnessed since. It is an era of 'decomposition', but in the most nourishing of senses. In any case, Eliot's religious view of the corrupt nature of humanity means that there can be for him no entirely sound social order, as there can be for the secular-minded Leavis. The civilisation of Dante may be exemplary, but it includes a lively sense of sin and damnation.

The protagonist of Eliot's thought from beginning to end is language – more specifically, the way in which its evolution reflects certain advances or regressions in the quality of feeling of a whole culture. Every development of language represents a shift of feeling and sensation as well. Thought can remain constant across different periods and languages, but the affective life is far more culturally particular. Sensibility alters all the time, Eliot points out, but it takes a writer of genius to invent the formal means of articulating these changes. (We do not need to inquire too deeply into who performs this task for the early twentieth century.) In some Jacobean dramatists, we witness 'that perpetual slight alteration of language, words perpetually juxtaposed in new and sudden combinations, meanings perpetually *eingeschachtelt* into meanings, which evidences a very high development of the senses, a development of the English language which we have perhaps never equalled' (SE, p. 209).

Sensory and linguistic development are sides of the same coin. It is as though these playwrights prefigure such modernist techniques as montage, elision, estrangement and ambiguity. Cyril Tourneur's *The Revenger's Tragedy* reveals 'a highly original development of vocabulary and metric, unlike that of any other play [of Tourneur] and every other dramatist' (SE, p. 186), as the horror of human existence finds exactly the right words and rhythms to reveal itself. (We now know that one reason why the play is unlike Tourneur's other work is because it was co-authored with his colleague Thomas Middleton.)

One might suggest, then, that Eliot's subject is less language in itself than language as a record of the history of sensibility. He is in quest of what Stefan Collini calls in a different context 'a *qualitative* history of experience'.[9] The business of criticism is to evaluate various nuances of feeling, whether 'decadent' or sentimentalist, ebullient or enervated, sardonic or sublime. Certain tones and cadences are signs of a distinctive sensibility. Eliot is more interested in 'the system of Dante's organisation of sensibility' (SE, p. 275) than he is, say, in his cosmological beliefs or theological idiosyncrasies. In this sense, his criticism belongs to a body of twentieth-century writing, one which stretches from I.A. Richards, F.R. Leavis and George Orwell to Richard Hoggart and Raymond Williams, which seeks to detect in the quality of language the quality of the civilisation from which it springs. It is a distinctively English preoccupation. Eliot's interest is not so much in what a poem says – indeed, he is often remarkably indifferent to what we normally call content – as with the 'structure of emotions' it embodies. We shall see later that the phrase 'structure of feeling' is central to the criticism of Raymond Williams, an adversary of Eliot in most other respects. What is at stake for both critics is not some shapeless sprawl of emotion but precisely organised patterns of feeling. It is a question of what Eliot calls a 'logic of sensibility' (SE, p. 269).

The home of feeling is language, at least when it comes to poetry. Language, writes Raymond Williams, 'is as much the record of the history of a people as political institutions and religions and philosophical modes'.[10] The task of the poet for Eliot is not quite to purify the language of the tribe, as Mallarmé proposes, but to preserve and enrich it so that it can offer a more sensitive, diverse range of tone and feeling. Language is like a living organism which is ceaselessly mutating as well as constantly being corroded, and the literary artist is engaged in an endless battle against this deterioration, as *Four Quartets* makes clear. One reason why a language declines as it evolves is because it offers only a limited range of literary possibilities, many of which will already have been exploited by past authors. Every modern writer is in this sense belated. So though language is the poet's medium, it is also his or her antagonist. At moments of seismic historical change, we need a form of speech which is 'struggling to digest and accept new objects, new feelings, new aspects, as, for instance, the prose of Mr James Joyce or the earlier Conrad' (SE, p. 327). In Eliot's own lifetime, the name of this upheaval is modernism, and only modesty forbids him from adding his own name to those of the authors he mentions. Yet though forms need to be broken and refashioned from time to time, language imposes its own laws and limits on such transformations, determining speech rhythms and sound patterns in a way which restricts the possibilities of innovation. We are the servants of our discourse, not its masters; and the poet is simply the instrument by which it may be bequeathed by one generation to the next in the sprightliest possible shape.

The verse of the era from Marlowe to Marvell has in Eliot's eyes a subtlety and complexity which remains unmatched. From there, however, it has been downhill all the way – or at least all the way until we arrive at Eliot himself and a clutch of his modernist colleagues. All ages may be corrupt, but linguistically speaking some are more corrupt than others. Blank verse degenerates from Shakespeare to Milton, becoming less capable of expressing shades of sense and intricacies of feeling. Milton, with his outlandish Latinisms, tortuous syntax, ritualised verse forms, remoteness from everyday speech and lack of sensuous specificity, wreaks a degree of damage on the English language from which it has yet to recover. He is a 'Chinese Wall' which blocks off our return to a time when we could feel our thought as immediately as the odour of a rose. Once again, it is not inconceivable that Eliot's hostility to this Puritan regicide is bound up with a dislike of his revolutionary politics. Yet here, too, form predominates over content. By the time of John Dryden, so Eliot declares with a typically magisterial flourish, 'the mind and sensibility of England has altered' (UPUC, p. 22). There is a decline in vigour from the writings of Montaigne to the style of Hobbes, and from there to what Eliot sees as the desiccated prose of Gibbon and Voltaire. Language and affect, however, are not always so closely coupled: in the eighteenth century, poetic diction becomes more urbane but the feeling it registers grows cruder, so that with poets like Thomas Gray and William Collins a sophistication still evident in the language has faded from the sensibility.

We are speaking, in other words, of what is probably Eliot's best-known article of faith: the 'dissociation of sensibility'. The idea was seized upon so eagerly by other critics that Eliot came to profess himself both bored and embarrassed by it. It is a dissociation which supposedly set in some time in the mid-seventeenth century, marking off writers such as the Metaphysical poets and Jacobean dramatists, who are able to invest their language with a complex unity of thought, feeling and sensory experience, from later, ill-starred authors who were incapable of achieving this fusion. It is the moment when literary art signals a more general Fall into the debased modern age. It represents the defeat of royalism, the rise of secularism, the triumph of scientific rationalism, the demise of the catholicity of the church, the loss of a sense of cosmic order and the emergence of an uncurbed individualism. A turbulent civil war had beheaded the monarch, lower-class Puritanism had disrupted the church, and while some poets could think but not feel, others, mostly labelled Romantics, could feel but not think.

Viewed in this light, it becomes easier to grasp how the literary tradition can be said to bypass some of the most renowned reputations. For what that tradition really signifies, as we have suggested already, is a specific *kind* of writing, one which reflects a supposedly non-dissociated sensibility. For Dante, medieval philosophy constitutes a system of ideas which are lived, perceived, felt on the senses. The Elizabethans and Jacobeans also reveal 'a quality of sensuous thought' (ASG, p. 19). By contrast, 'Tennyson and Browning are poets, but they do not feel their thought as immediately as the odour of a rose. A thought to Donne was an experience; it modified his sensibility' (SE, p. 287). In the drama of George Chapman, 'there is a direct sensuous apprehension of thought, or a recreation of thought into feeling' (SE, p. 286). Eliot's quest is for a marriage between two meanings of the word 'sense': as meaning, but also as sensation.

The most gifted writers of Donne and Chapman's period were equipped with 'a mechanism of sensibility that could devour any kind of experience' (SE, p. 287). It was a time when 'the intellect was immediately at the tip of the senses. Sensation became word and word became sensation' (SE, pp. 209–10). We gain a sense in these authors of the necessary difficulty of poetry in a diverse, fragmented age. Poetic obscurity is thus a historical product. 'The poet must become more and more comprehensive, more allusive, more indirect, in order to force, to dislocate if necessary, language into his meaning' (SE, p. 289). Poetic language becomes peculiarly condensed, vibrant and allusive, marked by a compacting of images and spawning of associations. Eliot is speaking here of the Metaphysical poets, but he might just as well be describing his own literary work, or indeed modernist poetry in general.

The Metaphysical poet, confronted with dissonance and dissolution, seeks to forge unities out of fragments; but he does so ironically, self-consciously, aware that in a disintegrating social order these resemblances are bound to seem arbitrary and inorganic. This is what we know as the Metaphysical conceit. There is a fine example of it in the opening lines of Eliot's 'Prufrock', which present us with a notoriously incongruous image: 'Let us go then, you and I, / When the evening is spread out against the sky / Like a patient etherised upon a table'. The simile asserts an affinity at the same time as it flaunts its oddness. There is no given correspondence between its two parts, unless they are meant to be linked by the colour red (sunset and blood). They are forced into alliance, but in a way which deliberately highlights their disparity. Or, to quote Samuel Johnson's legendary description of the Metaphysical poets, as Eliot himself does in his essay on these writers, 'the most heterogeneous ideas are yoked by violence together' (SE, p. 283). Part of the meaning of Eliot's image lies in the flagrantly synthetic way in which it is manufactured. It is an example of what Samuel Taylor Coleridge calls Fancy, as opposed to the organic unities of the Imagination. In the medieval world of Dante and Aquinas, at least in Eliot's rose-tinted version of it, reality is composed of certain divinely given correspondences on which the poet may spontaneously draw. In the modern era, however, this is no longer the case, so that all relations between things become fortuitous, products of the mind rather than inherent in reality. What holds the world together is a capricious act of consciousness, which is what we have in the Prufrock simile. It is worth noting, however, that in a statement in *On Poetry and Poets* Eliot seeks to have it both ways, announcing that art 'gives us some perception of an order in life, by imposing an order upon it' (OPP, p. 93). Perhaps he means that by organising the bits and pieces of human existence into a somewhat arbitrary shape, one can allow a deeper pattern to emerge, one which is somehow given. It is not a bad description of *The Waste Land*.

There is a historical subtext to the dissociation of sensibility thesis, though it is not one which Eliot himself spells out. In the modern age, with the growth of science, rationalism, technology, commercialism, bureaucracy and the dominance of utility, language is bound to become more abstract, and thus less hospitable to poetry. Yet this verbal anaemia also inspires a Romantic revolt, which can tip the balance too far towards the subjectivist and self-indulgent. The two tendencies are sides of the same coin. As Marx points out, Utilitarianism and Romanticism are terrible twins. What is needed, then, is a mode of feeling which is toughened by being sensuously objectified, as in the objective correlative, but also a form of thought which avoids the dryly conceptual by sticking close to the senses. Eliot's conservatism leads him to be distrustful of the purely cerebral (arid blueprints are for Jacobins and Stalinists), but also to keep his distance from undisciplined splurges of sentiment.

In the end, poets are distinguished not so much by a sense of truth or beauty but by the degree of sensitivity of their psychophysical constitution. One must do more than look into the heart; one must also 'look into the cerebral cortex, the nervous system, and the digestive tracts' (SE, p. 290). We shall see a similar neurological bias in the work of Eliot's friend I.A. Richards. We are speaking of the physiology of poetry, not simply of its extractable meaning. In a striking passage, Eliot comments that Dante's sensory images suggest that 'the resurrection of the body has perhaps a deeper meaning than we understand' (SE, p. 250). 'Nowhere in poetry', he adds, 'has experience so remote from ordinary experience been expressed so concretely' (SE, p. 267). By contrast, the verse of the Carolingian dramatist Philip Massinger, who writes after the Fall in Eliot's scheme of salvation, suffers from a certain verbal pallor. Literary style should chart 'the involutions of a mode of perceiving, registering, and digesting impressions' (SE, p. 211), whereas Massinger's work is 'not guided by direct communication through the nerves' (SE, p. 215). One thinks of a couplet from 'Prufrock': 'It is impossible to say just what I mean! / But as if a magic lantern threw the nerves in patterns on a screen'.

Poetry, then, works by sensation and suggestion, not by a bloodless rationalism. If it does involve ideas, they should be fleshed out in sensory form. There is a relation between this poetic creed and the nature of ideology. The most persuasive political creeds, though abstract enough in themselves, succeed by embedding themselves in men and women's lived experience. In fact, any ruling ideology which fails to accomplish this project is unlikely to survive very long. It is thus that power converts itself into everyday culture, so that we come to obey its edicts habitually, spontaneously, by custom rather than intellectual conviction. Assumptions that are felt, Eliot writes in *After Strange Gods*, are more compelling than those that can be formulated. It is a typical article of conservative faith – conservative, because if ideas and beliefs are as immediate as the smell of lavender, then they are far harder to refute than if they can be argued over. And this spontaneous acceptance of ideas can prove convenient for the ruling powers. In any case, the view that what matters most about poetry is its sensuous specificity should not pass unquestioned, as we shall see later in the case of F.R. Leavis. It is only really with Romanticism that it comes into its own. It is scarcely the first impression we are likely to gather from reading Horace, John Clare or Robert Graves.

If language is rammed up tightly against the world, then there would seem no room for it to act as a critique of it. A critique must establish a certain distance from its object in order to appraise it. So poetic language can represent experience or reality, but it cannot pass direct judgement on it. It cannot give us the world and evaluate it at the same time. In Eliot's poetry, the author's own attitudes must therefore remain for the most part implicit, hinted at by tone, rhythm, allusion, suggestion or ironic juxtaposition. They can be shown but not said. This is fortunate, since the modern age, fatigued by preaching and propaganda, will not take easily to conceptual or didactic literary art. Poetry has become the opposite of rhetoric. We moderns, Eliot argues, distrust the kind of verse which aims to edify, instruct or persuade. His colleague I.A. Richards observes that 'disordered feelings cannot be purified by preaching'.[11] As Barry Cullen puts it, 'the new poetry has to be a reflector of fractured consciousness, not a vessel of elevated sentiment'.[12] For a doctrinal author like Eliot, this might seem to pose a problem; but we are dealing with the doctrine of a conservative, who, as we have seen, is likely to be suspicious of abstract conceptions. A discussion of general ideas is siphoned off instead into his prose, leaving a curious contrast between it and the poetry. The difference comes through most notably as one of tone.

The poetry of an integrated sensibility is one in which language is wedded to its object. The two, so to speak, form an organic society in miniature. 'Language in a healthy state', Eliot writes in an essay on the poet Swinburne, 'presents the object, is so close to the object that the two are identified' (SE, p. 327). Signs cling to their referents, unlike in *Paradise Lost* – a work which Eliot believes you have to read twice: once for the music and once for the meaning. Words and things, seamlessly unified in the work of Shakespeare or Donne, have fallen apart in the modern era, and must be stitched together by a new poetic practice. Yet this is not quite consistent with Eliot's own early poetry. At that time he was influenced by the French Symbolist movement, from which many of his critical tenets are derived: the autonomy of the artwork, its multiplicity of meaning and resistance to everyday rationality, its evocative rather than declarative nature, the elusiveness of truth, the irrelevance of authorial intentions, the central role of myth, symbol and the unconscious, the poem as a fleeting revelation of some transcendent reality. We shall see later that most of these principles are vigorously rebutted by that most ferociously anti-Symbolist of critics, William Empson.

In the Symbolists' view, the sign or word is more or less autonomous – a material reality in itself, not simply the vehicle of a meaning. Accordingly, there are passages in Eliot's poetry which appear to refer to some object or situation but which are really just verbal concoctions, self-referential snatches of language with nothing in the real world to latch on to. In 'Gerontion', for example, we read of 'Hakagawa, bowing among the Titians', but we are not meant to inquire who Hakagawa is, or what he is up to bowing among the works of a Venetian master. In 'A Cooking Egg', we encounter terms like 'red-eyed scavengers' and 'penny world', phenomena which exist only at the level of language. Phrases like this have resonances rather than referents; and since they are relieved of the burden of denotation, they are free to breed among themselves to trigger fresh reverberations in the reader's mind. Yet since the word as a thing in itself is not the same as the word as wedded to an object, it is hard to make coherent sense of Eliot's aesthetics. Both techniques materialise language, but in quite different ways.

His reflections on the place of thought or ideas in poetry are similarly inconsistent. He maintains at one point that thought, feeling and sensory experience should blend into one, but argues elsewhere that poets do not think in their work at all. Instead, they express what he calls the emotional equivalent of thought. Art should not embody a philosophy or act as a medium for argument. Wisdom is more important than theory. Dante has a coherent system of thought behind him while Shakespeare does not, but from a poetic viewpoint the distinction is irrelevant. Neither author does any real thinking, since as poets this is not their job. Shelley is plagued by too many intangible ideas for Eliot's taste. It is their abstraction that he finds offensive, he insists, not the fact that most of them are politically repugnant to him, a claim that only the most charitable of readers is likely to credit. John Donne, by contrast, probably believed nothing at all, simply picking up 'like a magpie, various shining fragments of ideas as they struck his eye' (SE, pp. 138–9), but his work is none the worse for that. Yet though Eliot is sceptical of the role of ideas in poetry, his late masterpiece *Four Quartets* is hardly short of them, and we have seen already that he upbraids the work of D.H. Lawrence for being incapable of thought. He also maintains that *Agamemnon* and *Macbeth* are as much works of intellect as the writings of Aristotle, which is hard to square with the claim that poets do not think in their verse. There is a modernist poet even finer than Eliot – Wallace Stevens – whose poems are quite often about epistemology, hardly the sort of subject that one feels as palpably as the scent of perfume.

What matters, Eliot insists, is not so much an author's beliefs as his or her 'orthodoxy of sensibility and the sense of tradition' (ASG, p. 38). Yet a writer who values such things is likely to share a number of Eliot's own convictions in any case. The reader, he declares, need not agree with a poet's opinions in order to find their work persuasive; but in case this concession opens the floodgates to the writings of too many shaggy-haired Trotskyists, he also insists on a difference between mature, well-founded beliefs (whether one endorses them or not) and feeble or childish ones, which ruin one's response to the poetry. He does not seem to recognise that what counts as mature or childish is a controversial matter, as well as sometimes hard to distinguish from what you consider true or false. Detesting a poet's ideas, he holds, is bound to affect one's estimate of their art, as opposed perhaps to simply dissenting from such notions. No doubt he has such figures as Milton and Shelley in mind. It is impossible, he holds, to sever one's personal beliefs entirely from one's response to a work of art; and though one can of course grasp a poet's views without taking them on board oneself, it is likely that absorbing the poet's vision of things at the deepest emotional level will involve committing yourself to it morally and intellectually as well. There are times when beliefs in poetry strike Eliot as having a merely pragmatic value (do they enhance the overall poetic effect?), and other times when he warns that a writer must not adopt for purely poetic reasons a system of concepts he holds to be untrue. Dante the man is not identical with Dante the poet; but if we suspected that he thought the theology behind *The Divine Comedy* was nonsensical, our enjoyment of the work would be gravely diminished. And if the views poets advance are vile or meaningless, they are not writing poetry at all. One source of these discrepancies is a clash between Eliot's poetics, which as we have seen allots a lowly place to general conceptions, and his conservative politics, which make him ill-disposed to radical ideas in poetry and anxious to rebut them. But that means accepting that there is indeed thought in poetry, which in other moods Eliot is reluctant to accept.

One of the benefits of writing like Dante against the backdrop of a taken-for-granted creed is that it can do the work of believing for you, allowing you to get on with the business of poetry. As we have seen already, William Blake supposedly lacks 'a framework of accepted and traditional ideas which would have prevented him from indulging in a philosophy of his own, and concentrated his attention on the problems of poetry' (SE, p. 322). The classical work, as we have seen, depends on just such a community of conviction; and its absence in the case of Blake leaves his hands free for private fantasy and political mischief. In a culture in which values and principles are held in common, the poet is saved a tiresome amount of intellectual labour. In Eliot's view, Samuel Johnson is a critic bred in precisely such conditions, writing as he does in the 'settled' civilisation of Augustan England. In modern times, by contrast, sociology, psychology and kindred specialisms enlarge our sense of a poem's relation to the culture as a whole; but they also involve dispute and dissent, displacing our attention from the work itself.

Genuine criticism, then, requires a common culture. So Eliot argues in an essay on Johnson in *On Poetry and Poets*. Dante, he asserts, thought in a way that was shared by every cultivated individual of his time, a perilous generalisation. Yet in *The Use of Poetry and the Use of Criticism* Eliot appears to advance just the opposite case – that it is the breakdown of such common criteria which results in the rise of criticism in the first place. 'The important moment for the appearance of criticism', he writes, 'seems to be the time when poetry ceases to be the expression of the mind of a whole people' (UPUC, p. 22). In the case of Wordsworth and Coleridge, for example, certain deep-seated historical changes mean that the critic can no longer take poetry for granted but must look into its deeper social and philosophical assumptions. Theory emerges when practices find themselves in trouble. It is when a literary or social activity can no longer take itself as natural, but is forced by historical circumstance into a new kind of self-consciousness, that criticism or theory begins to take hold. Indeed, theory *is* that self-consciousness. We only need to think hard about things when they stop working as they should. Yet criticism, Eliot maintains, can also become a problem in its own right. In a liberal pluralist society, our aesthetic enjoyment of a literary work may be at odds with our ideological censure of it; a variety of viewpoints is bound to conflict; and the din of such critical contention may drown out the music of poetic art.

It follows from this argument that in a settled culture with common beliefs, criticism would wither away. The aim of critics, like that of political radicals, is to do themselves out of a job by helping to bring about the conditions in which they would no longer be necessary. Nevertheless, while criticism still exists, it represents a communal, collaborative enterprise, rather like language and civilisation themselves. As such, it provides an antidote to an atomised society. It consists in 'the common pursuit of true judgement' (SE, p. 45); and we shall see later that F.R. Leavis will pluck from this phrase the title of one of his most influential works.

More or less single-handedly, this mild-mannered ex-banker and churchwarden inaugurated a literary and critical revolution which still reverberates across the globe. If some of his social views are offensive, and some of his critical ideas are not to be probed too rigorously, it is with his reflections on literature that a distinctively modern criticism is forged. His recasting of the English literary canon is breathtakingly bold, his cosmopolitan breadth of knowledge remarkable, and his sensibility light years removed from that of the thin-blooded, straitjacketed verse he encountered on first coming to London. He moved from Missouri to Mayfair, literary Bolshevik to national institution, in a drastic shift of allegiance and identity; yet it is hard to shake off the suspicion that in all these roles he was a consummate performer, who, like the music-hall stars he admired, never ceased to keep a canny eye on his effect on an audience, and who could always be relied upon to produce a stunning impersonation of himself.

2

I.A. RICHARDS

In his *Selected Essays*, T.S. Eliot quotes from a writer he commends as 'one of the most acute of younger psychologists', and describes him elsewhere as 'of cardinal importance in the history of literary criticism' ('The Modern Mind', RC, p. 213).[1] The psychologist in question was Ivor Armstrong Richards, who took the Cambridge English Faculty by storm in the early 1920s. The son of a works manager who was also a chemical engineer, Richards had come to Cambridge from his private school intent on studying History; but he soon concluded (to use his own words) that history was something that ought never to have happened, and decided to study Mental and Moral Sciences instead. He was to retain his hatred of the past as a saga of cruelty and destitution for the rest of his life, a loathing which contrasted sharply with his optimism about the future.

The Cambridge English Faculty of the time was not exactly a hub of rigorous critical inquiry. Sir Arthur Quiller-Couch, who held the Chair of English, spent most of his time in the Cornish village of Fowey as commodore of the local yacht club, condescending to visit Cambridge for a few weeks each term. It was his custom to address as 'Gentlemen' a lecture hall containing a large number of women, before proceeding to rhapsodise for an hour or so about the twin mysteries of the soul within and the exquisitely designed universe without. He habitually lectured in morning dress. What mattered was literary gossip, good taste and elegant *belles lettres*, not disciplined critical intelligence. T.S. Eliot, hardly a fan of professionalism, comments on the 'British dislike of the specialist' as one cause of the nation's intellectual mediocrity.[2] Towards the end of the nineteenth century, the sociologist Émile Durkheim wrote that 'the time has passed when the perfect man was he who appeared interested in everything without attaching himself exclusively to anything, capable of tasting and understanding everything, finds the means to unite and condense in himself all that was most exquisite in civilisation'.[3] The age of the dilettante was drawing to a close.

It is scarcely surprising that in the genteel-amateur milieu of Cambridge English, the young I.A. Richards considered becoming a mountain guide in the Hebrides rather than throwing in his lot with academia. (He was a highly skilled mountaineer, and once had his hair set on fire by lightning during a climb. He also forced a bear in the Canadian Rockies to back off by urinating on it from a balcony.) He was diverted from spending his life scrambling up Hebridean rock faces by being invited to lecture in the English Faculty in 1919. Like his slightly younger colleague F.R. Leavis he was paid by the head, that is, according to the number of students who attended his sessions.

Two path-breaking works, *Principles of Literary Criticism* (1924) and *Practical Criticism* (1929), became world-renowned and established their author as an international star. One might claim that he more or less single-handedly professionalised a subject which until then had consisted largely in waffle, impressionism and textual scholarship. He was also well aware of his own significance in this respect. Some of his colleagues were averse to the whole idea of evaluating literary works, as opposed to a scholarly discussion of them. The Oxford English professor Helen Gardner described such evaluation as 'a folly, if not a crime'. Richards was also one of the earliest examples of what we would call today a literary theorist, which is to say someone who feels that most literary critics fail to reflect in any systematic way on what they get up to. 'Critics', Richards writes, 'have as yet hardly begun to ask themselves what they are doing or under what conditions they work' (PLC, p. 202). From the viewpoint of a theorist, critics do not start far back enough. Whereas the critic asks (for example) whether the poem is effective, the theorist wants to know what we mean by a poem in the first place, and by what criteria we judge its success.

Richards's lectures in Cambridge were so popular that he was sometimes obliged to deliver them out of doors, perhaps the first time the university had witnessed such an event since medieval times. He visited Japan and China, conducting courses on practical criticism in Beijing, and returned to China some years later before taking up a Chair at Harvard. His frame of mind, like that of his most eminent student William Empson, was decidedly cosmopolitan. On his first visit to the East, he and his partner Dorothy first climbed in the Alps, then visited Moscow where they met Sergei Eisenstein, took the Siberian Express to Vladivostok, travelled by ship to Japan and Korea and then set out overland to China via Manchuria. The couple picked up some basic Chinese in the course of their visit. Eliot's cosmopolitanism, by contrast, was mostly confined to Europe, along with a handful of ancient Sanskrit and Buddhist texts.

Richards's international outlook was shared to a lesser degree by the Cambridge English school of the time. The Faculty, as we have seen, emerged alongside the experiments of European modernism and was by no means insulated from them. Nor was it remote from new developments in American literature and criticism. Richards himself spoke up for modernism, and was one of the first critics to champion the poetry of Hopkins and Hardy. He once smuggled a copy of Joyce's *Ulysses* into the United States, while F.R. Leavis had his collar felt by members of the Cambridge constabulary for being in possession of the novel. The matter in Leavis's case went all the way up to the Home Office, who feared that anyone degenerate enough to read the book might be a corrupting influence on the young ladies whom he taught. Since Leavis had a low opinion of Joyce, whom he described privately as a 'nasty Irishman', the incident is not without irony.

For the last four decades of his life Richards abandoned literary criticism almost entirely, attending instead to problems of pedagogy (including in high schools), world literacy, the teaching of English as a foreign language, technology and communication. Among his many anticipations of the future was his founding role in today's global industry of English-language teaching. It was communication, not criticism, he remarked, which had been his concern from the outset; and it was by this route that he passed from literary criticism to international politics. Language was the nexus between the two, since a training in foreign languages, as well as in English as a foreign language, would in his view promote international peace and understanding in an era of aggressive nationalism. He paid little regard to the structural factors (material interests, for example, or the power of ideology) which disrupt dialogue and thwart consensus. He also believed that without literacy, men and women in weaker, poorer nations were condemned to social and economic misery. His work had a profound influence on education, both in schools and universities.

Much of his time he spent promoting so-called Basic English, a simplified form of the language invented by his colleague C.K. Ogden, and founded an institute in the United States, Language Research Inc, to help propagate it. It is probable that the sinister Newspeak of George Orwell's novel *1984* is a parody of the project. Ogden was a pacifist, feminist and collaborator with James Joyce, as well as a notorious Cambridge eccentric: he deeply disapproved of fresh air and exercise, and thought conversations could be conducted more efficiently if the participants wore masks. Richards's campaign for the role of Basic English in advancing mutual understanding on a global scale, which eventually brought him to the attention of both Churchill and Roosevelt, involved him in frequent international travel and negotiations with various governments. He was intent on nothing less than reversing the curse of Babel.

The crusade also took him to the Walt Disney studios in Los Angeles, where with the help of cartoonists he created the first simplified figures for language instruction manuals, to be used in a US Navy programme for Chinese sailors. It is hard to imagine, say, T.S. Eliot at work alongside the creators of Donald Duck. Bizarrely, Richards's Basic English version of Plato's *Republic* was distributed to US troops, while the CIA was later to make use of his techniques of close verbal analysis. He was also hired by the Rockefeller Foundation to draw up a statement on the practice of reading. This most worldly of dons had morphed from academic to global activist, speaking rather grandly of his desire to unify the planet. It was an admirable vision, though one which involved the liberal-rationalist mistake that conflict is essentially a matter of miscommunication. If only we understood each other better, we would abandon our antagonisms. Among other misconceptions, this fails to account for the fact that a good many adversaries understand each other only too well, indeed conflict with each other precisely for this reason. It was not misunderstanding that caused the Wall Street crash or the rise of fascism in Richards's own day. One of the drawbacks of social media is that there is too much communication rather than too little.

As a student at Cambridge, Richards was reputed to be some-thing of an anarchist, and became a member of the celebrated Heretics society. He was, in fact, not an anarchist but a liberal, for whom freedom was perhaps the most precious value, a case sometimes easy to confuse with a more militant libertarianism. Yet in some respects his liberal creed did indeed lead him to radical conclusions. He harboured a deep suspicion of English studies, not least as a subject fit for examination, and thought it 'iniquitous, profanation, to use literature for such purposes' (FA, p. xxxiv). He also believed that scholarly research in English was largely a waste of time, and wrote in a private letter that he despised literary types. In his view, English failed to provide sufficient discipline for the intellect, and his experiments with students' capacities for critical analysis, which we shall be touching on later, convinced him that levels of proficiency in reading were so dismayingly low as to render the subject pointless as a form of education. In fact, he came to regard academic criticism as his enemy, a view shared by his colleague F.R. Leavis, and announced that 'the worst threat to the world's critical standards comes just now from the universities' (CI, p. lx). He himself was a pioneer of so-called practical criticism, as we shall see later; but he was also a literary theorist, psychologist, philosopher of language, aesthetician, educationalist, cultural commentator and second-rate poet. Given this assortment of interests, English as Cambridge conceived of it struck him as lamentably parochial.

At the same time, Richards's intellectual interests proved useful to a Faculty in search of some rather more plausible way of legitimating English as an academic subject than Quiller-Couch-like appeals to the mysteries of soul and universe. Richards's work was vital in helping to put the subject on a sound disciplinary footing. Cambridge was accordingly grateful: a later English professor there, Basil Willey, describes him as the founder of modern literary criticism, and maintains that nobody since Samuel Taylor Coleridge had done such deep-seated thinking about the subject.[4] It is true that no English critic since Coleridge had brought such fundamental concepts, or such an armoury of theoretical instruments, to bear on the study of literary works. Richards had a most un-English interest in first principles. One might claim that his work constitutes the most systematic defence of poetry to be found in the English language. Coleridge, who had similar theoretical interests and on whom Richards wrote an impressive book, was one of his most vital sources of inspiration, as was, more remotely, Confucius. In fact, in the view of some commentators, the influence of Coleridge led Richards to abandon, or at least to modify, his Benthamite ethics. Critics in the future, he declared prophetically, would feel the need for theoretical resources not previously thought to be necessary, and he himself conducted a more or less single-handed campaign against the anti-theoretical literary scholars of his own day, prominent among whom was the Oxford medievalist C.S. Lewis. Lewis once sardonically handed Richards a copy of his own work *Principles of Literary Criticism* in order to help him get to sleep.

Seen from a traditionalist standpoint, Richards's views of language are startlingly heterodox. He rejects the idea of correct usage – 'this social or snob control over language', as he calls it (PR, p. 51) – insisting instead that how people actually speak and write is also how they ought to do so. If those around you habitually drop their aitches, then it is correct usage for you to do so as well. The precept that one should use a word in the way the 'best' writers do (but who decides who is best?) strikes him as the most pernicious dogma in the teaching of English. In *The Meaning of Meaning*, he denounces as 'the Proper Meaning superstition' the idea that words are in some sense part of what they stand for, or have a fixed meaning independent of their specific uses. There is no inherent relation between a word and a thing. To imagine that such a relation exists is a species of 'word magic' – the 'primitive' belief that a name is part of what it denotes, and can conjure it up like a spiritual presence. On this view, to manipulate words is to manipulate things. For Ogden and Richards, by contrast, words only attach themselves to objects within a specific context or situation. Only when this context is considered can the connection between sign and object be established. To demonstrate the point, Richards produces a famous diagram – a picture of a triangle with 'Symbol', 'Thought' and 'Referent' (or object) at its respective corners – to show that the relation between the first and the third is always mediated by the second. (The American philosopher C.S. Peirce anticipates this insight, referring to what Richards calls the Thought as the Interpretant.)[5] To put the point another way: the relation between language and reality is always a question of interpretation, rather than one which is given, natural, immediate or intuitive. Even so, the ancient idea of word magic lives on in Richards's view in the hypostasising of certain abstractions which have a formidable power to mould reality: Church, State, Order, Liberty, Leader, Nation, Democracy and so on. In Ken Hirschkop's judgement, 'The modern version of the sacred was, in short, politics, for there was where one found abstractions worth dying and killing for'.[6] In this sense, *The*

Meaning of Meaning folds a politics wary of idols and fetishes into its theory of meaning.

Whatever the grammarians may imagine, Ogden and Richards claim, there are many different grammars used for various purposes, and grammar itself can tell you nothing of the social situation or discursive context which gives rise to an utterance in the first place. Grammarians tend to treat their own classifications as fixed and absolute, and so do logicians. They do not recognise that how you classify depends on what you are trying to do. Notions such as subject and predicate, or universal and particular, are not inherent in human thought but convenient for certain ends. Our grammatical categories ultimately reflect the way we carve up the world as part of our struggle for existence, so that thought is rooted in our biology and language is part of our bodily behaviour. If we had different bodies and sensory organisations we would inhabit a different world altogether, as no doubt congers and kangaroos do; and if we happened to be congers and kangaroos who were able to speak, our language would no doubt be unintelligible to the creatures we are right now. Our feelings and attitudes are shaped by our social and physiological needs. For Richards as for Friedrich Nietzsche, the supposedly objective structure of the world is in fact a projection of our grammar, and a different grammar would yield us a different reality. Traditional grammar teaching, which fails to grasp this point, should be banned from schools. What should be studied instead is what Richards calls in *Speculative Instruments* 'the laws of the elasticity of language' (SI, p. 80), its supple, loose-limbed nature – though one might note that if a law is elastic enough, it ceases to be a law. As a liberal, Richards is hostile to all types of rigidity and conformism. Public opinion, 'good form', social codes and conventional moral norms are alike suspect.

There is more than a touch of the obstreperous young iconoclast about the early Richards. Existing linguistic theories, he airily announces, are almost all to be jettisoned. The whole aesthetic heritage from Immanuel Kant onwards is briskly discarded. Most critical dogmas of the past are either nonsense or obsolete, and far more of the great art of the past is inaccessible to us than we care to imagine. The fact that works of art are products of their historical moment may limit their durability, which for Richards (but not, as we have seen, for Eliot) is true to some extent of Dante. The greater part of ancient Greek tragedy, like almost all Elizabethan tragic drama apart from Shakespeare, should be written off as pseudo-tragedy. The belief that there is a special aesthetic state, one clearly distinguishable from the rest of our experience, is a 'phantom'. On the contrary, 'the world of poetry has in no sense any different reality from the rest of the world and it has no special laws and no other-worldly peculiarities' (PLC, p. 70). Works of art deal in commonplace pleasures and emotions. Artists may differ from their fellow citizens, but only because the experiences they share with them are in their case more delicately organised. It is a difference of degree rather than of kind. We shall see later that F.R. Leavis similarly dismisses the whole concept of specifically literary values.

Unlike Eliot, Richards is an egalitarian rather than an elitist, maintaining that 'no man should be so situated as to be deprived of all the generally accessible values' (PLC, p. 56). As we shall see, the influence of Utilitarianism underlies this conviction that everyone should count as one, and no more than one. The most complete mode of human utterance – poetry – must be made widely available, since 'the salvation we are seeking is for all' (SI, p. 71). Mass education may be our only hope; and if ordinary men and women find modern poetry unintelligible, it is the fault of a defective social and educational system, not the upshot of their own stupidity. When it comes to culture, there is a 'gulf between what is preferred by the majority and what is accepted as excellent by the most qualified opinion' (PLC, p. 34), and protecting such standards of excellence against the debased taste of the masses is one reason why criticism needs a dose of professional rigour. Yet Richards is insistent that this gap must be narrowed. He also takes leave to doubt whether those educated in the humanities are in general more morally admirable than those who are not. Still, to read well is to cultivate one's sensibility; and if this were to happen on a broader scale, one would expect it to breed positive social effects.

What makes Richards a genuinely radical thinker, however, is the fact that he is a self-avowed materialist, and this at a time when the literary air was heavy with pseudo-religious forms of criticism. Cambridge in the 1920s, however, was peculiarly hospitable to the scientific spirit, as Richards's work testifies. Emotion and imagination are for him matters of the brain and nervous system, not of the soul. All forms of Platonic Idealism – a belief in Beauty, Goodness and Truth, for example – are sent packing, along with such supposedly outmoded metaphysical notions as essences, natures, substances, attributes, universals, eternal verities, absolute values and the like.

Humanism is to be reconstructed on a secular, scientific basis. Deeply influenced by the philosophy of William James, Richards is a pragmatist whose habit is to ask not what things are but how they work. 'An idea, or a notion', he writes, 'like the physicist's ultimate particles and rays, is known only by what it does' (PR, p. 2). Truth in a broad sense is what promotes our interests and enhances our powers. Theories are to be regarded as speculative instruments rather than ends in themselves. One is always finally obliged to go beyond a set of ideas in order to make an existential choice (is this poem really as bad as I suspect it is?) which theory itself cannot make for us. All the same, Richards sees theory, at least of an embryonic kind, as implicit even in our most apparently raw perceptions. Unlike the empiricists, he does not believe that there is first of all sensory experience, and then a translation of it into concepts. On the contrary, interpretation is at work from the outset. It goes all the way down. Besides, our perceptions and responses are shaped by our entire history, not simply by what strikes the eyeball or the eardrum at any particular moment.

Criticism, likewise, has its limits. Nowhere but in poetry, unless perhaps in mathematics, do we confront ideas so closely packed and interwoven that any investigation of them is bound to prove interminable. Not even the finest of critical instruments can unravel the intricate interactions of sound, mood, feeling, tone, pitch, pace, rhythm, cadence and so on, each of which modifies the others to generate inexhaustible possibilities which cannot be schematised. The poem represents what Richards calls in *Practical Criticism* a 'fabulous complexity'. In this sense, a poetic text is never fully closed. There will always be a spectral swarm of potential meanings around any specific reading of it. 'Inference and guesswork!' Richards remarks. 'What else is interpretation?' (PR, p. 35). Our sense of value turns on differences and affinities too microscopic to be consciously perceived, and it is here that criticism must acknowledge its incompleteness. In the end, understanding is a hazardous, hit-and-miss process.

'Man', Richards writes, 'is not in any sense primarily an intelligence; he is a system of interests' (PLC, p. 299). Like Eliot, he downgrades the intellect while upgrading the nervous system. Before we come to grasp the meaning of a poem, we are already responding subliminally to the sound and texture of its words, to the feel of their movement, to their tones and rhythms, and all this before the mind has had time to spring into action. The parallel with Eliot's similarly neurological poetics is plain. The difference lies in the fact that whereas for Eliot the significant life of a poem is conducted at a visceral and neural level far deeper than the mind, the materialist Richards suspects that the mind and the nervous system are actually identical. We are our bodies – more specifically, our neurological constitution. In the teeth of the quasi-religious poetics of such currents as Symbolism, aestheticism and the American New Criticism, he is a thoroughly naturalistic thinker who places a supreme value on art while at the same time finding nothing in the least transcendent about it.

Poetry, then, is too unfathomably complex to be scientifically explained. But Richards does not rule out the possibility that when the science that matters to him most – psychology – has evolved from its currently rudimentary condition into a more sophisticated state, such comprehension might be in principle within our grasp. Literary criticism is, or should be, a branch of the science of psychology. Indeed, Richards seemed to believe that in the future the sciences may take over from the humanities, so that we might one day be able to lend our humanistic values a scientific foundation. All the same, poetry for Richards is a far richer form of communication than science, which is necessarily reductive. In fact, it is the finest form of communication of which we are capable. But this is not to endorse the churlish, sometimes snobbish distaste for science of the traditional humanist, traces of which can be found among the post-modernists of the present. By the early twentieth century, science had become such a dominant discourse in the West that some humanists felt obliged either to beat it or join it. F.R. Leavis chose the former strategy, while Richards, like the structuralists and semioticians some decades later, opted for the latter.

Psychology studies the mind, but how is the mind accessible to us? Richards's answer to this question is really Eliot's as well: in language. It is through language that we learn certain nuances of sentiment and desire, along with our concepts and values; and it is in language, with its intricacies and ambiguities, that we find the most faithful image of our minds. 'The whole abstract world of moral values', Richards writes in his essay 'Our Lost Leaders', 'is held for us by a framework of words' (CSW, p. 337). As the critic Joseph North puts it, 'language [is] the sediment of a collective historical effort to come to terms with the world'.[7] It encodes the ways in which humanity has classified and controlled its environment over the millennia, so that for Richards, as for his Cambridge contemporary Ludwig Wittgenstein, to imagine a language is to imagine a practical form of life. Language is the psychological record of humanity, the imprint of our history in sound and sign, rather as for Eliot it represents a storehouse of riches accumulated over vast tracts of time. And since other forms of continuity with the past (family, church, community and the like) are being undermined by modernity, language in Richards's view is rapidly becoming the main rapport we have with our ancestry. In his eyes, however, there is no one strand of continuity at stake here – no one venerable tradition *à la* Eliot, but a prodigal diversity of legacies. It is the difference between a liberal pluralist and a conservative.

Literary criticism concerns itself among other things with the evaluation of literary works. Yet how does one come up with a materialist concept of value? Formulating such a theory ranks among Richards's most innovative moves, though it is not, as we shall see, without its problems. Taking his cue in *Principles of Literary Criticism* from the ethical thought of Jeremy Bentham, founder of the creed of Utilitarianism in the late eighteenth century, he sees the human mind as divided between two different kinds of impulse: appetencies (or desires) on the one hand and aversions on the other; and whatever satisfies the former is valuable. To live well is a matter of ordering one's appetencies so that as many of them as possible can be gratified. Morality is essentially a question of organisation. Value is economy. Rather as a virtuous action for Bentham is one which promotes the greatest happiness of the greatest number of individuals, so for Richards an effective work of art is one which fulfils the greatest number of appetencies. One problem for Bentham is that ethics must necessarily be retrospective: you can only know how many people's happiness was promoted by looking back at the consequences of your action. This is not a problem for the Richardian critic confronted with a poem.

More precisely, what is valuable is what fulfils an appetency without frustrating some equally or more important want. Richards clearly needs to define the word 'important' in a way which avoids an appeal to some non-Utilitarian standard such as duty, the law of God, love of humanity, the ultimate Good, the revelation of some higher Truth and so on. He is impatient with terms like 'ought', 'must', 'right', 'wrong', along with most of the rest of conventional moral discourse. So the importance of an impulse is defined instead in terms of how far its non-fulfilment would frustrate other impulses – the damage, in short, that it would wreak within the whole system. It is, in effect, a quantitative ethics, though Richards denies this charge. The most desirable organisation is the least wasteful, meaning one in which least is sacrificed and suppressed and as much as possible of one's personality is realised. Fullness of life is Richards's moral ideal, as it is for F.R. Leavis. To live morally is to live not dutifully or self-denyingly but to flourish in the plenitude of one's powers. Immanuel Kant would have demurred, but Aristotle, Hegel and Marx would have largely agreed. 'The ultimate value of equilibrium', Richards writes in *The Foundations of Aesthetics*, 'is that it is better to be fully rather than partially alive' (FA, p. 77). The less lop-sided you are, the more experience you can savour.

What bearing does all this have on poetry, and more particularly on how good or bad a poem might be? The answer is that good poetry represents the finest, most delicate and efficient organisation of impulses available to humanity. Words, Richards observes, are not a 'medium in which to copy life. Their true work is to restore life to order' (PR, p. 90). In everyday existence, our impulses tend to be confused and disorganised, not least in the turbulent modern era; but in art they enjoy a complete systematisation, achieving an equilibrium which brings the whole personality into play. The result is a feeling of wholeness, fullness, clarity, unity, freedom, integration, poise, balance, stability and autonomy. Richards speaks of the 'organisation of our feelings', as Eliot writes of the 'structure of emotions' and Raymond Williams would later coin the phrase 'structure of feeling'. It is not hard in Richards's case to feel the influence of Confucius behind this poetics. Art is a form of mental hygiene. It allows us to maintain a certain poise and equanimity amid the shocks and buffetings of everyday life. In fact, the poise in question may be literal, as when Richards tells us with a straight face that to achieve balance in one area of one's life may have salutary effects in another, such as the ability to stand on one foot without unsteadiness. Reading Goethe can do wonders for your imitation of a stork.

Art, then, does not instruct us in how to live by what it says, but by what it shows – by its unity, harmony and equipoise. One might say that its very disinterestedness is didactic. The supreme value is to find oneself in a state of perfect self-possession and self-sufficiency, which Richards also regards as the highest form of freedom; and it is this that a successful poem or painting accomplishes. It is from its form rather than its content that we learn how to live. Richards is disdainful of what he calls 'message hunters', meaning those who raid literary works for their moral content. The moral lesson they fail to recognise is the poem itself. A poem is not a sermon or bulletin but an experience put into words; and in Richards's view its words are not just expressive of the experience but constitutive of it. It is as though the experience forms in the act of communication, and cannot be abstracted from it.

There are problems with Richards's Benthamite case, as there are with any ethical theory. It seems to assume, for example, that all our so-called impulses are inherently positive, and that only the frustration of them is wrong. William Empson, who accepted this view of value in general, inquires in his book *Milton's God* whether it applies to the desire to inflict pain. It is, in short, too innocent a view of the mind, compared, say, with the Gothic horrors that Freud excavates; but Richards, despite his Eliot-like belief that poetry springs from the deepest roots of the psyche, harbours a typically English scepticism of psychoanalysis, one common among academic psychologists both then and now. Yet if all our appetencies are intrinsically worthy, what of my overpowering urge to strangle my bank manager? Richards would retort that such an appetency is illicit because it thwarts a number of my other desires. But there is also the question of the bank manager's right to fulfil his needs, which would not be easy if he were dead.

Besides, it is strongly counter-intuitive to claim that, say, genocide is wicked simply because it throws us into psychic disarray. The theory is curiously self-centred. The fact is that genocide is immoral because of what it does to others, not primarily because of what it does to the perpetrators. Richards argues that unjust or aggressive behaviour deprives us of a whole range of important values, so that in behaving injuriously to others we inflict damage on ourselves. But not all those who harm their fellow humans are morally bankrupt themselves. There is always the case of the sensitive, compassionate con man. To commit a monstrous act does not necessarily mean that one is a moral monster. It is also far too convenient for the virtuous to claim that deep down the villainous are miserable because of their wickedness. Anyway, one could tolerate a spot of moral misery if it meant living for the rest of one's days off the proceeds of a lucrative bank robbery.

Would we say that Martin Luther King was morally admirable because he had satisfactorily organised his psychological impulses? We commend King because he dedicated his life to others, but this kind of value plays little role in Richards's system. He acknowledges the importance of friendly relations with others, but this does not take one far beyond the Senior Combination Room. It overlooks the fact that the deepest self-fulfilment is reciprocal, achieved in and through the self-realisation of others. The name we give to this mutuality at its most fruitful is love. The name Marx gives to it politically is communism. Richards's ethics, by contrast, are too individualistic to have such a rich social dimension, as indeed one might expect of a liberal thinker. He is adamant that each person's good is an absolute end in itself. He also opens the door to moral relativism by declaring that what is valuable for one individual may not be so for another. The case works well enough if one is thinking of, say, tennis or chocolate pancakes, but looks less persuasive if one has justice or truth-telling in mind. The argument applies to litera-ture as well. Different readers respond to the same poem in different ways, but they do so, Richards is careful to add, only within certain limits. Otherwise one is faced with the embarrassment of there being as many *Waste Lands* as there are readers.

Richards denies that his theory of impulses is calculative and mechanistic, but it is hard to see how he can plausibly do so. If impulses are to be in equilibrium, then this must surely involve some form of calculation. William Empson remarks in his facetious way that psychologically speaking we have about a million impulses a minute, so that the calculations involved might be pretty heavy. In any case, how does one identify an impulse? And how can it be 'satisfied' by a poem? One reason why Richards denies that appetencies are calculable is because he sometimes seems to think of them as innumerable, fathomlessly complex and intricately interrelated. But there may be two meanings of the word 'impulse' at work here: on the one hand, the common-or-garden sense of an urge to laugh or scream, and on the other hand the more technical sense of electric and chemical charges along the nerve fibres, which is presumably what Empson has in mind. Yet Richards, the champion of practical criticism, provides us with little actual analysis of poetry to demonstrate this theory of value, thus leaving a host of questions unresolved.

'Order' is a key term for Richards, as it is for Eliot. The most commendable individual is one who is stable, balanced, controlled and coherent. It sounds dismayingly like a British District Commissioner in Punjab. Along with these virtues goes a distaste for inefficiency, the vice of those who fail to coordinate their impulses in the most productive way. Perhaps one can detect the son of the works manager in this aversion to waste. In a calculatedly outrageous comment, Richards writes of John Keats that he 'is a more efficient poet than [Ella Wheeler] Wilcox, and that is the same thing as saying that his works are more valuable' (PLC, p. 182). It was remarks of this kind that inspired T.S. Eliot to write in the journal *The Dial* that Richards's system of thought was rather like a mental version of a Roneo Steel Cabinet. Yet why should order, balance and economy always be viewed as positive? Richards commonly writes as though the greatest danger to civilisation is chaos, a claim which is far from obvious. In his own time, a more immediate peril was posed by a pathological version of order itself – by the autocratic regimes of Hitler, Franco, Mussolini and other dictators, which were nothing if not highly organised. Scientology and the North Korean secret police are no doubt superbly organised as well, but this is no reason to admire them.

It is true that the young Richards was writing in the wake of the First World War, a period in which he feared that the whole fabric of Western civilisation was unravelling at the seams and heading for unprecedented catastrophe; but his contrast between order and chaos is far too simplistic. The economic depression of the 1930s certainly gave birth to a degree of disorder in Britain, not least in the form of hunger marches and political battles in the street; but much of this disorder was in a just cause, while the dominant social order was destroying livelihoods and entire communities. Richards, however, seems to have perceived only tumult and futility around him.

As for equilibrium, of which Richards never ceases to sing the praises, there is no great merit in striking a judicious balance between, say, racism and anti-racism. In this sense, disinterestedness itself can be covertly prejudiced. The centre ground is not always the appropriate place to stand, not least when it comes to the conflict between, say, oil companies and ecologists. Liberals like Richards tend to be wary of partisanship, as though all commitment is cripplingly one-sided. But liberalism itself champions freedom over tyranny, the diverse over the monolithic, flexibility over intransigence and so on. The French Resistance was quite properly partisan, and so are those who object to forced marriages and domestic violence. Richards, by contrast, sees poetry as the very model of disinterestedness, or 'impersonality' as he sometimes calls it, viewing an object from a diversity of angles, no more predisposed to one perspective than to another. But this is surely not true. A great many poems privilege one viewpoint over another, and may be quite right to do so. Tennyson's 'In Memoriam' does not regard a burst of uproarious laughter at the death of the poet's friend Arthur Hallam as just as appropriate as tears. And what of 'committed' art? Does Picasso's 'Guernica' portray the bombing of a Basque town in a soberly dispassionate way, or feminist theatre present a non-committal view of misogyny?

The well-organised, self-sufficient human subject sounds uncomfortably like Bourgeois Man. It is also a psychologised, 'scientific' version of a familiar form of classical humanism, for which the virtuous life consists of realising your various powers and capabilities in as full, harmonious and well-rounded way as possible. This, one presumes, is what the critic Geoffrey Hartman has in mind when he describes Richards as 'a classicist of the nervous system'.[8] He has dressed an antique ethics in modern scientific garb. The greatest Victorian advocate of this vision is John Stuart Mill, not least in his magnificent essay *On Liberty*. Yet the well-rounded individual is a specimen of humanity which the sociologist Max Weber fears is fading from the world, and one might wonder in any case whether well-roundedness is always worth aiming for. What of the individual who shuns all other activities in pursuit of a single goal, and in doing so produces the finest tuba playing or most spectacular snooker of their time? In any case, there is no reason to assume that our capacities are mutually harmonious. It is also a standpoint more appropriate to the contemplative rather than active individual, since action involves predilection, orientation, the exclusion of certain possibilities for the sake of others. The case does not fare particularly well if one starts from the self as agent. If the truth is one-sided, as Marx argues, so are our practical interventions in the world.

One might claim that Richards makes use of a radical theory, in the sense of a materialist one, for conservative ends: the need to preserve order. Like many a liberal (though a left-leaning one himself), he tends to assume that discord is inherently undesirable. This is why the supreme achievement of the poem is to reconcile antitheses and resolve contradictions. Yet some antagonisms are surely essential, and seeking to resolve them can be far from impartial. A struggle between democrats and neo-Nazis is unavoidable, as is one between patriarchs and feminists. Conflict can be productive as well as injurious, as with slaves who rise up against their masters. It is usually in the interests of those in power that such conflict should be quelled. No doubt it would come as a relief to Prince

Charles if his critics ceased to object to his pampered, petulant behaviour and were united in their esteem for his wisdom. Liberal thinkers like Richards tend to overlook the question of whose interests are served by order and reconciliation. Ideology has been defined as the imaginary resolution of real contradictions, and it is this, in effect, that Richards sees poetry as achieving.

The 1920s were this critic's most productive years, the period when he was at the peak of his form. Yet they were also a time when Europe had felt the impact of the various artistic avant gardes (Futurism, Constructivism, Dadaism, Expressionism, Surrealism and the like); and these groups were not out to resolve contradictions in the name of stability. On the contrary, most of them produced works of art which were dissonant, fragmented and self-divided, staging antagonisms rather than resolving them. Far from cultivating a sense of wholeness and serenity in an audience, they sought to shatter their routine certainties, and in doing so to place them in a more critical relationship to the prevailing social order.

In culturally traditionalist Britain, by contrast, there was little such artistic experiment, and Richards's criticism reflects the fact. Western civilisation, he held, was enduring its greatest historical change ever, with the development of science, technology, mass culture, secularism and global warfare; but human psychology has still to catch up with these transformations. This is not far from the vision of the various European avant gardes; but whereas they are intent on using their art to produce a revolutionised human subject, one adapted to a fragmented, strife-ridden world, Richards asks how the subject is to maintain its classical poise and balance in the midst of this historical upheaval. His answer, in a word, is poetry. Like the avant gardists, he calls for the evolution of a thoroughly modern mind, one with the suppleness to switch tack, process dissonant bits of sense data and undergo rapid shifts of stance; yet the point is to be capable of this while retaining one's composure.

It is important to see that Richards's notion of art is a non-cognitive one. It is not the function of poetry to yield us any kind of knowledge. It is more of a form of therapy than a mode of understanding. Tragedy, he remarks in a deliberately provocative comment, doesn't persuade us that all is right with the world, but that all is right with our nervous system. It does so chiefly by harmonising our antithetical responses of pity and fear. There is a sense, then, in which art never allows us to get outside of ourselves. In one sense, to be sure, poetry is something we use for real-life ends. It is not simply an end in itself, but shows us how to live. Yet it fulfils this function not by being didactic or moralistic but simply by being itself. It is its autonomy and self-completion which teach us how to be human, the aim of life being simply to realise one's being as fully as possible. The barriers between the aesthetic, the moral and the social are thus dismantled.

To call art non-cognitive means that though literary works appear to make propositions about the world, they really present the reader with what Richards calls pseudo-statements. Pseudo-statements may be true, as when a novel informs us that the port of Rijeka is in Croatia. But this is not the point. Propositions like this earn their keep in a work of art only by the part they play in releasing and organising our impulses – or what Richards calls our attitudes, meaning our disposition to act in a certain way. They are not offered simply as information, and neither are 'moral' statements such as 'All the world's a stage', 'A terrible beauty is born' or 'We must love one another or die'. The correct response to such assertions is not 'How true!' or 'What a load of rubbish!'. Instead, we are invited to grasp them as part of a larger poetic context in which our impulses are balanced and harmonised; and as far as that goes, a piece of blatant nonsense might do just as well. There can even be mutually contradictory references or systems of reference in a poem, since truth in the everyday sense is not at stake. Behind this case one can detect the presence of Matthew Arnold, who sought to combat the growing atheism of the Victorian masses by claiming that propositions such as 'There is a Divine Being' may be factually false, but that this is to mistake the force of such claims. Their purpose is to reinforce moral values such as reverence, awe and obligation. The socially disruptive consequences of religious scepticism might thus be avoided. Religion for Arnold becomes a species of edifying poetry, rather as for Richards poetry becomes a form of redemptive religion. The idea of pseudo-statements has its source in the Death of God.

On this view, the 'truth' of a poetic statement is measured by its internal appropriateness – by how it cooperates with other aspects of its context to evoke a certain response. The poet's control of our thoughts, Richards observes, is often his or her main way of controlling our sentiments. As with Eliot, the role of the intellect is played down, which is not to say that the meaning of a poem is unimportant. Its importance, however, lies in the way it can evoke feelings, just as rhythm, tone, rhyme, mood, metre and so on may do as well. Poetic language for Richards is emotive rather than referential. More precisely, it is language in which the latter is subordinated to the former. The emotive includes not simply feelings but moods, attitudes, appraisals and beliefs. You can have emotive beliefs, in the sense of convictions which satisfy some impulse or other, without assenting to such convictions intellectually. The cry 'Justice will be done!' is a way of stimulating certain passions and dispositions, not a verifiable or falsifiable prediction of what will happen. 'Referential' for Richards really means 'factual' or 'empirical', and the paradigm of this form of language is science. Scientific propositions are supposed to be emotionally neutral. Chemistry textbooks do not tend to provoke great surges of lust or loathing in their readers. In science, the mind is subjected to things, while in the emotive realm the mind moulds things to its own ends and desires.

Even so, Richards understands well enough that the neutrality of science is relative – indeed, we shall see later that he regards science as one myth among many. There are situations (performing brain surgery, for example) in which to be dispassionate is essential. The same goes for much that takes place in the laboratory. A lack of feeling is by no means always objectionable. One does not want one's dentist to become frustrated and enraged in trying to pull a tooth, placing a foot against your chest for extra leverage. Even so, science has an emotive and evaluative dimension. Brain surgeons would no doubt feel that they were wasting their time if they believed that human life was entirely worthless. In writing a scientific paper, one is providing factual information to others for certain purposes within a broader social context; the facts themselves are inevitably selective; and they are established only within certain conceptual frameworks which are historically specific. Besides, science (though Richards does not comment on the fact) reveals phenomena of breathtaking beauty, and can do so with something of the aesthetic elegance and imaginative brio of the finest works of art. There is, then, no hard-and-fast distinction between the emotive and the referential, and probably no purely referential statement. Simply to convey factual information raises the question of why you are doing so, what you hope to achieve by it, why you are choosing to focus on these facts and not others and so on.

All the same, there is a difference between saying 'It's just turned red' and 'He's a lousy Red'. There is a working distinction between the emotive and the referential, even if it is not set in stone; and for the pragmatist Richards, the fact that a distinction does some productive work is enough to justify its existence. The difference, however, is never an absolute one. In poetry, feeling and meaning are always mutually modifying. Perhaps this represents Richards's response to Eliot's dissociation of sensibility. In any case, it is not always easy to distinguish what we are thinking from what we are feeling, or to demarcate either from what we want to do. Most uses of language in Richards's view mix the emotive and referential (or 'symbolic', as he sometimes confusingly called it); and the purely referential, if there is such a thing, constitutes a minor part of our speech. We have, he remarks, enormously exaggerated the importance of factual propositions. Sentences like 'An irregular heart rhythm can be effectively treated by the judicious use of bisoprolol fumarate' are not typical of our daily discourse, not even in health centres. Ludwig Wittgenstein was another who saw the language game of reference as a misleading model for language as a whole, which is not primarily propositional. In most of our verbal activity, greeting, joking, thanking, cursing, questioning, disputing and so on tend to trump the indicative. Some commentators on Richards claim that he finally overcomes the distinction between the emotive and the referential by means of the Coleridgean idea of Imagination, which represents both an emotional revelation and a form of truth.

It is not true, then, that the world is carved down the middle between facts and feelings, or facts and values. This is not only because facts can be identified only within conceptual frameworks which are by no means value-free. It is also because there are argu-ably such things as moral facts, which constitute a category distinct from both scientific observations and emotional responses. Richards himself would not endorse this claim. When it comes to moral matters, he is a so-called emotivist who holds that moral values, far from being objective, simply register the way we feel about certain forms of behaviour. For an emotivist, there is a factual situation – let's say, a man hanging a child – and then a subjective response to it, such as 'This is wrong'. For a moral realist, by contrast, the wrongness of the action is not simply a question of what you and I happen to make of it. It inheres in the action itself. The moral realist might even be able to judge whether an action is moral or immoral simply by looking at a photograph of it – though in the case of someone hanging a child you would need to know whether he was of sound mind in order to call it a crime, which a photograph would not establish. On this theory, however, hanging a child remains immoral even if there is universal agreement that there can be no more supremely virtuous way to behave. On this (disputable) view, it is possible for everyone to be mistaken in moral affairs, just as everyone once believed that the world was flat. There was, after all, a time when torture was almost universally acceptable. To call an act 'murder' is to claim that it is a fact that it is murder. Murder is not just in the mind. It is not a question of a neutrally describable act plus a subjective evaluation of it. Fact and value cannot be neatly divided, as both the positivists and the emotivists claim from opposite sides of the fence.

For the moral realist, then, moral assertions can be said to be true or false, just like descriptive ones. There may be interminable debates over whether a particular piece of behaviour is reckless or prudent, generous or self-serving, but it is the facts we are wrangling about, not our feelings. It follows on this theory that when someone announces that 'A terrible beauty is born' it would make perfect sense to reply 'No, it isn't', just as 'Give me a break!' would be a coherent enough response to 'All the world's a stage'. It is part of the critic's task (though not in Richards's opinion) to pass judgement on such assertions – to inquire into whether a literary work reveals some important moral truths, which may be one reason why we rate it highly. Conversely, if a poem or novel strikes us as full of silly, vicious or wrong-headed moral assumptions, this might limit our enjoyment of it as much as would a supposedly realist work which for no obvious artistic purpose continually got the topography of

Liverpool grotesquely wrong. Richards concedes that a truly offensive moral statement can ruin the aesthetic effect of a poem, but maintains even so that a false moral assertion might serve to organise our psyches more efficiently than a true one. One of the most vital functions of poetry, he believes, is to deepen our sensitivity to language in an age in which advertising and political propaganda have grown insidiously powerful; yet this is ironic, since in advertising and propaganda what matters is not so much what you say as the emotive effects it produces, which is also true for the most part of Richards's conception of poetry.

There is a relation between Richards's concept of pseudo-statements and the nature of ideology, in the sense of a body of feelings and ideas which helps to support an objectionable form of power. Not all ideological statements are false: it is true, for example, that the Queen of England is a conscientious, hard-working woman, not much given to shoplifting and vandalising police stations. But someone who thought this point worth making would probably be using it to help justify the institution of monarchy, rather than simply providing a piece of information. As with Richards's pseudo-statements, it is the way the proposition behaves within a larger context which counts, not its inherent truth or falsehood. The slogan 'White Lives Matter' states a truth; but it is also racist, since it was dreamt up to denigrate the Black Lives Matter movement.

As a pragmatist, Richards believes that words signify nothing in themselves. Words acquire meaning only when they are used by speakers for a specific purpose. When it comes to language, he is also a resolute anti-essentialist: terms like 'poetry' and 'aesthetic', for example, have no fixed, inherent meaning but cover all the things known by those names for all kinds of reasons. The theory is technically known as nominalism, and involves various problems which Richards fails to address – one of the more obvious being why, if all the things we call elephants have nothing in common except the name 'elephant', we call them all elephants. Words for Richards correspond not to things, but to thoughts and feelings – or as the linguist Ferdinand de Saussure would put it, to signifieds (concepts) rather than to referents (objects or situations in the world). The study of signs, for which Richards uses the unlovely word 'semasiology', must be placed at the heart of science and philosophy, though the less ungainly term that would emerge some decades later was semiotics. In this way as in others, he is something of a prophet.

All meaning, then, is contextual: a single phrase activates the whole of language rather as a motion of one's hand involves nearly the whole system of muscles. Of no type of language is this truer than poetry, in which each word is shaped and sustained by all the others in a process that Richards, stealing a term from the poet John Donne, calls 'interinanimation'. Words, he believes, gain their effect from the multiple contexts in which they are used, so that they are the means by which different discursive powers exerted in different situations may be brought together. They are nodes of diverse forces. The philosopher Thomas Hobbes points out rather more pessimistically in his work *The Elements of Law* that because the contexts in which words occur are so variable, it is hard to rescue them from equivocation and ambiguity. One reason why Hobbes believed in an absolute sovereignty was because it was needed to determine precise meanings.

Richards distinguishes between four aspects of discourse: intention, feeling, tone and sense (or meaning). The first three he sometimes groups together as 'gesture', which can predominate over sense. By intention he seems to mean less a mental act on the part of an author than the way a piece of language is organised to produce an effect, which is publicly available to us in the way that a so-called mental act is not. The 'intention' of a chair is the way it is structured in order to be sat on. One may speak of the intentions of the poem itself – the way it deploys certain techniques to attain certain effects – but not in Richards's view of the poet, who may not remember what he or she intended, or who intended a number of different, perhaps mutually contradictory things, or who had nothing much in mind except the act of writing. The American New Critics, much influenced by Richards's thinking, would adopt this idea of intentionality. Tone is first defined as implying an attitude to the reader, but later expanded to include an attitude to the subject matter itself. In the case of all speech or writing, Richards insists, one must pay due attention to the mode, occasion, context and purpose.

In *The Philosophy of Rhetoric*, Richards argues that a piece of language can be understood only in terms of the complete utterance. It is not a question of understanding the meaning of single words and then building them like bricks into an edifice. 'Free, discursive thinking, and its expression', he writes in *Interpretation in Teaching*, 'are much more widely serviceable to us than the strict, explicit, checkable articulation of discrete, separately definable meanings' (IT, p. 302). Meaning, whether poetic or otherwise, results from 'the interplay of the interpretative possibilities of the whole utterance' (PR, p. 37). This includes words which lurk unspoken in the background, so that the meaning of a term, like the job of a doorman at the Ritz Hotel, may depend quite as much on what it keeps out as what it allows in. In fact, all signification involves such absence, since we understand a word by calling to mind some concrete context in which it makes sense but which is not present here and now. The word, so to speak, is an abridgement of this context, a sign standing for what is lacking. Even experiences can act as signs, in the sense that they, too, evoke past contexts.

In all these respects, Richards anticipates what would later be called discourse theory, as well as modern hermeneutics or the art of interpretation. He even prefigures the thought of Jacques Derrida in claiming that the meaning of words is always deferred or suspended, awaiting those phrases which come after them. Words have no meaning in isolation from other words; and if their sense seems stable, it is only because of the constancy of their contexts. It is context alone which lends meaning some firm foundation, a view which is at least as old as the thought of St Augustine. The same applies to feelings and attitudes. But contexts themselves are not always easy to determine. In which of a host of potential settings should one situate a word, and where do such settings begin and end? Context can sometimes be called upon to do too much work, as in such familiar self-apologias as 'The phrase "disgusting little hypocrite" that I used of you was taken out of context'.

It belongs to the nature of a sign to be portable, capable of being shifted from one location to another; and the fuzziness of meaning which can result from this, far from being a defect, is part of what makes it work. In his *Philosophical Investigations*, Ludwig Wittgenstein compares speaking a 'pure' language to trying to walk on ice, and recalls us instead to what he calls the rough ground of our everyday speech. (There are, incidentally, a good many points of contact between Richards's ideas and Wittgenstein's, though Richards, who found Wittgenstein's autocratic manner distasteful, denies that he was influenced by him.) In his study of Coleridge, Richards speaks of the 'roominess' of certain meanings, a theme which runs throughout his work. He is interested in how certain key terms like 'being', 'cause', 'have', 'same' and so on shift their meanings – an interest which, as we shall see, is inherited by William Empson in *The Structure of Complex Words*, as well as by Raymond Williams in his *Keywords*. Meaning is fluid, diverse, multiple and sometimes impossible to pin down. We find ambiguity almost everywhere. There is no one correct construction of any sentence, since its sense depends on its various uses. In fact, Richards published a popular work, *How To Read A Page*, devoted to this subject.

Perhaps Richards, like the post-structuralists who follow in his wake, makes too much of semantic instability. Against the phantom of immutable meanings he wields his doctrine of Multiple Definition, and there are times when this is obviously appropriate. The word 'lunette', for example, can mean an arched aperture or window in a domed ceiling, a crescent-shaped or semi-circular alcove containing a painting or statue, a fortification with two faces forming two flanks and a projecting angle, a holder for the consecrated host in a monstrance or a ring on a vehicle by which it can be towed. Yet words like 'marmalade' or 'myxomatosis' are a lot less pliable. Besides, if words completely changed their sense when shuttled from one context to another, it is hard to see how a small child could learn to speak. Children pick up language not by learning words in isolation but by grasping how they are deployed in certain practical situations; but if there were no continuity across such situations, they would surely be at a loss. Language involves both identity and non-identity, as is evident enough when we claim that the same word is used in different ways. Pure difference would be no more intelligible than pure identity.

As Michael Moriarty remarks, 'one wonders how the sign could be adapted and its novelty in context assimilated if there were not some relatively stable unit there to be recognised on the semantic level'.[9] In 'The priest placed the host in the lunette' and 'the mechanic looped the tow-rope through the lunette', the word 'lunette' alters its meaning entirely. Yet this is not the case with 'The finest marmalade on the market is undoubtedly Frank Cooper's Oxford thick cut brand' and 'In a moment of madness he would come to regret, he emptied the jar of marmalade down the police officer's trousers'. The importance of context is a matter of degree. Nor do all contexts carry equal weight. 'Dog' can mean all sorts of things, but its most common reference is to a species of animal.

Language, Richards argues, 'is the supreme organ of the mind's self-ordering growth . . . an instrument for controlling our becoming'

(SI, p. 9). It is the means of all our distinctive development, 'of every-thing in which we go beyond the other animals' (PR, p. 88). Elsewhere, he calls it 'man's chief coordinating instrument of the service of the most integral purposes of life' (CI, p. 176), and announces that linguistics is the most extensive and fundamental of all inquiries. Statements like these are typical of what one might call the linguistic revolution of the twentieth century, one which may well have inflated the role of language in the act of stressing its centrality. The other animals live primarily by their sensory experience, but it is a mistake, Richards rightly considers, to think of language in these terms. Sensory images, for example, are not essential for verbal communica-tion. Those who think so fall victim to the picture theory of language. But what picture pops into your head when someone says 'Hi there!' or 'Can you come back next Wednesday?' What visual image is conjured up by 'To be or not to be, that is the question'? There are, however, what Richards calls 'tied' images, meaning those which are produced by the physical process of language, its sounds, rhythms and textures. An 'auditory' image is the sound of words in the mind's ear, while an 'articulatory' image is the feel of how it would be to speak them, the sensation they make in the mind's lips, tongue and throat. Other forms of imagery he calls 'free'. As far as the physical process of language goes, it is worth noting that Richards was said to be one of the most superlative speakers of verse of his time. There is a contrast between his talent in this respect and his charmless, rather bloodless prose style.

Richards's reservations about sensory images came at a time when there was much literary preoccupation with the sensuous or concrete. One thinks of the Imagist poets, Eliot's poetics or the criticism of F.R. Leavis. On this view, language is at its most forceful when it appears as dense and palpable as things themselves, conveying their distinctive flavour and texture. But it is not a defect of the word 'apple' that it does not convey the tang and chunkiness of the fruit itself. It is not supposed to. Words are not to be mistaken for things. Richards also points out that the concrete, which we usually imagine as simple and immediate, is in fact complex. It derives from a Latin word meaning 'to grow together', and signifies the convergence of a number of different features. Thus what makes a piece of paper a 'concrete' entity rather than an 'abstract' one is the fact that it is square, pink, flimsy, lightweight, semi-transparent and so on. The abstract, by contrast, is a more simple notion. This, as it happens, is precisely the definition of the concrete offered by Karl Marx in his *Grundrisse*, a work that was still undiscovered when Richards was writing.

There is, then, no need for language to evoke visual, aural or tactile images in order to work. Indeed, words represent the meeting-point of types of experience which in some cases could never be combined in sensation or intuition. You can have a garbage can which makes an excellent prime minister at the level of language, but not in the everyday sensory world. In this sense, language frees us from being imprisoned within our senses by opening up possibilities which a slug could not imagine. In fact, a slug cannot imagine very much at all, since to dream up alternative scenarios depends on having language. Even so, slugs have their own form of intelligence, which may lack a certain Einsteinian grandeur but which Richards ought to take note of more than he does. This is because he contends at one point in his work that there is no such thing as non-verbal intelligence. Perhaps he never encountered a spaniel or a one-year-old child. The linguistic views of a number of modern philosophers may have been shaped by the fact that they had little or no acquaintance with children. It is also true that the body has its own intelligence, of which the mind may know nothing.

Richards has a pioneering approach to the concept of metaphor. Far from treating it as a mere embellishment, or as a deviation from a normative use of language, he regards it as the 'omniscient principle of language' (PR, p. 61). 'We all live, and speak', he writes, 'only through our eye for resemblances' (PR, p. 59). All intellectual operations, he maintains, are described in language drawn from the physical, and are in that sense metaphorical. Thought itself proceeds by difference and comparison, so that metaphor is of its essence. Besides, everything is apprehended under some sort of category, so that seeing is always 'seeing as', and this, in a broad sense of the word, is a metaphorical activity. We transpose an individual object to the class to which it belongs, whereas (to borrow an example from Martin Heidegger) a lizard does not see the rock on which it is lying *as* a rock. The rock is part of its perceptual world, but not part of a world of meaning. Metaphor, which fuses two or more thoughts or images together, is a microcosm of the pluralistic nature of language as such. It consists in Richards's view of a 'tenor', which is the underlying idea or subject; a 'vehicle', which is the mode in which the tenor finds expression; and a 'ground', which denotes whatever the two have in common. Thus 'warrior' might be a tenor, 'tiger' its vehicle and 'strength or courage' the ground which connects them. Tenor and vehicle constantly interact, as sometimes the one is thrust to the fore and sometimes the other. A tenor can have a single vehicle or a multiplicity of them, and a tension or contrast between the two may be as significant as a fusion. The two aspects may also cooperate to produce a more powerful, diverse meaning than either of them taken in isolation. In this sense, metaphor is a transaction between contexts, since like all terms tenor and vehicle are only intelligible as part of a wider linguistic landscape. One metaphor, as in some of the richest passages of Shakespeare, can be 'mounted' on another, and that on another, without the whole self-generative process ever, so to speak, touching down on non-figurative terra firma.

This sense of a ceaselessly creative process is vital to Richards's conception of poetry. A poem is essentially meaning in motion, and the motion (rhythm, pace, metre and so on) can either enhance the meaning or work against it, running counter to the sense or reflecting it. In his later work, as the influence of Coleridge becomes more deep-seated, Richards continues to see the poem as a structure of harmonised impulses, a view which Coleridge holds as well, but also as an organic growth – one which the reader 'realises' in the sense of recreates, and in doing so realises his or her whole personality. The final goal of reading is self-creation. Readers become aware that they are bringing the poem into being at the same time as they are exploring, 'becoming' or comprehending it, and the ambiguous verb 'to realise' captures both of these activities. We are so intimately bound up with the work that it becomes impossible to say where it stops and we start, or whether we are producing it or it is producing us. Knower and known, or knowledge and being, are identical. There is a hint of Confucius behind this doctrine, which represents a momentary surrender by a materialist critic to a semi-mystical idea. There is also an anticipation of late twentieth-century reception theory.

Metaphor for Richards is more than a verbal device. There are times when he uses the term as synonymous with 'myth', meaning the way our minds model the world and render it intelligible. We project certain metaphors onto reality in order to make sense of it; but reality is itself already metaphorical, since it is the result of previous such projections. Metaphor, then, for Richards as for Friedrich Nietzsche and Jacques Derrida, goes all the way down. You cannot peel it off, layer after layer, to arrive at a brute reality. All you can do is overlay one set of metaphors with another. To put the point more technically, Richards is a materialist in so far as he believes in a Nature which is independent of the mind; but he is not a philosophical realist, in the sense of one who maintains that this world can be known as it actually is. We ourselves project values, meanings and sentiments into the inert stuff of reality, so that all we can ever truly know is ourselves. Nature is always Nature-for-us. The constructive activity of the mind enters into the simplest-seeming sense data, so that there is nothing which is simply given. It is a view typical of philosophical Idealism, with its belief that the mind creates the world, and so would seem to be at odds with

Richards's materialism. Yet the mind for Richards is itself material, more or less identical with the nervous system.

What we live by, then, is myth, meaning a specific way of ordering reality which allows us to adapt to it and therefore to flourish. Indeed, science itself in Richards's eyes is simply our latest form of mythology, one which organises the world in ways which enhance our control over it. Yet though we need the myth of science for our practical existence, we need other forms of fiction for our spiritual well-being. Through such life-giving fables, 'our will is collected, our power unified, our growth controlled'; without it, 'man is only a cruel animal without a soul' (CI, p. 134). Such myths unify our existence, endowing us with a wisdom of which science is incapable, and binding us to a Nature with which we are rapidly losing touch. In fulfilling these functions, modern myths inherit the role of previous fictions (metaphysics, absolute moralities, a faith in tradition and authority) and above all religion – so that there is a sense here, too, in which Richards, like Nietzsche, is a Death-of-God thinker. How are we to maintain order and value in a world from which the Almighty has vanished, and which no longer puts its faith in moral absolutes? T.S. Eliot, unusually for a modern writer, moves from atheism to Christianity; Richards finds a form of ultimate value in the progress of humanity; William Empson (to anticipate a little) hates God as though he believes he existed; F.R. Leavis discovers a surrogate for him in the vitalism of D.H. Lawrence; while Raymond Williams, who refused the church ritual of confirmation as a child, is indifferent to the whole issue.

I.A. RICHARDS

Richards's response to the disappearance of the Deity is unequivocal: the most effective way of creating stability and significance in a post-theistic universe is poetry. Poetry, he insists, in a comment probably meant to scandalise and certainly intended to be quoted, 'is capable of saving us; it is a perfectly possible means of overcoming chaos' (*Science and Poetry*, in PLC, p. 330). It is the most remarkable example of mental and emotional order that we have, and 'the necessary channel for the reconstitution of [social] order' (CI, 174). Poetry will remake our minds, and with them our civilisation. As with Matthew Arnold, the poet now assumes the mantle of the prophet or priest. T.S. Eliot, who as a Christian scorns any attempt to substitute art for religion, comments sourly that this is like saying that the wallpaper will save us when the walls have crumbled. The idea that poetry, which involves only a minuscule fraction of the population, will redeem us from the 'chaos' of modernity is so absurd as to be mildly comic. At least religion, whatever its crimes and delusions, has secured the allegiance of billions of ordinary men and women throughout the world. Richards, as we have seen, hopes to disseminate the study of literature more widely, but even then it is likely to remain a minority pursuit.

Poetry, he argues, might seem inferior to religion, morality, science or metaphysics since it is simply a fiction. Once, however, we recognise that religion, morality, science and metaphysics are fictions as well, we can lay this prejudice to rest. Besides, poetry is self-consciously fictional, which is what any authentic myth must be. Myths must be aware that they are mythical, and so must those who place their faith in them. Their relation to them must thus be ironic, a question of believing and not believing at the same time. Otherwise we are in danger of mistaking the work of our own hands for absolute reality, which is a form of idolatry. In *The Sense of an Ending*, the critic Frank Kermode distinguishes between myths, which regard themselves as true, from fiction, which does not. Myths are fictions which take themselves as fact. Richards must proceed here with caution: he was a liberal who proclaimed the need for myth in a fascist age, and myth in fascistic hands was rapidly becoming noxious. Men and women must therefore lend only a limited credence to their symbolic worlds, refusing to grant exorbitant authority to any of them. It is not obvious that people can really live like this for any length of time. Othello believes that Desdemona is faithful to him and disbelieves it at the same time, but this is the sign of a mind in pieces, not of an ironist.

We must, then, create a kind of second Nature, given that Nature itself, in the sense of things as they really are, is impenetrable to us. This second Nature is the practical domain in which we conduct our daily lives, a world of passions and values, actions and perceptions; and scientific inquiry represents only a small sector of it. Science can't satisfy our metaphysical questionings, which to Richards's mind is no great loss since he believes that metaphysics is bogus; but it does represent certain affective needs which must be satisfied, and this is the function of art and culture. Through language, we construct a reality to satisfy our needs as a whole, so that 'the fabrics of all our various worlds are the fabrics of our meanings' (PR, p. 12). Far from constituting a solid fact, reality is a product of our conventions, which vary from place to place and time to time; and the arbitrariness of these conventions is obvious enough if one encounters a culture sufficiently alien to one's own, as Richards did when he visited China. This, he admits, is an unsettling truth to digest, since it seems to mean that our existence lacks a sure foundation. He is what we would call today an anti-foundationalist thinker, as well as a precursor of some other aspects of postmodernism. Cultural relativism is one of them.

If the world is a projection of ourselves, then so, inevitably, must be the poem. Like some later reception theorists, Richards maintains that much of what we regard as being 'in' a literary work is actually put there by the reader. For perhaps the first time in the history of English criticism, the underprivileged reader emerges from the wings and is placed at the centre of the literary stage. The literary text is a transaction with a reader, not a stable object. Nor is it to be treated as part of its author's biography, a form of criticism which Richards distrusts. He is a forerunner of semiotics, discourse theory, hermeneutics, neuroscience, post-colonial studies and so-called close reading; but he is also one of the first practitioners of what would later become known as reception or reader-response theory, and his enormously influential book *Practical Criticism* is one of the great classics of that current even before it had properly got under way. Just as reception theory examines the activity of the reader in helping to construct the literary text, so Richards argues that all interpretation involves our filling in connections which are not made by the work itself, and that in the case of poetry our freedom to forge these relations is the primary source of the work's power. No writer can supply the full context of what he or she says, so that readers will bring their own frame of assumptions to it, each of them rather different from the others. Beauty, for example, lies in the eye of the beholder. As in the case of pseudo-statements, what looks like a statement about an object turns out to concern the subject. As far as beauty goes it is a convincing enough case, given how much of what counts as beauty alters from one time or place to another, though whether rape and torture also lie in the eye of the beholder is a problem we have glanced at already.

Generally speaking, Richards thinks that what we say of a poem is really shorthand for describing its effects on us. We may speak of a piece of verse as having a jocular tone or a clunky rhythm, but for him this is a consequence of the way we read it, not a quality of the work itself. The sense of equilibrium which a successful poem creates lies in the reader's mind or nervous system rather than in the words on the page. The plot of a play or novel is simply 'a series, an intricately wrought system, of thoughts, feelings, expectations, surprises, desires, hopes, disappointments and the rest' (CSW, p. 161). Rhythm is similarly a matter of surprises, anticipations and so on. So plot and rhythm are just in the mind as well. Is there anything in a literary work which isn't? The black marks on the page, perhaps. But to identify something as a black mark involves an act of inter-pretation, so is this simply a mental event as well? Even literary judgements for Richards tell you more about the readers – their past history, current interests and so on – than about the work at hand.

The fact that there is no beauty, envy, agony, commas, apostro-phes or line-endings in a work without an interpreter doesn't mean, however, that to describe a poem is to describe the reader. The opposition between what is given by the poem and what is constructed by the reader is a misleading one. When we say that the word 'mother' is 'in' the poem, we don't mean that it is in it in the way that brandy is in a bottle. We mean that in the English language these six black marks are commonly agreed to have a specific meaning or cluster of meanings, and that the reader cannot simply decide that they mean 'porridge' instead. So meaning is in this sense objective. You can be wrong about it, just as you can be wrong about whether a narrative features a character called Julia or how many words there are in a line of verse; and this is one sense in which such matters are not purely subjective. (Though you can be wrong about the subjective too – not in the sense that you don't know whether you are having a particular experience or not, but in the sense that you may, say, take it for anger when it is actually fear.)

Even so, meaning is not objective in the sense that waterfalls are. Waterfalls would exist even if human beings didn't, but meanings would not. Mount Etna does not exist simply because we all agree that it does, whereas if we did not agree that six black marks have a certain meaning, they would not do so. Perhaps in some other language they mean 'tractor'. Some things are part of the world's furniture, whereas others are not. There is nothing in Nature called 'property', which is purely a social construct, but there are things in the world called trees, a few of which might belong to me. In his work on Coleridge, Richards seeks to resolve the conflict between what is given in a text and what we project into it with Coleridge's notion of a 'fact of mind', which involves an interaction of subject and object.

Richards sees a poetic work as the way in which the poet conveys an experience from his or her own mind to the mind of the reader. But this is a strange way to think of it. Take, for example, the opening of John Milton's *Paradise Lost*:

Of Man's First Disobedience, and the Fruit
Of that Forbidden Tree, whose mortal taste
Brought Death into the World, and all our woe,
With loss of Eden, till one greater Man
Restore us, and regain the blissful Seat,
Sing Heavenly Muse . . .

What experience are these lines trying to communicate? And how would we know that what we experience as we read them is what Milton was experiencing when he wrote them? The fact is that the passage does not present us with an experience which could be described independently of its words. It offers us instead a set of meanings – and meaning is not an experience, any more than promising, intending or expecting are experiences. One can speak, to be sure, of the experience of words – of the way their sound, shape, rhythm and texture reverberate in the mind – but the words are not simply a medium for an experience which lies 'behind' them. What is the experience behind 'We've just run out of sardines'? One is tempted to say that the whole idea of experience is misleading in this context, a hangover from an empiricist tradition that tempts us into modelling non-sensory activities on sensory ones. I could say that I had the experience of shutting a drawer, but all I mean by this is that I shut a drawer. There is another residue of the empiricist legacy in the way that Richards speaks of a poem as a 'mental state' (CSW, p. 230), and of meaning as a mental process. But a poem exists on paper, not in the first place in the mind. It is in our minds that it comes alive, to be sure; but would we call a conversation a mental state just because it involves our minds? Might a crafty defence counsel get his client off by describing his act of chewing someone's ear as a mental state?

As for meaning, Wittgenstein points out that it is a social practice, a way of doing things with words, not an invisible occurrence in our heads. Because meaning is a social affair, 'There's a maniac with a blood-stained machete creeping up behind you' means what it means whatever happens to be going on in my head as I pronounce the words. Of course the words of a poem may give us what we might call a virtual experience, so that we seem to feel the sensuous delights of reclining in a leafy bower sipping a glass of Chardonnay and stroking a cat; but this experience is not separable from the language of the poem, and it does not matter whether the poet actually had it or not. For all we know the poet might be a teetotaller with a pathological aversion to touching animals.

It has been claimed that Richards was the first critic to attend to tone in poetry, tone being one of the chief ways in which feeling enters into language. It is also an exemplary case of the point we have just tried to make. Tone is not objective in the sense that a semi-colon is. We can argue over the tone of a passage, but not over whether it contains a semi-colon. Yet it is objective in the sense that we cannot just read any old tone we like into a series of words. It would be perverse, though not impossible, to hear Lear's 'I am a very foolish fond old man' as jovial or sarcastic. This is because feelings are in one sense as social as meanings. 'In one sense', because some of our emotions are also natural. Feeling your military honour to be impugned is a purely cultural sentiment, but it is natural for human beings to grieve over the death of their loved ones, panic when falling accidentally from high buildings or scream when under torture. These are not simply cultural matters, as some theorists would claim. Some of them, like how people laugh or grieve, are natural but with different cultural inflections, while others are more or less universal. How Canadians scream under torture is pretty much how Cambodians do. But just as we learn gradually how to mean, so we also learn conventionally established names for our 'private' emotions, which is how we come to identify them not only to others but to ourselves. We also learn what it is culturally appropriate to feel in particular circumstances. We can still argue over tone, as we can argue over meaning: are Lear's words, for example, to be taken as poignant or self-pitying? But it would be odd to claim that they should be delivered as though the king is stifling a fit of giggles as he speaks them, unless one is playing him as completely out of his mind.

In 1932, Richards published a book entitled *Mencius on the Mind* which encapsulates a good deal of his thought. Mencius was an ancient Chinese philosopher, second in intellectual stature only to Confucius, and with some assistance from Chinese colleagues Richards was able to decipher a portion of his writings. In some ways he felt more at home in China than he did in Cambridge, and at one point considered taking up a permanent academic post there. He was not immune to certain sentimental illusions about the despotic Chinese regime, remarking in 1968 that the country's people had a deeply ingrained horror of violence and were closer to achieving the good life than their Western counterparts. This observation was made only two years after Mao Zedong launched the Cultural Revolution, in which a great many Chinese citizens were murdered, driven to suicide or otherwise ruined, and only a decade after the so-called Great Leap Forward, which resulted in one of the most terrible famines in modern history.

Even so, the Mencius book represents a fascinating encounter between one of the West's leading intellectuals and a very different culture, one whose distinctive style and structure of thought he is eager to grasp. Different peoples, Richards thinks, may have vastly different mental constitutions, and the findings of Western psychology might be far more culturally specific than we are aware. He does not seem to find such cultural relativism as much of a problem as one might expect, given his goal of greatly improved international communication. There is a danger, he believes, of forcing a Western mentality onto modes of thought to which it is inappropriate, a viewpoint that anticipates some post-colonial theory. What he calls 'nationalism in thought' (MM, p. 90) is to be avoided. He was a strong supporter of the League of Nations (the precursor of the United Nations), advocated world government and was deeply committed to international understanding. With these new forms of internationalism came a need for mutual comprehension on a scale never previously envisaged, so that questions of interpretation had now become thoroughly political.

Perhaps one thing Richards thought the West could learn from China was how to cultivate order without the need for a religious foundation. What also attracts him to Chinese writing is the fact that it seems not to be governed by an explicit logic or clearly articulated syntax; and this, he believes, yields us an insight into the workings of language in general, allowing as it does for a number of different interpretations, no one of which can be said to be definitive.[10] It is as though he has stumbled upon a language which practises what he has always preached. There is a fluid, unstable quality to Mencius's work which Richards, with his distaste for the clear-cut and rigidly classified, finds especially gratifying. Whole sentences in Chinese can have an indefiniteness of expression, so that their meaning is not settled. Concepts have a vagueness which lends them power and coherence, and the language, he considers, pays no attention to certain distinctions crucial to the West. Mencius, much to Richards's approval, steers clear of metaphysical notions, dispensing with universals, particulars, substances, attributes, essences, classes and the like. An interest in what a thing is in itself, as opposed to what moral and social significance it may have, strikes Richards as a recent, Western-based style of thought. He also claims that in Mencius's writing the emotive takes precedence over meaning, as it does for Richards in poetry, and that in the Chinese language more generally we sometimes have to choose between the different possible senses of a term according to their emotional resonances. Words do not behave as fixed, independent units of discourse, and meaning seems highly context-dependent. What matters, as in the Western tradition of rhetoric, is the force or 'gesture' of an utterance, the purpose it seeks to achieve, rather than the bare proposition; and this means in Richards's view that verbal forms have to be grasped in terms of the effects and intentions of a piece of language, not the other way round.

In all these ways, Richards the pragmatist finds Mencius's work congenial. His arguments seem to turn on practical interests directed to specific ends. Among these ends is the maintenance of social order, which as we have seen is one of Richards's own most precious values. A certain system of social practices, involving honour, respect, hierarchy and so on, is taken for granted, and the aim of an utterance is how to sustain it. What matters is not that a statement is in accord with the facts, but in accord with such facts as are compatible with the governing social structure. This, Richards suspects, might also be truer of Western psychology than it cares to acknowledge. Mencius's primary concern is not knowledge or reflection but virtuous action. What looks at first glance like referential language is really 'a series of overt or disguised imperatives' (MM, p. 64).

Disturbingly, Richards seems thoroughly to approve of this subordination of truth to power, examples of which could be found in abundance in the fascist regimes of the time. They are also increasingly apparent in advanced capitalist ones. What we need, he remarks, is a 'fictional account of human nature in the interests of a finely ordered society and of reasonably unwasteful living' (MM, p. 66). We should harness psychology (by which he really means manipulate the mind) to the cause of social stability, which is to say that psychology should become ideology. For this purpose, he distinguishes between the concept of equilibrium, which is profoundly disinterested and predisposes you to no one course of action over another, and the notion of harmony, which coordinates one's impulses in such a way as to bring about beneficial action. The beneficial action both he and Mencius have upmost in mind is the maintaining of social cohesion. So harmony is a question of partisanship, given that social cohesion is usually in the interests of our rulers. There is a tension, however, between the conservative politics implicit in this case and Richards's interest in ambiguity, since ambiguity is in a sense the opposite of authoritarianism. It is probably no accident that at a time when political nationalism was on the rise, the topic of ambiguity should play so crucial a role in the work of Richards, Empson and others. Among other things, ambiguity can be a coded kind of anti-chauvinism. To be hospitable to different meanings may involve being open to a diversity of cultures.

It would seem a far cry from the Mencius study to Richards's most celebrated work, *Practical Criticism*. Yet there are important connections between them. The latter book is the record of a legendary experiment which Richards conducted with a group of Cambridge students, in which he handed them poems without informing them of their authors or contexts, and asked them to analyse and evaluate them. It is worth noting that although Richards's name is therefore indissolubly linked with so-called practical criticism, a term he actually invented, he does rather little of it himself in his published writing. It is a form of inquiry which involves so-called 'close reading', which is not to suggest that every critic before Richards read only an average of two or three words a line. You can read a work with scrupulous attention and then proceed to waffle about it. A barrister reads a brief carefully, but not usually in the sense of grasping its layout on the page, or the odd piece of alliteration or assonance, as part of its meaning. Close reading in criticism means the kind of reading which clings tenaciously to the shape of the sentences – to their rhythm, sound, tone, texture, syntactical form and so on – and comes up with judgements and interpretations on this basis. Some traditionally minded critics at the time denounced the approach as too myopic, missing the wood for the trees. It was too much like what Eliot called 'lemon-squeezing', offensive to one's sense of decorum and proportion. A gentleman like Quiller-Couch relaxed with a book rather than scrutinising it like an officious ticket inspector.

The general response to the handed-out passages was one of dismal ineptitude. One critic characterises Richards's report as a modern *Dunciad*. It would seem that what was traditionally the most literate section of the population was effectively unable to read. Richards speaks of the 'reckless, desperate' nature of some of the contributions, and comments with a mildly mischievous air that they are the work of expensively educated students. (There were, however, some reasonably perceptive insights, perhaps in part because William Empson and F.R. Leavis were among the participants.) A number of myths have clustered around this project, one of the few attempts to turn literary criticism into a collaborative enterprise. First, Richards himself did not invent practical criticism. It had already been part of the Cambridge English Tripos for some time, though it was Richards who put it on the map. Second, he did not believe that reading a work in ignorance of its author, circumstances and historical context was the ideal critical method, as did most of the American New Critics who came under his influence. He withheld these reference-points from his students not because he thought them irrelevant but in order to demonstrate how ready his guinea pigs were, once deprived of such pointers, to mark up a piece of slipshod Victorian sentimentalism while marking down Donne and Hopkins.

Thirdly, Richards did not regard the exercise as being primarily about criticism. He saw it rather as about communication, and described it somewhat obscurely as 'a piece of field-work in comparative ideology' (PC, p. 15). The only goal of criticism, he insisted, was to improve communication. He wanted to know more about the chief impediments to it, and his students provided him with an embarrassing profusion of evidence. It is the idea of communication which links *Practical Criticism* to *Mencius on the Mind*, since mutual understanding between two very different cultures seems as hit and miss an affair as a group of tin-eared students' understanding of a poem. Indeed, in Richards's view it is misunderstanding which is the norm and understanding the exception. Rhetoric is chiefly the study of misinterpretation. His case is confirmed by those modern linguisticians for whom human language is so complex, and the factors involved in decoding it so numerous, that any act of comprehension would seem like a small miracle.

Practical Criticism uses the material it gathers to examine certain common causes of misapprehension: stock responses, excessive literalism, purely subjective associations, emotions inappropriate to the occasion and so on. Some of this Richards attributed to the baleful influence of mass culture, which in his day meant for the most part film, radio, popular fiction and popular newspapers. A pervasive decline in the quality of speech, along with a 'levelling down' of sensitivity and critical intelligence, was under way, with potentially disastrous historical consequences. One wonders what he would have made of the so-called social media. There was a 'deliquescence' of traditional culture. A secular, scientific, urban and industrial society had 'neutralised' Nature. It had also invalidated traditional notions of the universe and of humanity's place within it. The human psyche had accordingly been thrown out of kilter, but no new vision had emerged to rebalance it. It was essential, then, to cast off the last vestiges of religion, metaphysics and philosophy, accept that God is dead, and place the psyche on a firm foundation by turning to a discourse that was as emotionally potent as religious belief but without its gross improbabilities. That discourse was of course poetry. It was a pity (though Richards does not exactly say so) that hardly anyone read it, and that the majority of people were deprived of the means to appreciate it. It was also untrue that secularisation had spread as widely as Richards imagined. Millions of his fellow citizens still believed in God, not to speak of societies elsewhere in the world in which religion remained solidly entrenched as an everyday practice. There was one such nation only a few miles to the west of Britain.

Richards, then, shares much of the cultural pessimism of Eliot and Leavis. He speaks of the 'sinister potentialities of the cinema and the loud-speaker' (PLC, p. 35), not as absurd a statement as it sounds if one thinks of the uses to which the Nazis put such technology a decade or so after Richards was writing. The masses are assailed by advertising, propaganda, popular journalism, radio and cinema, with a consequent cheapening of their experience. The less well-educated, he believes, inhabit chaos, thereby posing a threat to social stability in an age of political turbulence. Richards is aware of the extraordinary capacity of language to manipulate the mind, and like Wittgenstein sees it as capable of exerting a bewitching power over us. Words, he believes, are the most conservative force in the world, and the mass of citizens must learn how to break their spell. It is not enough that a cultivated elite remains immune to their seductions. Poetry, as we have seen, will play a major role in this transformation. To suggest that only those who are sensitive to poetry are morally admirable in everyday life is clearly too elitist a claim, so Richards admits that one can be a sensitive reader but unpalatable as a person. Yet if he presses this point too far, he would undercut the need for poetry's supposedly redemptive power; so he also maintains that there is a certain correlation between fineness in criticism and fineness in life.

This largely negative stance to contemporary culture leads to the occasional outbreak of nostalgia. The ceaseless roar of modern transport, he remarks, 'replacing the rhythm of the footstep or of horses' hoofs, is capable in many ways of interfering with our reading of verse' (PC, p. 306). He also observes that 'there are plenty of individuals, of course, whose lives are fairly stable and consistent, whose desires are orderly and whose outlook is clear. But this, in most cases, is because they are not really contemporary with the automobile and the radio' ('Why I Am A Literary Critic', CSW, pp. 164–5). Despite his fondness for the clopping of horses' hoofs, however, Richards, like Raymond Williams, is a thoroughly modern thinker in a way that Eliot and Leavis are not. He does not believe with Eliot that human nature is unchangeable. A new social order must emerge, which will in no sense represent a mere return to the old. The critic must be midwife to this new dispensation, and psychology and the study of language must provide us with a new comprehension of and control over our minds. Such an understanding would then allow us to reconstruct education and achieve a saner, richer and more stable culture – one which would not only be strong enough to withstand the forces working against civilisation, but harness them to our service. He is prepared, in other words, to use a scientifically based psychology to counteract the more degrading effects of a scientific-technological society.

The latter emphasis is what truly distinguishes Richards from the cultural pessimists. The new technologies are not to be written off as simply oppressive; instead, in the spirit of the European avant gardes, productive uses must be found for them. Richards's own career is testimony to his faith in media technology, mass communication and institutions of learning. There is more than a dash of Enlightenment rationalism to his trust in the mind, education, scientific inquiry and the possibility of transforming our environment. It is an affirmative spirit which is shared in different ways by William Empson and Raymond Williams. Yet Richards combines it with a sense of cultural decline which is closer to the thought of Eliot and Leavis. The more widely communication spreads, he warns, the more levelling down there will be. Writing in 1974, he maintains that the literature of the time represents a drastic falling-off from that around 1920.[11] A gradual climb back, however, is not out of the question. Science has for centuries been constrained by religion, ethics and the humanities, and needs to be given its head. Properly understood, it is an emancipatory force.

Richards is surely right that over the course of British history it is science, by and large, which has promoted the cause of social progress, and the humanities which have acted often enough as a bulwark against it. The postmodern scepticism of science is simply the latest manifestation of an age-old historical prejudice. In any case, Richards's rationalism, as we have seen, has its limits. Though he is much given to listing, classifying and diagram drawing, this rigour is the service of an end which it knows is bound to elude it: an exhaustive explanation of the work of art. What the painstaking analysis of a critic devoted to order finally reveal is the fluid, unstable and indefinite. In one sense, perhaps, this is not as paradoxical as it seems: for the science of the time, not least as it was practised at Cambridge, the notion of indeterminacy played an important role.

Few critics have been both as wide-ranging and tightly focused as Richards. On the one hand, his work spans what was later to become a growing gulf between literary and scientific cultures, roaming across literature, rhetoric, psychology, aesthetics, philosophy, linguistics, educational theory, cultural diagnosis and some hair-raising accounts of his mountaineering exploits. On the other hand, no aspect of a poem is too microscopic to merit his attention. He is probably the first literary critic to have paid attention to the actual look of the poem on the page – to the role played in its overall effect by typographical devices such as fonts, line breaks, spacing and the visual character of words. His pupil William Empson inherited only part of his teacher's intellectual versatility, but pressed his techniques of close analysis well beyond anything Richards accomplished himself – indeed beyond the constraints of any previous critic. It is to the work of this *enfant terrible* that we may now turn.

3

WILLIAM EMPSON

'Anyone who reads me also reads Richards', writes William Empson.[1] There is a curious echo in these words of Jesus's 'Whoever has seen me has seen the Father', a suggestion that this embattled atheist would no doubt have found grotesquely inappropriate. He also states in a note to the most ambitious of his works, *The Structure of Complex Words*, that Richards, his teacher at Cambridge, is the source of all the book's ideas. The more senior critic, however, didn't always return the compliment. Whereas Empson's allusions to Richards's work are respectful even when he radically disagrees with him, a few of Richards's references to Empson are only grudgingly complimentary. Maybe the master felt overshadowed by the brilliance of his former pupil, perhaps the cleverest critic England has ever produced.

Empson's father was a Yorkshire landowner in possession of over 2,000 acres, while his mother, in his own words, was a 'terrific classaddict', so that he could only bring home upper-class friends whom she approved of and he himself didn't like.[2] Perhaps this was one reason for what might have been his unconscious wish to see her ripped to pieces, which we shall be noting later. This son of the squirearchy attended one of the most prestigious of English private schools, Winchester College, which by being so ostentatiously privileged helped to move him to the political left. Indeed, this is perhaps the only worthwhile function such places have ever served. From there he won a place at Magdalene College, Cambridge to study mathematics, later abandoning the subject for English. As a student, Empson published poems which won the praise of F.R. Leavis, became interested in Marx and Freud and helped to run an experimental literary journal which had the distinction of turning down a poem by Ezra Pound. Like his mentor, he was a member of the Heretics society, of which he became president, and knocked around with an assorted bunch of rebels, misfits and eccentrics.

Empson was expelled from Magdalene for being found with contraceptives in his room, and, furnished with a modest financial allowance from his father, conducted a hand-to-mouth existence in London, enjoying some riotous nights on the town with T.S. Eliot, Dylan Thomas, Stephen Spender, Louis MacNeice and other literary luminaries. Eliot proved to be a generous patron, inviting him to review for the *Criterion*. At the age of 24 he published one of the greatest critical works ever to appear in English, *Seven Types of Ambiguity*, some of it cobbled together from his undergraduate essays. It was hailed by the American critic John Crowe Ransom as the most imaginative account of reading ever published. Its author was scruffy, shy, kind-hearted, free of airs and graces, and lived in squalid conditions that Robert Lowell described as having a certain 'weird, sordid nobility'. He was also an alcoholic, actively bisexual, experimented with opium and lived in an open marriage with the South African sculptor Hetta Crouse, who was a member of the Communist Party. Their home in London became something of a bohemian commune, frequented by literary and political dissidents as well as those simply in search of a drink.

From 1931 to 1934, Empson taught at the Japanese National University in Tokyo. His time in Japan was not without a touch of drama: trying to climb into his hotel through a window one night while hopelessly drunk, he got stuck and had to be hauled out by his legs. He also smuggled a friend out of a Japanese prison by disguising him in sunglasses and a false moustache. He was thrown out of the country for making a pass at a male taxi driver, implausibly maintaining in his own defence that he found Japanese men and women hard to tell apart. From 1937 to 1939 he was a professor in Beijing, where his drinking gained him revered status as one of a classical tradition of intoxicated Chinese poets. His educational work in the country, to which he returned some years later, deeply shaped the future course of English studies there, and he was said to be a devoted teacher both in China and in Japan. He was robbed by bandits in China, developed a passionate interest in Buddhism and enthusiastically witnessed Mao Zedong's triumphal entry into the capital.

During the Second World War he returned to England and worked as a propagandist alongside George Orwell at the BBC, later becoming the Corporation's Chinese editor. He thought Orwell's novel *1984* 'horrible' since it underrated the power of the human

144

mind to withstand the manipulations of authoritarian language. The novel, in short, offended his rationalist faith. His war work led him to feel a certain affinity with the otherwise detestable God of *Paradise Lost* ('a pompous old buffer', as he called him in *Milton's God*), whom he saw as essentially a propagandist. In 1953 he was appointed Professor of English Literature at Sheffield University, a post he accepted partly because the city was in his home county of Yorkshire. He was knighted in 1979, five years before his death.

Empson and Richards are alike in many respects, though there are divergences between them as well. Empson shares his mentor's progressive view of history and rejects the Eliotic theory that a dissociation of sensibility had led to a decline in literature and civilisation since the seventeenth century. In fact, he explicitly and unfashionably embraces the so-called Whig theory of history, which sees English history as a steady expansion of liberty, prosperity and enlightenment. It is not true, he argues, that things have been constantly growing worse, a belief which for many intellectuals of the time was almost an article of faith. Like Richards, Empson taught for a while in Eastern Asia, and was fascinated by Buddhist thought. He considered his book on the subject, *The Face of the Buddha*, one of the best things he had written.[3] An interest in Eastern thought marks much of the modernist period. Empson was also an advocate of Basic English, and as cosmopolitan in outlook as his teacher. On his return from China, the Eng. Lit. establishment in Britain struck him as stuffy and parochial. Yet he did not learn any Chinese or Japanese while abroad, and was later to regret that he had not integrated more fully into Chinese society. He was always at some level the Englishman abroad. His range of literary reference, like Richards's, is almost exclusively English. In fact, of the five critics considered in this book, only Eliot roams habitually beyond the confines of English literature, while F.R. Leavis gives the impression that the only non-English-language work he ever read without boredom or displeasure is Tolstoy's *Anna Karenina*.

Like Richards, Empson is a rationalist who has a briskly dismissive way with Symbolist, Imagist or New Critical notions of the poem as a self-enclosed object cut adrift from everyday life and language. He is a relentless demythologiser of such doctrines, presenting himself in one critic's words as 'the bluff squire, with his keen English nose for nonsense'.[4] He is no fan of the aesthetic, as his own depthless, off-hand prose style bears witness. Poetry must be judged by the same rational standards of argumentation that we draw on in daily life. There is nothing mystical or transcendent about it. Its truth, whatever Eliot and the Symbolists may consider, does not finally elude language. Empson's first and most famous book, *Seven Types of Ambiguity*, received a fair amount of flak from critics and reviewers for this plain-minded approach. He was clearly out of step with the literary orthodoxy personified by Eliot, taking issue with the whole modernist programme of poetry as portraying states of feeling with sensuous particularity, or of using language to gesture beyond itself. Like Richards, he plays down the 'visual image' idea of poetry. A poem in his opinion is as open to being paraphrased as a piece of legislation, a case which smacks of heresy for the Symbolists and American New Critics. Paraphrasing a poem may mean losing something of its unique effect, but it may also allow us to return to the work with a deeper, richer sense of its meaning. Whereas Eliot added notes to *The Waste Land* simply to fill in a few blank pages, and perhaps to bamboozle the reader even more thoroughly, Empson sometimes appended notes to his own poetry in order to elucidate its meaning for the reader. He was not afraid of desecrating the mystery of his art by explaining what it means in prosaic terms.

This, then, is a critic who places his trust in rational argument, critical reason and open public debate. If he revels in the technical intricacies of a Donne or Marvell, another side of him is thoroughly at home in the eighteenth century, which he sees as the very sanctuary of rationality. To paraphrase the critic Christopher Norris, he works on the assumption that the human mind, however complex, baffled and self-divided, is essentially sane; and to interpret a text is to make as large-minded, generous an allowance as one can for the way in which a particular poetic mind, however broodingly idiosyncratic, is striving to work through and pluck some sense from its conflicts.[5] Any contradiction, Empson maintains, is likely to have some sensible interpretation. It is the critic as therapist, approaching knotted meanings and fractured images while coolly maintaining his own good sense as a tacit example of the well-ordered human mind. Science, he remarks, has held a monopoly on reason in the modern era, yet the belief that reason should be brought to bear on the arts is as old as criticism itself, and is fundamental to its workings. Analysis is only the refuge of the emotionally sterile when it is poorly performed. Given enough practice, you can respond simultaneously to the music and the meaning of a poem, which in Eliot's terms is the mark of an undissociated sensibility.

No explanation of a literary work can be exhaustive, but vigorous arguments over it are still worth conducting. The fact that there is no ultimate truth does not mean that there is no truth at all. It is worth recalling that Empson lived through the barbarous irrationalism of fascism, in the light of which a trust in the fundamental rationality of men and women becomes an implicit form of politics. Like Freud, he is aware of the limits of reason – of the conflicts and chronic illusions of the human mind – without ever losing faith in its sense-making capabilities. The problem is how to acknowledge the muddled, contradictory nature of human affairs without devaluing reason and thus selling the pass to a motley array of irrationalists: Symbolists, neo-Christians, the 'loathsome' Imagists, intuitionists, Romantic sentimentalists and other reach-me-down Empsonian bugbears. And just as Empson puts his trust in the sanity of the mind – its ability to stretch itself around any situation without losing its integrity – so he has a belief in the vigour and resilience of language which is very far from the distrust of the word typical of modernism.

When confronted with a literary work, Empson appeals to what philosophers call the principle of charity – the assumption that a piece of language, however tortuous or obscure, is trying to say something which makes sense. 'We could not use language as we do', he writes, 'and above all we could not learn it . . . unless we were always floating in a general willingness to make sense of it; all the more, then, to try to make a printed page mean something good is only fair' (MG, p. 28). In this sense, understanding is both a moral and a cognitive act, as well as a fundamental disposition of our being. Before we come to grasp anything in particular, we are always in a state of what one might call pre-understanding. All good poetry, Empson considers, requires an active effort of intellectual sympathy on the reader's part, so that the act of knowing is also an exercise of feeling. Pleasure and cognition go together: 'unless you are enjoying the poetry', Empson insists, 'you cannot create it, as poetry, in your mind' (STA, p. 248). Without some affection for a work, you don't really get to understand it. You must also rely on it to show you the way it is trying to be good.

The critical act, then, must be both affective and analytical, so that in this local sense at least, Eliot's dissociation of sensibility is overcome. In an excessively charitable gesture, Empson argues that 'a student of literature ought to be trying all the time to empathise with the author' (UB, p. viii). The case is an ancient one: St Augustine, for example, believed that understanding is a form of love – of being emotionally engaged with what you are seeking to grasp. If one's empathy were to be complete, however, one would lose one's capacity to judge, which requires a certain reflective distance. Besides, to empathise is not necessarily to sympathise, in the sense of regarding an author's feelings as valid. You can empathise with a torturer. Even so, a poem, Empson considers, must be thought worth the trouble of being carefully examined, and examining it carefully allows you to know more about what it is worth. Fact and value conspire together, each enhancing the other.

Empson's concern with sense and argument in poetry is at odds with Richards's view of it as a form of pseudo-statement – as emotive rather than cognitive. For Empson, as we have just seen, thought and feeling work together in the process of criticism; indeed, the semantic (what the text means) has primacy over its formal aspects, since the latter have significance only in the context of what the work is trying to say. We wouldn't, for example, see disjointed syntax as symptomatic of an unhinged mind unless we knew from the poem's content that this was what it was trying to convey. In any case, emotions, far from being the opposite of rational propositions, implicitly contain them: I am afraid of this animal because I know that it is hungry, that it is notorious for eating humans, that it has a particular hankering for the flesh of people like myself from the north-west of England and so on. Much of what we call 'feeling' in poetry is in Empson's view an elaborate structure of interrelated meanings; and with this idea he anticipates Raymond Williams's concept of a 'structure of feeling'. A central aim of *The Structure of Complex Words*, as the book's title suggests, is to investigate what one might call the inner logic of certain key words, the structural relations between their various senses; and if it is this inner logic which sometimes matters, then Empson is bound to reject Richards's view that all meaning is determined by its linguistic context.

Empson is a realist who believes in trying to understand the world as it is, whereas Richards, as we have seen, is sceptical of such naive objectivism, as he would no doubt regard it. When Empson writes in *Seven Types* that 'the object of life, after all, is not to understand things, but to maintain one's defences and equilibrium and live as well as one can' (STA, p. 247), he is momentarily ventriloquising his master in a way which seems untrue to his genuine beliefs. He is also out of step with his mentor on the question of order and unity, of which, as we have seen, Richards makes something of a fetish. The younger critic, by contrast, reveals a certain indifference to order in the shapeless, digressive nature of his prose style. (When asked how he came to write so slackly, he blamed it on beer. One visitor to his rooms in Cambridge found him patiently sucking beer stains from the carpet, no doubt at a time of day when the pubs were closed.) He admired what he called a certain 'productive looseness' in a work of art, which allows it to gather into itself various disparate elements that have been contained in tradition. He even uses the homely image of a stew, in which various chunks of stuff are suffused in the same medium. You know what words have gone into the making of a poem, but each of these words floats in language as a whole, rather as the ingredients of a stew are mixed with each other in a juice which envelops them; and just as one does not know how these different bits of the stew are combined or held in suspension, so it is hard to know how words take their flavour from the nature of language as a whole. Language for Empson is a kind of social unconscious, the deep resources which underlie a specific word or lurk in the background of a phrase, but which are hard to dredge to consciousness. He speaks cryptically but suggestively in *Seven Types* of 'the poet's sense of the nature of a language' (STA, p. 6), and of 'meanings latent in the mode of action of the language' (STA, p. 7). Writers are those who need to have a language in their bones if they are to use it effectively. They have somehow to be attuned to its deep structures and typical modes of operation, rather than simply be able to turn a fine phrase.

Empson's casualness about unity is evident in *Some Versions of Pastoral*, a work so broken-backed in structure, ranging from proletarian literature to *Alice in Wonderland*, that any coherent conception of what it means by pastoral has to be assembled largely by the reader. The book's own form thus suggests a disunity which pastoral itself is supposed to overcome, with its harmonising of the social classes. It is a deliberately perverse text, a smack at academic decorum which can be found almost everywhere in Empson's work. In fact, one critic regarded the book as a joke. In *Seven Types of Ambiguity*, the seventh ambiguity to be examined is one reflecting a fundamental rift or self-division in the poet's mind; and though Empson allows that this contradiction may be resolved in some larger context, he also claims that the task of reconciliation falls heavily on the reader. One such fissured mind, as we shall see, is that of John Milton; but it is a self-division whose effects Empson admires rather than laments, just as he finds Othello all the more plausible because of his conflicting motives. The fact that Milton seems to believe different things at the same time makes *Paradise Lost* a lot more interesting than it might otherwise have been.

In explicating the various possible meanings of a text, Empson does not seem to mind that they may be mutually incompatible, nor does he try to synthesise them into a whole. Indeed, he expressly denies that this is the poet's task, and neither need it be that of the critic. Great poetry, he believes, is usually written against a background of discord. 'Human life', he remarks, 'is so much a matter of juggling with contradictory impulses . . . that one is accustomed to thinking people are sensible if they follow first one, then the other, of two such courses' (STA, p. 197). In a note to one of his poems, he claims that life consists of maintaining oneself among contradictions that can't be resolved by analysis. In the words of his biographer, he is a 'connoisseur of conflict',[6] who declares himself enthralled by the way in which, at the end of Shakespeare's *Henry IV, Part 1*, Falstaff, Harry Percy and Prince Henry 'in a series of lightning changes, force upon the audience in succession their mutually incompatible views of the world' (STA, p. 116). Discussing the tension in Gerard Manley Hopkins's poem 'The Windhover' between joy in physical beauty and the urge to spiritual renunciation, he sees it as a case of ambiguity in which 'two things thought of as incompatible, but desired intensely by different systems of judgements, are spoken of simultaneously by words applying to both; both desires are thus given a transient and exhausting satisfaction, and the two systems of judgement are forced into open conflict before the reader' (STA, p. 226). Unity can be the enemy of diversity: Empson believes that 'the way in which opposites can be stated so as to satisfy a wide variety of people, for a great number of degrees of interpretation, is the most important thing about the communication of the arts' (STA, p. 221). Elizabethan drama has to gratify both courtiers and groundlings, and so must accommodate alternative viewpoints and levels of interpretation. The device of a double plot, to which a chapter of *Some Versions of Pastoral* is devoted, is one way of doing so.

What Empson finds most impressive about the literature of the Elizabethan period is that the conflicting nature of human sympathies was somehow obvious to it, which he thinks is less true of the post-Restoration era. As with Eliot and Leavis, though in less doctrinaire a manner, there is a wistful sense of history having lapsed from a more sound condition in the past. In the so-called Age of Reason of eighteenth-century England, unruly emotions which could previously be incorporated into literary works are increasingly split off from them, until by the time of Lewis Carroll's Alice books virtue, intelligence and natural feeling, personified by Alice herself, are isolated from the chaotic forces she observes around her. Only the child – a semi-outsider – can now be the bearer of 'normal' values in an anarchic society.

The mind, Empson remarks in *Some Versions of Pastoral*, is complex and ill-connected like a theatre audience, so that it is as surprising in the one case as the other that some kind of unity can be produced by a play. Good literature has to work successfully for readers who don't share its viewpoint, and two individuals may have very different experiences of the same work of art without either of them being unequivocally wrong. We have seen that Richards is also an advocate of diversity, but for him it must be compatible with order. Politically speaking, it is a standard liberal case. His tidy mind is uneasy with the unfinished and unresolved, as Empson's disorderly imagination is not. In fact, the latter's discussion of various kinds of ambiguity in *Seven Types* traces what he calls 'stages of advancing logical disorder' (STA, p. 48). It is not that he objects to a reconciliatory art – pastoral, he thinks, is a prime example of it – but that he is less insistent on it than most of the critics around him. The point of a work of art is not so much to resolve antagonisms as to perform the process of working them through, as well as to allow the reader to participate in this activity. At one point he speaks of a poem as the expression of an unresolved conflict. Where Empson does find common ground with Richards is on the question of the

154

value of literature, the study of which he thinks is frivolous unless it helps us to decide which attitudes and world views are preferable to others. In practice, however, he is not much concerned with ranking literary works on a scale of excellence. This is partly because his impulse is to be inclusive and generous-minded, without being in the least scatterbrained or sentimental.

While Cambridge philosophers like Bertrand Russell and the early Wittgenstein were in search of a purely logical form of language purged of equivocation, it is for his work on ambiguity that Empson is probably best known; and an ambiguity is by definition irresolvable, at least if one lifts it out of context. He defines it as 'any verbal nuance, however slight, which gives room for alternative reactions to the same piece of language' (STA, p. 1), which suggests that the issue is in the hands of the reader rather than the writer. A writer may not regard what he or she has written as ambiguous, but in the end it is for the readers to decide, just as some of them may detect an irony while others do not. Like Richards, Empson sees the reader as playing a key role in the constitution of the poem. Readers will think up a range of reasons why (for example) apparently unconnected items in the work should go together, even if this process is largely unconscious. Empson's sixth type of ambiguity occurs when a statement really says nothing, being a tautology or contradiction, and readers are forced to come up with statements of their own which are liable to be at odds with each other.

Yet Empson's definition of ambiguity may need some modifying. One can contrast ambiguity with ambivalence, which also gives room for alternative reactions, yet which usually consists of two opposed but determinate meanings. One can feel ambivalent about the automobile, for example, which has proved wonderfully convenient but has also brought countless human lives to an abrupt halt. (When the first fatal car accident occurred in Britain in 1896, a shocked Lord Mayor of London remarked that he hoped such a thing would never happen again.) In *Dombey and Son*, by contrast, Dickens is not sure whether the recently established railways are a 'black monster' or a triumph of modernity. It is when alternative meanings or attitudes merge to the point where we no longer know what to think, or what is intended, that ambivalence slides into ambiguity in the richest sense of the term; and this in Empson's view lies at the root of poetry. What catches his eye is what one commentator calls poetry's 'weft and warp of mixed meanings'.[7]

Even when a poem focuses on something definite, it implicitly appeals to a broader, vaguer backdrop of human experience which is all the more intrusive because it cannot be named. Any language gives us a rich, obscure practical knowledge which can be felt hovering in the background of whatever is actually articulated. Poets do not need to be in full control of their experience to write effectively: Empson's fifth ambiguity is a matter of 'fortunate confusion' or 'fruitful disorder', when authors are in the process of discovering their meaning in the act of writing, or not holding all of it in their mind at once, or are in transition from one idea to another. Truth is dishevelled, and so is inimical to rigid conventions or images of an ideal order. Artists, Empson believes, generally live in a muddle (he certainly did himself, as we have seen already), whereas Richards's goal is a life of equipoise.

Empson shares Richards's view that metaphor is the normal condition of language, and agrees that words resonate with past contexts and usages. Yet whereas Richards's interest in language is primarily philosophical, Empson's aim is to put social history back into speech, as he does most memorably in *The Structure of Complex Words*. He also endorses his teacher's Benthamite ethics. He, too, holds that the greatest variety of satisfactions is central to the good life. Given its pursuit of self-gratification, Benthamite morality has sometimes been accused of egoism; but Empson, commended by his friends and colleagues as a man remarkably free of ego, seeks to turn this apparent defect to advantage. He believes that others are satisfied when one satisfies oneself, not least because the latter involves acting out a number of generous impulses, with which he considers human beings to be plentifully equipped. You fulfil more impulses of your own, he claims, if you have a tendency to fulfil those of others. The great adversary of the Benthamite view, he argues, is Buddhism – not because it lacks a belief in value, but because it lacks a belief in the individual. Since he was deeply attracted to Buddhism, this may be an example of holding two contradictory views in creative tension.

Artists, Empson holds, must state unashamedly what they like and want, and only by virtue of this selfishness can they be of use to their fellows. It is a way of combining two strands of Empson's temperament: his liberal individualism, amounting at times to a kind of devil-may-care anarchism, and the social conscience which led him to call himself a socialist. In part, perhaps, that conscience is a matter of *noblesse oblige*, the belief that social rank brings with it responsibilities. Combining self-fulfilment with a concern for others is also a way of avoiding what he sees as the morbid cult of self-sacrifice of Christianity, while at the same time not lapsing into mere disregard for other people.

Empson has sometimes been accused of overlooking questions of literary form in his pursuit of ever finer nuances of meaning. But this is at best a half-truth. It is true that he has little to say about the overall structure of a literary work, partly because he rejects the modernist conviction that such structures can be present to the mind as a whole. Dismissing this 'spatial' view of a poem or novel, he views the work instead as a process in time, but generally doesn't have room in his writing to track this sequence step by step. His blow-by-blow account of *King Lear* in *Complex Words*, and of *Paradise Lost* in *Milton's God*, are notable exceptions. It is also true that he is mostly silent about tone, except to remark that striking the right one is more important to writing criticism than one might suppose. The mood, texture and atmosphere of a piece are similarly underplayed. He does, however, make some brilliantly perceptive comments on sound, grammar, syntax, rhythm, rhyme, pace and the like. He speaks of 'ambiguities of grammar' and 'subtleties of punctuation' (STA, p. 51), and in discussing Andrew Marvell's poem 'On a Drop of Dew' writes of 'the delicious weakness and prolonged hesitation of [the poem's] syntax' (STA, p. 80). As for rhythm, it 'allows one, by playing off the possible prose rhythms against the super-imposed verse rhythms, to combine a variety of statements in one order' (STA, p. 30). The effect of reading a particular sonnet is 'a general sense of compacted intellectual wealth, of an elaborate balance of variously associated feeling' (STA, p. 57). He speaks of a Shakespeare sonnet as 'glowing and dancing with [the author's] certitude' (STA, p. 138). A passage in *Paradise Lost* 'has the squalid gelatinous effect of ectoplasm in a flashlight photograph' (SVP, p. 127). None of this is the language of a critic who is intent simply on extracting the sense of a piece of writing. What he has to say in *Seven Types* of the stanzaic structure of Edmund Spenser's *Faerie Queene* is a masterpiece of formal analysis.

Unlike Richards, Empson was a superbly accomplished poet. Robert Lowell considered that almost no praise was too high for his verse. This current of imaginative creativity also runs beneath his critical language and occasionally erupts into it. So it is that he can describe George Herbert's poem 'The Sacrifice' as displaying a 'monotonous and rather naive pathos, of fixity of doctrine, of heartrending and straightforward grandeur' (STA, p. 231), where the various adjectives seem in tension with each other, so that the curious phrase 'straightforward grandeur' is almost an oxymoron or contradiction in terms. He also writes in similar style of an anonymous verse that 'the whole charm of the poem is its extravagant, its unreasonable simplicity' (STA, p. 49). Discussing Macbeth's words 'If th'assassination / Could trammel up the consequence, and catch /With his surcease, success', he speaks not only of those sinisterly hissing *s* sounds but also, in an extraordinary moment, of '*catch*, the single little flat word among these monsters . . . it is a mark of human inadequacy to deal with these matters of statecraft, a child snatching at the moon as she rides thunder-clouds' (STA, p. 50). He means that Macbeth's bungled attempt to assume regal power is as futile as a child (but why a girl?) reaching for the moon, and that both figures are at the mercy of forces ('thunder-clouds') which they are helpless to control.

Where this outlandish image drifts up from is a mystery. Nobody, including Empson himself, could imagine that Shakespeare himself had such an uncanny idea in mind. It is rather that the critical commentary enlarges and enriches the poetry, borrowing some of its creative energies and thus establishing a kind of solidarity with it. Asked whether his breathtakingly ingenious readings of literary works involved too much 'reading in', Empson retorted that unless a critic 'reads in' he or she would have nothing to say. He meant, presumably, that unless you draw out what strikes you as the implications of a work, which are not actually articulated, all you can do is repeat the work itself. The line between reading in and spelling out is not always exact. We generally argue not over the meaning of the actual words of a literary text but over their interpretation, and such argument has no obvious bounds.

Richards and Empson are both enthusiasts of science; indeed, Empson regards it as the finest imaginative achievement of the modern age. Criticism, however, should be a social rather than a scientific affair. In this sense, his old teacher is too much of a rationalist for him; yet in so far as Richards proposes an emotive theory of poetry, he is not rationalist enough. Both men are secular humanists, though Empson was a militant atheist whereas Richards was not. The Christian God, Empson observes with grim relish, is 'the wickedest thing yet invented by the black heart of man' (MG, p. 251). In fact, he spent much of the last 30 years of his life propagating a lurid caricature of this deity, one which no moderately intelligent theologian would have trouble in dismantling. If he was remarkably large-minded, he could also ride hobbyhorses. Both men also regard any absolute truth about a literary work as unattainable. Final judgement, Empson remarks, is something that must be indefinitely postponed.

More generally, they agree on the need for cultivating fictions to sustain human existence. We have seen this already in the case of Richards, while Empson considers that the real difficulty of the modern age is that 'true beliefs may make it impossible to act rightly; that we cannot think without verbal fictions; that they must not be taken for true beliefs, and yet must be taken seriously' (A, p. 198). A prosperous human life thrives among other things on a carefully cultivated pretence: 'The feeling that life is essentially inadequate to the human spirit', he comments, 'and yet a good life must avoid saying so, is naturally at home with most versions of pastoral' (SVP, p. 95). This vein of pathos or wry disenchantment runs throughout his work. 'It is only in degree', he writes, 'that any improvement of society could prevent wastage of human powers; the waste even in a fortunate life, the isolation even of a life rich in intimacy, cannot but be felt deeply, and is the central feeling of tragedy' (SVP, p. 12). It is an unusually despondent remark from a man in his early twenties.

Richards and Empson differ sharply on the relevance of authors' biographies and intentions to the interpretation of their work. Empson grew increasingly interested in writers' lives as his career progressed, and published a late work entitled *Using Biography*. As we have seen already, Richards was wary of such recourse to an author's life experiences, not least because it can be bound up with psycho-analytic criticism, which he deplored. Empson's work, as we shall see, is more hospitable to psychoanalysis (there is a scintillating Freudian analysis of *Alice in Wonderland* in *Some Versions of Pastoral*), though as a rationalist he, too, is rattled by some of its darker findings. One might claim that Richards is concerned with academic psychology, whereas Empson, with his extraordinary astuteness about human motives and self-deceptions, is an inspired amateur at the game.

As for the question of how far the author's intentions matter in determining the meaning of a literary work, Empson takes a briskly commonsensical view. He accepts that writers may have uncon-scious intentions, that they can mean more than they know, and that readers can legitimately find in their work meanings which they did not have in mind; but he also insists that there are times when we need to respect what an author is intending to say, even though establishing what this is may involve a degree of guesswork on our part. Yet it is not just a shot in the dark either. History, for example, places limits on interpretation. When W.B. Yeats writes in his poem 'Lapis Lazuli' that those who rebuild ruined civilisations are gay, he cannot have meant that they are homosexual. The imme-diate context may be important, too: when W.H. Auden in his elegy for Yeats asks Time to 'pardon him for writing well', we assume that he means pardon him because he was a great writer, not pardon him for being a great writer. As Empson points out in *Argufying*, we assess other people's intentions all the time without engaging in some complex reflection on the fact, rather as playing catch doesn't require a theory of dynamics.

Perhaps the most obvious contrast between the two critics is that Richards is a full-blown theorist whereas Empson is not. The latter takes a breezily pragmatic attitude to theory, believing that one should accept any theoretical approach which happens to prove productive, however mutually conflictive such methods might be. For the most part, however, critics should just follow their nose. Theories tend to restrict one's potential range of insights. When T.S. Eliot remarks that the only critical method is to be very intelligent, he could have found no finer illustration of this than his drinking mate Bill Empson. At the same time, what we might call everyday sensibility is in Empson's view a tissue of what was once conscious theory, now become unconscious and habitual. What began as a concept ends up as a custom. So theory has at least that much importance. One should also point out that *The Structure of Complex Words* is a major work of linguistic theory. Empson's prejudice against theoretical speculation also springs from the bluff, no-damn-nonsense country squire aspect of his personality. He scornfully writes off the work of a modern French philosopher known to him as 'Nerrida', a slip which might have interested Freud. Even so, there is a quality of wisdom about him lacking in many literary theorists, one which is by no means so evident in his mentor.

We have seen that Richards was a left-leaning liberal, whereas Empson was firmly ensconced on the left. He was a lifelong socialist, and remarked in the 1930s that he would have liked to be able to write poetry like the then-Marxist Auden and his Communist Party colleagues. At the same time, he dismissed the charge that poetry that was not politically engaged was necessarily escapist. He thought that the Auden group were right to demand socialism and a welfare state, and was to this extent a communist fellow traveller. He also took the side of the workers in the General Strike of 1926, at a time when a number of Oxbridge students acted as strike-breakers, and was later to proclaim his solidarity with the Chinese Revolution. He was always at odds with orthodoxies, and admired those who were regarded as traitors by their colleagues. In fact, he was just the kind of eccentric upper-class renegade whom one could imagine secretly working for the Soviets, if he had not been such an unswerving critic of Stalinism.

The finest literature, he maintains, tends to display a dissident streak. Its grandest theme, he writes in his *Essays on Renaissance Literature*, is the way in which individuals can become morally independent of the society which formed them. Works of art can afford the public some nourishment because they do not conform to conventional moral codes, and so, in pressing men and women beyond their usual boundaries, allow them a more critical view of these beliefs. It is hard to see that this is true of Pope or Goethe. The main purpose of art, Empson declares, is to allow us to encounter codes and customs different from our own. It is a worthy sentiment, but also a standard piece of liberal wisdom. Is this really the main purpose of Austen's *Emma* or Beckett's *Endgame*? One wonders why it is art, and not, say, anthropology or travel writing which is allotted this task. One also trusts that Empson, in a moment of what might now be seen as post-colonial sentimentalism, does not regard the customs of other cultures as invariably valuable, any more than our own are.

Empson sees Milton's Satan as a kind of patrician rebel, rather like himself. It is also likely that he detected a fascist or Stalinist leader in Milton's God, as did F.R. Leavis. When it comes to oppressive political regimes, he supported the communist takeover of China but harboured no illusions about the brutal reign of Mao Zedong. In this sense he was more hard-headed than the dewy-eyed Richards. Later in life he supported the Campaign for Nuclear Disarmament and opposed the United States' war in Vietnam. Yet he was also curiously tolerant of the right-wing views of a number of modernist writers, and seems at times to support an idealised version of the English class system, as well as to display a muted strain of nationalism. He writes of pastoral literature as assuming a proper and beautiful relationship between rich and poor, and observes that every nation with a strong class system needs an art form that makes the classes feel part of a larger unity or simply at home with each other. It is, however, a unity one has to work for, since pastoral displays a clash between different modes of feeling, as well as a contrast between its simple themes and complex styles. In *Some Versions of Pastoral*, published in 1935 in the throes of political and economic crisis, he appears to distance himself from what he calls 'the communists', and was never a card-carrying one himself. As we have seen already, he also remarks that there is only a limited extent to which any improvement in society can prevent tragedy, so that even the most radical politics can never be enough to repair suffering or evil altogether. Reviewing Raymond Williams's *Keywords* in the 1970s, he refers to the book's socialist arguments as 'propaganda'. Yet he did not regard propaganda as inherently objectionable, so he may not be using the term pejoratively. Nor does his sense of the limits of political change dim his enthusiasm for social progress.

If Empson considered himself on the far left in his later years, however, it is unlikely that he would have accepted a knighthood or written a masque for the Queen, as he did when she visited Sheffield. All the same, he is more 'modern' than Richards, and certainly more so than Eliot, in his cheerful acceptance of the style of such popular newspaper headlines as ITALIAN ASSASSIN BOMB PLOT DISASTER, which not only provide rich meat for his appetite for ambiguity but which strike him as an effective mode of writing. Unlike Leavis, he believes it might be to the benefit of civilisation, rather than its ruin, if such uses of language caught on more generally. As far as being up to date goes, he was also a fan of the Beatles, though he mixed this appetite for the new with the more traditional pastime of playing shove ha'penny in pubs.

However stubborn a nonconformist he was, Empson never ceased to be a member of the English gentry, precisely because such nonconformism ran deep in its veins. Patricians behave as though they are a law unto themselves, which makes them hard at times to distinguish from anarchists. Empson is reported to have acted like this in everyday life. A certain errant individualism may be expected of those who do not have to conform to the conventions because they set them themselves. Empson invested a great deal of value in independence of mind, which set him at odds with the ruling social orthodoxies at the same time as it made him suspicious of 'tribal' loyalties such as communism. In the familiar tradition of the English upper classes, he

166

was quirky, unruly, forthright and sometimes curmudgeonly; but he also displayed a certain aristocratic spirit of geniality and affability, the irony and good humour of those who enjoy an easy authority.

This is one reason why he was wary of tragedy, despite the fact that several commentators have detected an undertow of fear, gloom and anxiety in his writing. The gentleman associates seriousness with the earnest, self-important language of the puritanical middle classes, and is out to deflate it whenever he can seize the chance. He also has an affection for the rogue or underdog, being something of an outsider himself, and this, as we shall see, is one of the themes of *Some Versions of Pastoral*. The landlord has a sneaking regard for the poacher, as opposed to the respectable gamekeeper. Empson particularly admired the eighteenth-century novelist Henry Fielding, who was in some ways his alter ego: upper-class, genial, ironic and generous-spirited, yet a shrewd judge of men and women with no illusions about human nature. *Using Biography* contains a fine essay on Fielding's *Tom Jones*.

Much of Empson's patrician background is captured in his prose style, which is jaunty, idiomatic and occasionally flippant. It is the facetious, mildly knockabout style of the wayward aristocrat who disdains the high-mindedness of the bourgeoisie. There is also a strain of Yorkshire bluntness about it, an impatience with fuss and nonsense. The gentleman can dispense with decorative language because he knows nobody is going to mistake him for a plumber. He remarks in *Argufying* that the seventeenth-century poet John Wilmot, Earl of Rochester, could talk in a plain-man way because he was a great lord and a favourite of the king. Yet his own laid-back, eminently readable prose is packed with subtleties of insight which place a heavy demand on the reader. As Michael Wood puts it, 'the double effect of high-powered thought and offhand statement is spectacular'.[8] Or, one might say, the combination of common sense and sheer idiosyncrasy. It is hard to see how any form of writing can be at once so lucid and so intricate. Like Empson's own definition of pastoral, it puts the complex into the simple.

He can also be funny in a way unlike the other critics discussed in this book. He writes with Freudian scepticism of the first line of Keats's 'Ode on Melancholy' – 'No, no; go not to Lethe; neither twist . . .' – that 'somebody, or some force in the poet's mind, must have wanted to go to Lethe very much, if it took four negatives in the first line to stop them' (STA, p. 205). (Empson no doubt has in mind here Freud's concept of denegation, meaning that an overemphatic denial implies an unconscious affirmation.) In *Milton's God*, he imagines a sadist who might live in fear of hell being welcomed instead into heaven, since the saved, according to one Christian tradition, reap malicious pleasure from the torments of the damned. 'Settling down to hold kind God's hand for all eternity', he watches 'old mother being ripped to pieces so much more satisfyingly than he could ever have imagined' (MG, p. 250). Empson, John Haffenden remarks, is 'a great entertainer'.[9]

The best way to convey something of the flavour of Empson's criticism is simply to quote him. We can begin with this celebrated passage from *Seven Types*, in which he examines the first four lines of Shakespeare's Sonnet 73:

That time of year thou mayst in me behold
When yellow leaves, or none, or few, do hang
Upon those boughs which shake against the cold,
Bare ruin'd choirs, where late the sweet birds sang.

The bare boughs are like ruined choirs, Empson claims,

> ... because ruined monastery choirs are places in which to sing, because they involve sitting in a row, because they are made of wood, are carved into knots and so forth, because they used to be surrounded by a sheltering building crystallised out of the likeness of a forest, and coloured with stained glass and painting like flowers and leaves, because they are now abandoned by all but the grey walls coloured like the skies of winter, because the cold and Narcissistic charm suggested by choir-boys suits well with Shakespeare's feeling for the object of the Sonnets, and for various sociological and historical reasons (the protestant destruction of monasteries; fear of puritanism) which it would be hard now to trace out in their proportions; these reasons, and many more relating the simile to its place in the Sonnet, must all combine to give the line its beauty, and there is a sort of ambiguity in not knowing which of them to hold most clearly in mind. (STA, pp. 2–3)

Nobody had ever read poetry as closely as this before, and certainly nobody from the landed gentry. Empson himself claimed that he had inherited the technique from the poet Robert Graves; but one of the works by Graves which influenced him in this respect was co-authored with Graves's partner Laura Riding; so that one of the originators of close reading, a method which has sometimes been seen as 'masculine' on account of its clinical, toughly analytical approach, was actually a woman.

There is something of the precocious undergraduate show-off in the passage just quoted, as there is in the book in general. Empson takes a sly pleasure in discomforting the reader, as when in a later work, *Argufying*, he interprets the last line of Shelley's 'Ode to the West Wind' – 'If Winter comes, can Spring be far behind?' – as meaning 'Though the Bourbons have got back their thrones, which is bad, the resulting exasperation will bring world revolution all the sooner, which is good' (A, p. 323). He had later to cut out of *Seven Types* what he felt were a number of tedious witticisms, and there is a sense in which the nonchalant brilliance of his virtuoso reading of the Shakespeare sonnet is itself a joke at the reader's expense, relentlessly piling one meaning on another (some of them brazenly fanciful) and gleefully anticipating the reader's incredulous response ('surely Shakespeare can't have intended all that!'). The book's title is also a kind of joke: since seven is traditionally a magic number, from seven dwarfs to seven sacraments, it seems to have some portentous significance, but Empson's division of types of ambiguity into seven categories is in fact fairly arbitrary.

The casual slinging together of one clause after another in the Shakespeare commentary is not only a classic example of Empsonian bravura, but – since it forms a single sentence – suggests that the author, enraptured by his own imaginative fertility but trying not to betray the fact, could go on forever. There is something implacable about the way the passage refuses to take a breath. There is also a comic or ironic disproportion between this single line of poetry and the surplus of critical insight it evokes. The critic is in danger of 'drowning in his own incontinence', as John Haffenden puts it (A, p. 4). It is as though the commentary, instead of subjecting itself to the work it examines, is trying to outdo it with its own imaginative acrobatics at the very moment it seems to stay tenaciously true to the words on the page. If it pays homage to the work, it also risks putting it in the shade. Yet the more meanings the commentary plucks from the line, like a magician conjuring doves from thin air, the more it suggests how miraculously condensed it must be, and so the more compliments it implicitly pays it. By the time we arrive at the end of the passage, we are meant to understand that this pyrotechnic display is not simply a matter of the critic revelling in his own exuberance but an attempt to understand why the image is so hauntingly beautiful. In the end, the intellect is in the service of the emotions; but at the same time beauty is treated as something that can be analysed and argued over, rather than as a mystery which slips through the net of language.

Seven Types also contains an analysis of some lines from T.S. Eliot's *The Waste Land*, beginning 'The Chair she sat in, like a burnished throne . . .'. Part of Empson's commentary on the passage runs as follows:

What is *poured* may be *cases, jewels, glitter*, or *light*, and *profusion*, enriching its modern meaning with its derivation, is shared, with a dazzled luxury, between them; so that while some of the *jewels* are pouring out *light* from their *cases*, others are *poured* about, as are their *cases*, on the dressing-table. If referring to *glitter*, *poured* may, in any case, be a main verb as well as a participle. There is a more trivial point of the same kind in the next line, where *glass* may stand alone for a glass bottle or may be paired with *ivory* ('vials of glass'); and *unstoppered* may refer only to *glass*, or to *vials and glass*, or to *vials of glass and of ivory*; till *lurked*, which is for a moment taken as the same grammatical form, attracts it towards *perfumes*. It is because of this blurring of the grammar into luxury that the scientific word *synthetic* is able to stand out so sharply as a dramatic and lyrical high light. (STA, pp. 77–8)

He continues along these lines for quite a while. It is a masterly demonstration of how you can derive a rich cluster of ambiguities from grammar and syntax alone. Yet it is typical of Empson's approach that he says almost nothing about the atmosphere of the piece – the sense of a cloying exoticism, one also to be found in the sumptuous language of Shakespeare's *Antony and Cleopatra*. (The Eliot passage is a pastiche of some lines in the play.) The language achieves its effect partly by playing off a sense of splendour against a disquieting whiff of decadence. If it manages to create an effect of genuine beauty, it also intimates that there is something unnatural and claustrophobic about it. Like Miss Havisham in Dickens's *Great Expectations*, this woman seems not to have put her head out of doors for several decades, and (so one feels) might disintegrate if she did, though it is true that a breeze is blowing through her window. One might also have expected a comment on the fact that the lines constitute a single sentence, with its various clauses linked by commas, semi-colons and a dash, and that this creates a feeling of sensory overload, as one opulent effect is heaped lavishly on another without giving us time to pause and digest them. The word 'synthetic' hints at a negative judgement on all this extravagant artifice, and perhaps on the pampered woman at the centre of it. The passage occurs in a section of *The Waste Land* which denigrates women in general, so that there is an ironic quality to its apparent relish of the richness it portrays.

Empson does indeed comment from time to time on mood and emotional texture, but much of the time these matters are edged aside by his focus on meaning. Another example of his eye for different shades of sense are his observations on John Donne's enigmatic phrase 'Weep me not dead' in his poem 'A Valediction, of weeping', which Empson thinks may mean

> do not make me cry myself to death; do not kill me with the sight of your tears; do not cry for me as for a man already dead, when, in fact, I am in your arms; and, with a different sort of feeling, do not exert your power over the sea as to make it drown me by sympathetic magic . . . (STA, p. 144)

Turning to George Herbert's poem 'The Sacrifice', he quotes the following verse, in which the speaker is Christ:

> Oh all ye who pass by, behold and see;
> Man stole the fruit, but I must climb the tree,

The tree of life, to all but only me.
Was ever grief like mine?

Empson's extraordinary reading of this stanza runs as follows:

> [Christ] climbs the tree to repay what was stolen, as if he was
> putting the apple back; but the phrase in itself implies rather
> that he is doing the stealing, that so far from sinless he is
> Prometheus and the criminal. Either he stole on behalf of man
> (it is he who appeared to be sinful, and was caught up the tree)
> or he is climbing upwards, like Jack on the Beanstalk, and
> taking his people with him back to Heaven. The phrase has an
> odd humility which makes us see him as the son of the house;
> possibly Herbert is drawing on the medieval tradition that the
> Cross was made of the wood of the forbidden trees. Jesus seems
> a child in this metaphor, because he is the Son of God, because
> he can take apples without actually stealing (though there is
> some doubt about this), because of the practical and domestic
> associations of such a necessity, and because he is evidently
> smaller than Man, or at any rate than Eve, who could pluck the
> fruit without climbing . . . on the other hand, the son stealing
> from his father's orchard is a symbol of incest; in the person of
> the Christ the supreme act of sin is combined with the supreme
> act of virtue. (STA, p. 232)

'I must climb the tree' means 'I must ascend the Cross'; but the Cross
is traditionally associated with the tree in the Garden of Eden from

which Eve plucks the fateful apple, so that the Redemption happens on the same spot as the Fall. In an imaginative *tour de force*, Empson sees Christ's ascending the Cross as being at the same time his climbing the tree of Eden in order to replace the apple which doomed the human race, thus undoing the Fall; and this goes hand in hand with his redemptive act on Calvary. Yet he also seems to be imitating Eve's action through his close association with lethal apples and cursed trees, and is thus a thief or outlaw himself. This is appropriate, since the crucified Christ is indeed a kind of criminal – both because he was found guilty of a crime by the authorities (though of what crime we can't be sure), but also because according to St Paul he was 'made sin' on the Cross in order to become representative of human sinfulness, and thus to redeem it by his Resurrection. So Christ is redeemer and reprobate together, rather like the Prometheus who stole fire for the sake of humanity, and incestuous to boot. He is a child because he is innocent, but also because he is a mischievous little scamp who knocks off other people's property.

Empson completes his remarks with a flurry of paradoxes: '[Christ] is scapegoat and tragic hero; loved because hated; hated because godlike; freeing from torture because tortured; torturing his torturers because all-merciful; source of all strength to men because by accepting he exaggerates their weakness; and, because outcast, creating the possibility of society' (STA, p. 233).

This, which is far more theologically perceptive stuff than the image of God as Stalin, neatly encapsulates the essence of Empson's next book, *Some Versions of Pastoral*, which for all its differences from *Seven Types* has a latent continuity with it. The quotation also suggests how Christian in spirit the pastoral book is, disgusted though its author would have been to hear it.

Some Versions begins with another of Empson's legendary bouts of brilliance, this time inspired by a verse from Thomas Gray's 'Elegy Written in a Country Churchyard':

> Full many a gem of purest ray serene
> The dark, unfathomed caves of ocean bear;
> Full many a flower is born to blush unseen
> And waste its sweetness on the desert air.

Gray has in mind talented men and women who, because of their humble social circumstances, will never have the chance to excel in the world's eyes. What this means, Empson remarks,

> . . . is that eighteenth-century England had no scholarship system or *carriere ouverte aux talents*. This is stated as pathetic, but the reader is put into a mood in which one would not try to alter it. . . . By comparing the social arrangement to Nature he makes it seem inevitable, which it was not, and gives it a dignity which was undeserved. Furthermore, a gem does not mind being in a cave and a flower prefers not to be picked; we feel that the man is like the flower, as short-lived, natural, and valuable, and this tricks us into feeling that he is better off without opportunities. The sexual suggestion of *blush* brings in the Christian idea that virginity is good in itself, and so that any renunciation

is good; this may trick us into feeling it is lucky for the poor man that society keeps him unspotted from the World. The tone of melancholy claims that the poet understands the considerations opposed to aristocracy, though he judges against them; the truism of the reflections in the churchyard, the universality and impersonality this gives to the style, claim as if by comparison that we ought to accept the injustice of society as we do the inevitability of death. (SVP, pp. 11–12)

There are one or two doubtful moves here: the idea that Christianity regards virginity as a value in itself is debatable, and if a gem does not mind being in a cave because it is not aware of the fact, it is hard to see why an equally insensate flower should object to being plucked. Even so, Empson superbly demonstrates how the tone and feeling of the verse are subtly undercut by its imagery – how a lament over the condition of the poor is qualified by the implication that nothing can be done about it. It is as though the poet identifies with the plight of the lowly, yet at the same time uses tropes which imply that it is inevitable in the very act of seeking to dignify it.

Some such ambiguous relationship lies for Empson at the heart of pastoral literature, in his own idiosyncratic use of the term. Pastoral presents us with both aristocrats and peasants, courtiers and rustics; and the aristocrats must acknowledge their difference from ordinary people while being mindful of the humanity they share in common. It is sometimes a good thing, Empson argues, to stand apart from your society so far as you can. This is his nonconformist persona speaking, disdainful of conventions and herd-like consensus. Like the face of the Buddha, the ideal is to be both blind and all-seeing – blind to tribal prejudices, but therefore able to expand and enrich the self in an openness to the reality of others. 'Some people are more delicate and complex than others', he writes, and 'if such people can keep this distinction from doing harm it is a good thing, though a small thing by comparison with our common humanity' (SVP, p. 23). The last phrase evokes the more sociable, socialistic Empson; so that it is a question of affirming individual difference and independence while continuing to prize what we share in common. Pastoral is among other things about this equipoise, which we shall find in a different form in the work of F.R. Leavis. The nobleman not only finds himself reflected in the rustic, but can also learn from him in a spirit of humility. Empson imagines him thinking:

> I now abandon my specialised feelings because I am trying to find better ones, so I must balance myself for the moment by imagining the feelings of the simple person. He may be in a better state than I am by luck, freshness, or divine grace . . . I must imagine his way of feeling because the refined thing must be judged by the fundamental thing, because strength must be learnt in weakness and sociability in isolation, because the best manners are learnt in the simple life. (SVP, pp. 22–3)

Empson learned from Buddhism the value of an organic relationship to Nature, an affinity with the world which prefigures today's ecological thought; and this he considered the only tolerable philosophy, one sharply at odds with what he regarded as the vile Christian cult of sacrificing Nature, or various parts of it, to a vindictive God. In the latter case, the One (Christ) is sacrificed to the Many, destroyed for its sake, while in pastoral the One contains the Many, rather as the all-seeing artist does. The scapegoat, who is sacrificed on behalf of the people as a whole, thereby unites the One and the Many, and like Christ is both high and low, unique and representative, victim and redeemer, hero and swain. Empson also learnt from Buddhism a way of balancing the claims of individual freedom with social responsibility. The Buddha is sufficient to himself yet full of universal charity. Individual distinction and common humanity, which in the process of living are a matter of constant trade-offs, compromises and contradictions, are reconciled in this utopian vision.

Pastoral is among other things Empson's warning to himself of the dangers of being too clever. The canny common sense of the peasant must keep the speculative intellectual in check. The class system is thus both challenged and upheld: patricians see the peasants as their equals or even as their betters, yet they cannot pretend that they themselves are simple rustics, which would be like the bad faith of middle-class authors who write about the proletariat while imagining that they are part of them. There were plenty of such types around at the time the book appeared. Effective proletarian literature, Empson considers in an enigmatic chapter on the subject, is a version of pastoral, airily passing over the fact that such writing is usually dedicated to dismantling the very class system on which pastoral depends.

Pastoral, then, is a matter of irony: the rich are richer than the poor, but they are poorer as well. The two social groups clash, but an equivalence is established between them all the same, rather as an ambiguity involves a convergence of conflicting meanings. It is hard not to see all this as an allegory of the relationship between the artistic (or critic) and the general public, rather as Stefan Collini sees the key terms examined in Empson's next study, *The Structure of Complex Words*, as all relating in some undeclared way to his own critical process.[10] The artist, Empson maintains, is never at one with any public – a reckless generalisation, to be sure, one truer of modern Europe than of some pre-modern cultures. The same goes for critics, whose specialised intelligence (not least if it is as adroit as Empson's) estranges them from the mass of people. Yet the paradox of literary art is that it deals in complex, sometimes highly technical ways with feelings and situations which are shared for the most part by humanity as a whole. It is, so to speak, both amateur and professional, complex and simple, elevated and mundane. The American critic R.P. Blackmur describes it as 'the formal discourse of the amateur'.[11] Empson himself was an academic and professional literary critic, yet he does not have a special field in the usual manner of scholars, roaming in the style of an erudite amateur over the whole of English literature. Unlike brain surgery, literary criticism is something that anyone can have a stab at. Anyone can say whether they enjoyed a book or not, or pass a few mildly intelligent remarks about its plot, characters and so on. Empson, of course, is a lot cleverer than this, but it is the kind of cleverness to which we feel we ourselves might aspire, the shrewdness of someone better versed in our common wisdom than we are ourselves. He has a kind of flat common sense pushed to the point of genius.

The writer or critic, then, is aristocrat and peasant in one body – both complex and simple, isolated yet in solidarity with others.

We need subtle and delicate instruments to investigate works which concern our common condition, but the problem is that these very instruments risk alienating us from that condition. This is one sense in which pastoral is an ironic mode. In the political climate of the 1930s, the fraught relations between the intelligentsia and the masses was a contentious issue on the left; and although Empson does not appeal explicitly to that context, it can be felt hovering somewhere in the background. For the upper classes to go to school with the lower orders is part of what he means by pastoral 'putting the complex into the simple' (SVP, p. 25). There is a coexistence in the form of the elevated and the mundane, rather as there is in the Incarnation, where God becomes a homeless Jew in an obscure corner of the Roman Empire. Putting the complex into the simple also means that in this vein of literary art, so-called rustics are made to speak the formal, elaborate language of the court, which teeters on the brink of being funny. This has the effect of bringing the two ranks together, thus buttressing the class system, at the same time as the homely wisdom of the lower orders can act as a critique of the sophisticated learning of the higher ones. One might say that the two classes converge in verbal form but conflict in moral content.

Yet if this ideal of harmony might be unsurprising in a man who was reared on a large country estate, and who was himself artist, critic and gentleman rolled into one, there is another, more subversive side to pastoral, as there is to Empson himself. For one thing, if the rustics are equal to their rulers in the ornateness of their speech, the class system is levelled as well as reinforced. If the complex can be put into the simple, then the simple cannot be as simple as all that. At the same time, the lower classes are superior to the upper classes because they retain an honesty, dignity and simplicity which can show up their rulers as artificial and insincere. Empson himself, it may be worth noting, was brought up to respect manual labour in the countryside. The pastoral assumption, he writes, is that you can say everything about complex people by a complete consideration of simple people. To this extent, it is an egalitarian form as well as a hierarchical one.

The artist, critic, child, aristocrat and intellectual are all in their different ways outsiders. The aristocrat may stand at the apex of society, but this can be a lonely place to be. The fool, clown, rogue and scapegoat are also outsiders, and they, too, at least in Empson's sense of the term, are pastoral figures. In this sense, the low reflects the high, and the high finds a parody of itself in the low. The same happens in the double plots of some Elizabethan plays, to which Empson devotes a chapter of his book. The clown, he remarks, 'has the wit of the Unconscious; he can speak the truth because he has nothing to lose' (SVP, p. 18). His own work was described as 'clownish' by some disapproving colleagues. The Fool, who sees all because he lurks on the margins of society as a satirical spectator, has more sense than his social betters and a firmer grasp of fundamental truths. The fact that he knows he is a Fool, in contrast with apparently sensible folk who are unaware of their own folly, lends him a kind of wisdom. In a similar way, the rogue has a fuller understanding of law and authority than those who formally dispense justice.

Children have yet to be fully inducted into the conventions of society, and are thus less ready to take them for granted. On the contrary, they may well find them pointless and farcical, as Alice does in Wonderland, and may therefore act as critics of social orthodoxy. Alice, Empson remarks in his chapter on her in this work, is 'the free and independent mind' (SVP, p. 210), a no-nonsense rationalist like Empson himself, and thus something like the ideal literary critic. Yet the irony is that free-wheeling individuals are fundamentally reliant on the social system to which they stand askew, and may feel this to be a form of bad faith. If everything is fundamentally one, then their autonomy is an illusion; yet standing alone can still yield them some insight into the essential arbitrariness of social conventions, as it does in the end with Alice. So there is something to be said for contrarians, however morally compromised they may be. In any case, the very idea of an individual is a case of ambiguity, since you become one only through dependence on a form of social existence. The word originally meant 'inseparable'.

Part of what the free mind discerns is the fallibility of the human condition, and this, too, is a 'pastoral' feeling. By grounding himself in common humanity, the nobleman can engage with an earthy wisdom which is tolerant of human weakness and all-encompassing in its sympathies. It is a capacious, good-humoured way of seeing which knows when not to ask too much of others. We must admire the high heroic values of truth, goodness and honour, but we should not use these ideals to terrorise others in a way which makes them painfully conscious of their own frailty. Empson's own relaxed, companionable prose style is a version of pastoral in just this sense. It is the style of a humanist – but in an ironic rather than triumphalist sense of the term, which is to say one who embraces humanity in a wry awareness of its deficiencies. There is a 'flatness' about pastoral, in the sense of a scepticism of high-pitched pretensions. Empson finds this quality in the eighteenth-century scholar Richard Bentley's plain-minded commentary on *Paradise Lost*; in Alice's brisk, very English common sense in her dealings with the freakish denizens of Wonderland; and in the clear-eyed, disenchanted view of polite society of the underworld of *The Beggar's Opera*. The higher you aspire, the further you have to fall: this is part of the warning of the speaker of Shakespeare's Sonnet 94 to the young courtier he is addressing. Those who, like the young man, are most detached from everyday sensual appetite are most likely to come a cropper when confronted with it, which is why lilies that fester smell far worse than weeds. The same could be said of Angelo in Shakespeare's *Measure for Measure*.

There is an arithmetical subtext to the work of this former mathematician. We have seen already that the notion of pastoral is bound up in Empson's thought with the idea of the One and the Many, which he derives for the most part from Eastern thought. Ambiguity can roll a multiplicity of meanings into a single term, and the same is true, as we shall see later, of what Empson calls 'complex words'. Pastoral stages discordant voices and contending modes of feeling, but it does so within an all-inclusive vision. The Milton of *Milton's God* is a single author split in two by his conflicting religious and humanist sympathies. The Buddha is one, but in what Empson sees as his 'ironic magnanimity' he presents to the world a multiplicity of faces. Both the king and the Fool are individuals, but they are also representative of more than themselves – the king, hero or nobleman because he incarnates in his person a whole social order, the Fool because he typifies our shared infirmities. Both contain multitudes, and there is a secret handy-dandy complicity between them. So is there in the fact that anyone who wants to be a king must be out of his mind, as Shakespeare's history plays might testify. There is also a link between these figures and the artist, critic or political rebel, who is similarly an outsider, but who just on this account can see further than many an insider. Thus the Adam and Eve of *Paradise Lost* are pastoral types in their harmonious relation with Nature, but Satan, as a critic of Creation, is a pastoral figure in a different sense.

Another such character is the scapegoat, who like Christ is an individual, but who bears on his innocent shoulders the sins of the whole of humanity. He is thereby allied with the villain or criminal, another outsider who can see through the elaborate pretences of social existence. Christ the One descends to share the destiny of the Many, which is an instance of the complex thing, spiritually speaking, setting up home with the simple. He is the single swain tending his multiple flock, but he is also portrayed as a lamb himself. The high must stoop to the low not only to redeem it, but to become part of it and learn enduringly from it. Despite Empson's near-pathological abhorrence of the Judaeo-Christian God, whom he compares in *Milton's God* to a Belsen commandant, the pastoral vision is at its most Christian in its faith that strength is rooted in weakness, and that the sublime thing (salvation) must be judged by the mundane thing (giving someone a cup of water). It is on such bathos that the Christian Gospel turns.

The most refined desires, Empson comments in both Freudian and pastoral vein, are inherent in the plainest, and would be false if they weren't. As F.R. Leavis puts it in his own distinctive idiom, 'humane culture, even in its most refined forms, [must] be kept appropriately aware of its derivation from and dependence on the culture of the soil'.[12] If you press this case too far, however, you end up with a vulgar Freudian reduction of all values to base instinct, a case of which the rationalist Empson is deeply wary. It accounts for why he finds Jonathan Swift 'blasphemous', with his brutal hacking down of the spiritual to the physical. To see the noblest desires as inherent in the plainest is not to rewrite every generous motivation as crass appetite. Despite these reservations, perhaps the most fundamental aspect of literary art in Empson's eyes is its awareness of the limits of the human situation – of loss, waste, fragility and failure. In this way, his humanism has a tragic inflection.

What Empson detests most about Christianity is the idea of sacrifice. God, he holds in a remarkably crude piece of theology, slaughters his own Son while reaping some grisly satisfaction from the fact.[13] Such barbarism must be distinguished from the non-sacrificial solidarity with others which pastoral involves. Selflessness is to be commended, but self-sacrifice is not. What this overlooks is that those who devote themselves selflessly to the cause of the 'swains' – the obscure and inconspicuous of this world – are quite likely to end up as sacrificial victims of the political state. Indeed, this is part of the central message of the Christian faith. Empson himself prefers those tragic heroes who give their lives for others to those (Hamlet, Macbeth, Othello, Coriolanus) whose heroic stature isolates them from humanity at large. It is good to stand a little aside – how else can one be a critic? – but not to the point at which one becomes sterilely self-enclosed.

Some Versions has a discussion of Shakespeare's much debated Sonnet 94, in which the speaker urges a narcissistic friend to persevere in his distasteful state of self-absorption, if only because there is no other way in which he might avoid succumbing to some ruinous temptation. Ironically, the speaker tries to make his plea more persuasive by comparing his friend's 'unnatural' estrangement from Nature to the innocence of a flower, which similarly lives only for itself. Humanity's separation from Nature is itself made to seem natural, rather as it is in Andrew Marvell's poem 'The Garden', to which Empson devotes a magnificent chapter. There is an ironic relationship between consciousness and the world, since the mind both is and is not part of its material surroundings; but this tension can itself be accommodated within the bountiful spirit of pastoral. It is a poetic mode which knows a moment of potentially tragic separation between mind and world, the cultivated and the simple, self-reflection and spontaneity; but it includes this insight within a richer, more complex vision which recognises that the intellectual must go to school with the masses, that there can be no fine things without humble things, and that the mind is an outcrop of Nature, not simply distinct from it.

Some critics read *Some Versions* as recording the decline of the pastoral form, claiming that this makes some sense of its odd assortment of topics.[14] In the sixteenth and seventeenth centuries, with their rock-solid class systems, pastoral could draw assuredly on a fixed gulf between peasants and aristocrats. In post-Restoration

England, however, the artifice of the form, in which rustics speak like noblemen, becomes more obvious, not least to a Puritan sensibility that finds it pretentious, so that pastoral begins to veer into mock-pastoral. John Gay's *The Beggar's Opera* is Empson's prime example of this shift, as the criminal orders continue to hold a mirror up to the morally disreputable aristocracy, but in a knowing, self-conscious way. Pastoral has lost its innocence, and with *Alice in Wonderland* can recover that naturalness only in the world of the child. In this sense, the story of pastoral is bound up with the evolution of English class society.

Empson was stung by the accusation that his approach to poetry in *Seven Types* was unhistorical; and though *Some Versions* is not much of a historical inquiry either, it is certainly more social and political than the former work. In general, Empson moves throughout his career from close poetic analysis to a more historically sensitive, socially responsive approach. Ambiguities which in *Seven Types* were mostly verbal become in the later book the claim (for example) that the poor are both richer and poorer than the rich. It is in *The Structure of Complex Words*, however, a work he himself justly describes as 'wonderful' and 'magnificent', that the linguistic and historical finally converge, to the point where Empson can be classified not only as a literary critic but as a historical linguist. In the case of ambiguity, different meanings clash to the point of indeterminacy; what concerns Empson here, however, is the interaction between different but determinate meanings within a single word. This means seeing certain key words as nodes or clusters of sense, or, if one prefers, as miniature texts. And since these terms change over time, capturing shifts in social and moral attitudes, we can speak of this form of inquiry as historical. Words, in C.S. Lewis's term, have 'biographies'. Stefan Collini points out that whereas an ambiguity for Empson is a device contrived by an individual writer, the structure of a complex word is a fact of the language, part of the established verbal currency.[15]

Empson describes these words as 'compacted doctrines', given that they can be unpacked into a number of claims or propositions, not all of them mutually compatible. Thus Macheath the highwayman in *The Beggar's Opera* uses the word 'honest' in a hearty, raffish style, which implies a certain cavalier contempt for social convention, while for the tradesman Peachum in the same play the term has a more respectable resonance. It is as though the sign becomes a site of social conflict. Words of this kind are mini-systems containing what Empson calls 'equations' between their various senses. There can be an equation between two meanings of the same term; an equation between a word and one of its implications; an equation between the sense of a word and the feeling it evokes; or an equation between a so-called head meaning (i.e. the primary sense of a term) and a chief meaning, which is to say one demanded by a specific context. You can also bring two terms together under the heading of a third, so that, for example, 'sense' in Wordsworth can mean both sensation and imagination. This suggests a certain relation between the two in reality, and hence constitutes a proposition or 'doctrine'. Finally, there are identities such as 'God is Love', 'Might is Right' or 'Time is Money' which can be major sources of delusion, and which sail close to what is commonly described as ideology. Despite these speculations, much of the book consists of literary criticism rather than linguistic theory, as Empson illustrates his complex words in a set of coruscating chapters on 'Fool in Lear', 'Timon's Dog', 'Honesty in Othello', 'Sense in Measure for Measure' and so on. They are among the most masterly pieces of literary analysis he produced.

Since most of the key words Empson has in mind – arch, dog, fool, rogue, wit, sense, honest – also have a bluff, no-nonsense, 'earth-touching' air about them, this is yet another example of locating the complex in the simple, and thus an extension of pastoral thought. There is, Empson comments, 'a sweetness or richness in the simple thing' (SCW, p. 170), a wealth of felt implication which can be spelt out in a relatively systematic way. Hence the word 'structure': we are speaking not just of a random scatter of associations but of the evolving inner logic of certain terms, which is rooted in turn in the logic of a specific form of social existence. They are 'complex' words because they crystallise a collective social wisdom. It is worth noting that *Complex Words* appeared only two years before Wittgenstein's *Philosophical Investigations*, which takes a broadly similar attitude to language.

The simple and the complex are related in the sense that to call a man a dog is to ascribe a fundamental sincerity to him which can then become the material basis on which a more refined version of humanity may be constructed. Indeed, only on such a modest foundation can anything valuable be accomplished, which is another of Empson's unwitting acts of collusion with Christianity. Life itself is a kind of double plot, since you can build yourself into a tolerable human being only on the basis of being a mortal, vulnerable animal. As Christopher Norris writes of Empson's complex words, they have 'a down-to-earth quality of healthy scepticism . . . which permits their users to build up a trust in human nature on a shared knowledge of its needs and attendant weaknesses'.[16] It is a materialist form of ethics, as opposed to the idealising view of humanity which can only end in bitter disenchantment. It belongs with an ironic awareness of one's own limitations, as well as a mutual forbearance and tolerant sense of human infirmity, all of which goes to constitute the pastoral sensibility.

The opposite of this ironic vision (though the point remains largely implicit in Empson's work) is ideological absolutism, which in the form of both fascism and Stalinism bulked large in the period during which he produced his first two major works. When *Complex Words* appeared in 1951, fascism had only recently been defeated, and the world was becoming locked ever deeper into the Cold War. In this sense, all of these studies have a political subtext. We have seen already that the openness to different meanings typical of ambiguity is at odds with the strict determinacy of sense to be found in fascist regimes, with their rigid signifiers of *Führer*, State and Fatherland and censorship of subversive speech. It also runs counter to the prevailing philosophical fashion of the day, which from Frege and Bertrand Russell to the early Wittgenstein and A.J. Ayer was in search of a language which would be entirely rational and transparent, purged of all fuzziness and imprecision. What countered this fantasy was literary criticism, which turned from the pure ice of linguistic philosophy to the rough ground of everyday life.

We have seen that pastoral can act as a form of social critique, as the values of the patricians are tested against the wisdom of the peasants. The politics of complex words are rather similar, since many of these terms belong to a colloquial language at odds with official morality. They represent the idiom of what one might call a counter-public sphere, drawing upon a repository of largely unconscious habits of mind which has its roots in what people actually think, feel and do, rather than in what they are supposed to think, feel and do. We are witness here to the birth of a secular, rationalist climate increasingly at loggerheads with religious orthodoxy. In fact, in Empson's view, that orthodoxy is the paradigmatic case of ideology. When he speaks in *Milton's God* of 'the lethal convictions which so often capture our brains' (MG, p. 169), it is this which he has in mind. Yet *Paradise Lost* stages a struggle against ideology rather than cravenly capitulating to it, which is part of what Empson finds so magnificent about it. 'The root of [Milton's] power', he writes, 'is that he could express and accept a downright horrible conception of God and yet keep somehow alive, underneath it, all the breadth and generosity, the welcome to every noble pleasure, which had been prominent in European history just before his time' (MG, pp. 276–7). He finds the work both wonderful and atrocious, appealing because of its moral incoherence rather than in spite of it. The text puts up some vigorous resistance to its own official standpoint.

This is a strikingly original position to take up in the thick of the Milton wars, which had been waged ever since Eliot turned down his imperial thumb, and which we shall see re-emerge in the criticism of F.R. Leavis. Empson deplores Milton's formal beliefs but finds his art full of poetic beauty. In a splendidly even-handed sentence, he describes it as a 'world of harsh and hypnotic, superb and crotchety isolation' (MG, p. 126). As a stalwart rationalist himself, he also admires the vigorously argumentative way in which the poet tries to make some tolerable sense of the indefensible. Milton's decent impulses ('decent' is a typical Empsonian term) refuse to be entirely suppressed by his theological dogma.

Even so, the opposition between ideology and humanity in *Paradise Lost* is surely too simplistic. The liberal is accustomed to viewing systems of ideas as impediments to the free play of the mind, restraints on our spontaneous humanity. Yet liberalism itself, as we encounter it in the work of John Locke or John Stuart Mill, as well as in its more everyday guises, is a system of sorts, privileging certain meanings and values over others, excluding as illicit whole ranges of behaviour (slavery, socialism, authoritarianism, censorship and so on) while acclaiming others. If liberalism is a reasonably coherent set of beliefs, yet also plays a vital role in the fostering of human liberty, then system and freedom cannot be everywhere in conflict. There are emancipatory theories such as feminism, which engage in the systematic analysis of patriarchy in order to be free of it. As a regicide and radical republican, John Milton placed some of his theological doctrines at the service of a revolutionary politics. Those who see other people's views as ideological and their own as simply human, pragmatic or commonsensical may be in the grip of an ideology which has survived for so long that it has become well-nigh invisible. And to become invisible is the aim of any ideology intent on enduring.

We have seen that Eliot was pained by the language of *Paradise Lost*, and we shall see shortly that the same was true of F.R. Leavis. If

Empson had no such complaints, it is partly because both Eliot and Leavis had a normative conception of the English language, whereas Empson did not. He did not believe, as they did, that there is a particular use of English which is somehow more native, authentic and loyal to the spirit of the language than others. Nor was he much taken by the idea of a literary tradition, a preoccupation which for Eliot and Leavis was closely bound up with the normative stand-point. Tradition for them consisted of those authors who use the language 'authentically': Donne rather than Milton, Marvell rather than Dryden, Keats rather than Shelley, Hopkins rather than Tennyson. It is to Empson's credit that he spurned this prejudice, as did I.A. Richards – not only because of its inherent defects, which we have glanced at already, but also because an extreme version of it was to breed some sinister consequences in mid-twentieth-century Europe. For the philosopher Martin Heidegger, the German language was the true home of Being, the locus of the Spirit of the People. There is, to be sure, a world of difference between this Nazi dogma and Leavis's preference for the kind of palpable, earth-bound poetry which when read out loud sounds rather like chewing an apple. Both, however, are types of spiritual chauvinism, even if Heidegger was thinking of the Third Reich and Leavis of the England of Morris dancing. Empson has been called the chief English literary critic of the twentieth century.[17] But he is also to be admired for his liberal rationalist habit of deflating and demystifying portentous nonsense; and in a dark political age in which exorbitant rhetoric could maim and murder, this was a more urgent task than it usually is.

4

F.R. LEAVIS

William Empson detested F.R. Leavis, not an uncommon sentiment in the literary world of the time. T.S. Eliot felt much the same. Leavis nursed a similar antipathy to Empson. 'If you want a character study of Empson, go to Iago', he is said to have remarked.[1] In many respects, Empson and Leavis were antitypes: whereas the former was cosmopolitan, non-moralistic, upper-class, humorous, versatile in his literary interests and bohemian in lifestyle, the latter was provincial, austere, moralistic, largely humourless (at least in print), intensely serious, lower-middle-class in origin, rigorously exclusive in his literary sympathies and conventional in his way of life. It was a classic case of the Cavalier versus the Roundhead. There were deeper differences too. If Empson was a rationalist, Leavis was attuned to a depth in humanity which he called religious, though he was by no means an orthodox believer.

We have seen that Empson was an inveterate nonconformist, and the same can be said of Leavis. In fact, he was easily the most controversial English critic of the twentieth century, revered by a faithful band of followers and reviled by a good many of his academic colleagues. For all his maverick ways, however, Empson slotted easily into the metropolitan literary establishment, while Leavis doggedly refused to do so. Empson was more eccentric than subversive, and did not attack the literary canon or the social and cultural establishment in the manner of Leavis. Partly by choice, and partly because of the rancour he provoked, Leavis was an outsider in a way that Empson was not. He was the victim of prejudice and discrimination, as well as an object of odium and derision, in a way which was by no means so true of his fellow critic. Both men occupied marginal positions within academia for some years: Empson, as we have seen, taught in East Asia, remote from the charmed circle of Oxford, Cambridge and London, while Leavis spent much of his early career as a part-time, freelance teacher in Cambridge with no official status. He gained a full university appointment only at the age of 50, was belatedly elected to a fellowship of a college, and was appointed to a readership in the English Faculty only three years before his retirement. He then became a visiting professor at the University of York; but it was Cambridge whose recognition he sought, at the same time as he never ceased to decry much that it stood for.

Though he maintained that all serious intellectual work took place on the margins of academia, Leavis was by no means entirely gratified to be consigned to that borderland himself. His partner and closest collaborator, Queenie Dorothy Leavis, was never granted any official academic status: she was turned down for a college fellowship, and was later refused a university lectureship. Neither of the Leavises, however, did themselves much good by their habit of denouncing imaginary conspiracies against them (there were some real ones, too), or by their vituperative onslaughts on their colleagues. It was a classic case of what one might call the Rousseau complex: the paranoiac who happens to be genuinely persecuted. (Rousseau compounded his problems by being a hypochondriac who was always ill.) Empson, by contrast to Leavis, spent his later years occupying a professorial Chair and was esteemed throughout the literary world, whereas Leavis continued to be both execrated and admired. As far as formal public recognition goes, it would be hard to imagine Sir Frank Raymond Leavis, though he did, rather surprisingly, accept the award of Companion of Honour, the highest of British civil honours, not long before his death.

Leavis was born in Cambridge in 1895, the son of a dealer in musical instruments whose ancestors were rural craftsmen. Apart from a spell as a medical orderly with a Quaker ambulance unit during the First World War, he lived in Cambridge all his life, first as a pupil at a grammar school, then as a student of History and English at the university and finally as a teacher of English in the same institution. He spoke throughout his life with a Cambridge accent, but one typical of the town rather than the university. In contrast to the footloose, adventurous Richards and Empson, very little happened to him. He was neither attacked by Chinese bandits nor erotically attracted to Japanese taxi drivers. He did, however, turn Cambridge into the hub of a campaign whose influence was to spread throughout the world, and which transformed the nature of English studies.

If T.S. Eliot had already redrawn the literary map, Leavis pressed this project further. He was continually charting, connecting, comparing, contrasting, tracing lines of continuity, inquiring where this comes in relation to that – an activity which he termed 'placing'. In fact, he pushed Eliot's project to the point where not many venerable reputations are left standing. The only truly great English novelists are Jane Austen, George Eliot, Henry James, Joseph Conrad and D.H. Lawrence, two of whom were not English at all. Dickens is first spurned and later exalted. The medieval period is almost wholly ignored, though Leavis recorded his preference for Chaucer rather than Dante, partly perhaps as a put-down of Eliot and partly as a patriotic smack at Continental Europe. Edmund Spenser is decisively dethroned. English literature, then, effectively begins with Shakespeare. Leavis shared Eliot's high estimation of the Metaphysical poets and Elizabethan and Jacobean dramatists; he also launched an assault on Milton a good deal more bare-knuckled than that of his more kid-gloved colleague. (There is, incidentally, an irony in this onslaught, given that Milton and Leavis were both militant, patriotic, Puritan-minded, dissident public intellectuals.)

Dryden and the Restoration yield little of value, though John Bunyan is an author to be admired. Whereas Eliot was for the most part lukewarm about the eighteenth century, Leavis praised Pope and (more equivocally) Swift, as well as Samuel Johnson and a range of more minor writers of the time. As we shall see later, he had reason to admire the so-called Augustan age, while Eliot did not. Like the latter, he charted what is for the most part a deteriorating history of sensibility from the seventeenth century to the present;

but it is a less drastic decline than Eliot's, since the latter largely disregarded the Romantics, who were uncongenial to his classical temperament and offered few resources for his own poetic practice. He also seemed uninspired by the nineteenth-century novel. Leavis, by contrast, found a good deal of merit in both. As poetry lapses into languor and sentimentalism in the nineteenth century, one of the finest of all European literary creations, the realist novel, moves to the fore. It is Eliot's apparent indifference to this genre which deepens his literary pessimism. In fact, though it is Leavis who is usually accused of being excessively narrow in his tastes, there is a sense in which Eliot was even more exclusive, at least when it comes to the literature of his adopted country.

If Eliot paid little heed to the Romantics, Leavis discriminated scrupulously among them. Wordsworth, Coleridge and Keats are mostly in, while Byron and Shelley are unquestionably out. From then on, there is really no truly outstanding poet to be found in the barren wastes of Victorian verse until we arrive at Gerard Manley Hopkins, who was scarcely a name to conjure with in the literary climate of the time. Nor, indeed, was that of T.S. Eliot, of whose early poetry Leavis was one of the first champions. He was also an early advocate of W.B. Yeats. Ezra Pound's *Hugh Selwyn Mauberley*, then a little-known work, is acclaimed, but his *Cantos* are savaged. James Joyce's *Ulysses* also comes in for some rough treatment. Virginia Woolf and her Bloomsbury colleagues are spurned as a tribe of precious aesthetes and social parasites, while W.H. Auden and his associates are arraigned for their modish Leftism. The finest novelist and literary critic of the modern age is without question D.H. Lawrence. There is a robust poetic tradition running from Shakespeare, Ben Jonson, the Metaphysical poets and Jacobean dramatists to Pope, Wordsworth, Keats, Hopkins and Eliot, as well as a largely sterile legacy which passes from Spenser and Milton to Shelley, Tennyson and Swinburne.

The parallels and differences between Leavis and Eliot are interesting to note. Leavis borrows from Eliot the doctrines of impersonality and the dissociation of sensibility, as well as the idea of tradition – though his tradition is less of a quasi-mystical entity than Eliot's, and greater weight is assigned to the individual author. Both men saw tradition as value-laden, a selection of ancestors shaped by the needs and proclivities of the present, rather than as a neutral chronicle of past authors. Both critics saw the whole of English literature as forming an organic unity, and were sensitively attuned to its social and historical context. They shared a belief that writers must be fully alive to their own time, inventing techniques which are adequate to contemporary habits of feeling and forms of experience. It is this that Leavis believes Eliot to have accomplished in his early poetry.

Eliot was not an academic, and Leavis, though a member of the tribe himself, viewed the literary scholar as the enemy of the literary critic. In his view, the intellectual habits bred by scholarly research are incompatible with the imaginative, subtly perceptive mind. Both thinkers were cultural pessimists, bearing witness to a Fall from a social order they admired into a corrupt modern age, though they located their ideal civilisations in different centuries. Both men were concerned with language and sensibility, though Leavis placed more weight than Eliot on the role of moral values in literary art. If he derived many of his critical ideas from the latter, much of his moral vision was shaped by D.H. Lawrence. As we have seen, he was more open than Eliot to Romanticism and the realist novel, while Eliot was more receptive than Leavis to the medieval period, modernist experiment and the literature of Continental Europe. Both critics saw the language of poetry as a sensory, almost physiological affair which resists rationalist abstraction. Neither was enamoured of general theories. Leavis, however, was a liberal humanist, whereas Eliot was neither liberal nor humanist. If the conservative Eliot was preoccupied with social order, the passion of the liberal Leavis was for personal fulfilment. Eliot believed in God, whereas Leavis placed his faith in a secularised version of the Deity known as Life.

By what criteria does Leavis make his remarkably assured judgements? The answer lies partly in his distinctive view of the English language. It is, he believed, a linguistic form to which the concrete, palpable and sensuously particularised are somehow natural, and which is averse to the abstract, general or theoretical. At its finest, which is to say at its most poetic, English does not simply indicate things but embodies or 'enacts' them. It performs what it speaks of, creates what it communicates, so that you cannot slide a cigarette paper between the words and the experience they record. As Leavis observes of some lines by John Donne, they seem to do what they say. It is what Leavis calls a 'creative-exploratory' form of writing, as opposed to one which seems merely to reflect whatever it is about. Change the words and you change the meaning or experience, which is not the case with 'Please Use The Rear Exits'. You could rewrite this as 'Kindly Make Use Of The Back Exits' with no loss of sense. Poetry is what can't be paraphrased. Leavis is thus at odds with Empson, who sees nothing indecorous about spelling out the meaning of a poem. He is also guilty of what Ogden and Richards call 'word magic', meaning a belief in the fusion of word and thing.

A persuasive example of this crops up in Leavis's analysis of Keats's 'To Autumn' ode, in which the poet writes of the allegorical figure of Autumn:

And sometimes like a gleaner thou dost keep
Steady thy laden head across a brook

In stepping over from one line to the other, Leavis argues, we are made to enact the balancing movement of the gleaner herself. A rather less persuasive example from the same passage is his comment on the phrase 'moss'd cottage trees':

the action of the packed consonants in 'moss'd cottage trees' is plain enough: there stand the trees, gnarled and sturdy in trunk and bough, their leafy entanglements thickly loaded. It is not fanciful, I think, to find that (the sense being what it is) the pronouncing of 'cottage trees' suggests, too, the crisp bite and the flow of juice as the teeth close in the ripe apple. (CP, p. 16)[2]

One feels like responding that if this isn't fanciful, then neither are alien abductions. Rather more suggestive is his insight into a line from Samuel Johnson's poem 'The Vanity of Human Wishes' – 'For such the steady Romans shook the world' – of which he remarks: 'That "steady" turns the vague cliché, "shook the world", into the felt percussion of tramping legions' (R, p. 118).

What Leavis does is to select a particular kind of English – racy, sinewy, earthy, muscular, idiomatic – and find in it the very essence of the language, so that those who write in this vein are commended and many of those who do not are cast into the outer darkness. For him, poetry is what St John calls in a more lofty context 'the Word made flesh'. His conception of the language, in other words, is normative rather than simply descriptive. There are a whole set of value judgements built into it from the outset. What one might call sensuous specificity has indeed come to be prized in poetry; but as we have seen in the case of Eliot, this is truer of the Romantic and post-Romantic period than it is of the age of Gray's 'Elegy', and to require it of poetry or language as a whole is surely unreasonable. Samuel Johnson thought that the particular was relatively insignificant and the general of supreme interest.

The work of Thomas Wyatt, John Clare, Arthur Hugh Clough or Christina Rossetti is not especially racy or sinewy, but neither is it intended to be. Whereas Keats uses elaborate adjectives like 'cool-rooted', John Clare would probably just write 'red'. Hopkins lets his verbal lushness run riot, while Yeats is spare, with a limited vocabulary consisting largely of non-sensuous words like 'bread', 'fool', 'stone', 'bird', 'cold' and so on. He is no lesser a poet for that. A good deal of English culture has indeed been averse to the abstract and theoretical, as its tradition of empiricist philosophy would suggest, but this is by no means always a virtue. For the nineteenth-century critic William Hazlitt, it means wallowing pig-like in the trough of one's senses, unable to rise to the dignity of an idea. Even so, there is indeed a vital heritage of vividly sensuous poetry in English, of which Leavis is a superb analyst.

There are, so he implies, other languages which simply indicate objects and experiences rather than 'enacting' them. One suspects that it is French that he has mostly in his sights, an ill-starred language which is unable to perform what it proposes. The French novel from Balzac to Proust is effectively written off. There is, in other words, a certain linguistic chauvinism at work here, which is one of several ways in which Leavis is a self-avowed Little Englander. The fact is that what he calls the 'creative-exploratory' use of language is true to some extent of language in general, if by this one means that words play a crucial part in constituting an experience or state of mind rather than merely reproducing it. It is as true of 'To be or not to be, that is the question', where the language is tactfully unobtrusive, as it is of 'Nay, but to stew in the rank sweat of an enseamed bed', where the stabbing monosyllables and hissing *s* sounds convey a sense of anger and disgust, and the whole effect is heightened by the closely packed, densely textured vowels. It is true that this kind of language seems to make us feel what it conveys, as 'When shall we three meet again?' or 'Try and get some sleep' do not. Yet to describe this effect in mimetic terms, as the words somehow 'embodying' or 'enacting' a situation, is misleading. What is actually happening is that the materiality of the language itself – the effort needed to pronounce so crammed and jagged a line, the labour of lips, tongue and voice organ it requires – puts us in mind of the materiality it describes. It is a question of analogy, not enactment.

Poetic language, then, must not be simply indicative, like a set of instructions for repairing a washing machine. (It is, however, a sign of Leavis's flexibility of mind that he regarded Samuel Johnson's poem 'The Vanity of Human Wishes' as a great work, even though Johnson has in his view no sense of the creative-exploratory use of words, and the style of the piece is accordingly one of statement, reflection and exposition.) The most effective literary art must be actual rather than nebulous, richly realised rather than vaguely suggestive, poetic rather than poetical. Language as gesture and performance is what wins this critic's approval. He speaks of the 'body and action' of words, remarking of Gerard Manley Hopkins that 'his words and phrases are actions as well as sounds, ideas and images, and must . . . be read with the body as well as with the eye' (NB, p. 172). A similar exploitation of the 'whole body' of language can be found in T.S. Eliot. In fact, this view of poetry is deeply influenced by Eliot's own criticism. It is a lack of body or 'cerebral muscle' which accounts for the supposed spiritual and intellectual anaemia of so much Victorian poetry. Yet to press this case too far is to risk selling the pass to the aesthetes, formalists and Symbolists, focusing on the words themselves rather than on what they seek to record. It is this which Leavis finds so deplorable in Milton, whose language, by drawing such ostentatious attention to itself, intervenes between the reader and the meaning or experience. Tennyson and Swinburne are also rapped over the knuckles for revelling in the musicality of words for its own sake, which the puritanical streak in

Leavis (one of which he was moderately proud) finds distastefully self-indulgent.

So the word cannot be transparent – a mere vehicle or medium of the meaning – but neither can it be autonomous and self-involved, cut off from real-life experience. There are times when Leavis prefers the former to the latter, as when he writes of the kind of poetry which has such life and body 'that we hardly seem to be reading arrangements of words' (LP, p. 108). Language, like a well-trained courtier, would seem to be at its best when it effaces itself. In similar vein, he remarks of a passage in Milton's *Comus* that the words seem to withdraw themselves from our attention and we are 'directly aware of a tissue of feelings and perceptions' (R, p. 49). Most of the time, however, Milton has a feeling *for* words rather than feeling *through* them, as in the supposedly laboured, pedantic diction of *Paradise Lost*. What is amiss with the poem is the fact that what Leavis suggestively calls the 'steep cadences' and 'slopes and curves' of its language cease to be expressive of the experience, and function instead by rote, as though they were on automatic. It is as if the words moved at one level and the meaning at another. Language has been cut off from its living source in the speaking voice. Though one sees what this means, it seems odd to upbraid a poet for having a feeling for language.

This is not the case with Alexander Pope, above whose every line 'we can imagine a tensely flexible and complex curve, representing the modulation, emphasis and changing tone and tempo of the voice in reading; the curve varying from line to line and the lines playing subtly against one another' (R, p. 31). It is a superlative piece of analysis. Milton, by contrast, has renounced the English language – which is to say, Leavis's own partisan version of it. With the stilted gestures, predictable thuds and monotonous ritual of his verse, he demonstrates an insensitivity to the 'intrinsic nature' of the English tongue, handling it from the outside rather than grasping it as expressive of lived experience. Leavis even compares its supposedly mechanical way with words to bricklaying.

How then to avoid a language which merely indicates or refers to the world, while steering clear of one which has cut adrift from it? The answer lies in the type of poetry in which the full body of the language expresses the full body of the experience. It is this which Leavis means when he speaks of a poem or novel as fully *realised*. Words must be subtle, sensuous, sinewy and densely textured – but these qualities derive from the experience or situation to which they give voice, not simply from their own substance. There seem to be two views of poetic language here, which are not easy to reconcile with each other. On the one hand, such language is essentially expressive, which implies that it must cling close to the experience and act as its faithful medium; on the other hand, poetic language is creative-exploratory, which means that the words actually constitute the experience. 'A man's most vivid emotional and sensuous experience', Leavis writes, 'is inevitably bound up with the language that he actually speaks' (NB, p. 82). It is not as though Shakespeare, in writing *King Lear*, had a thought that can be described as 'How shall your houseless heads and unfed sides, / Your looped and windowed raggedness, defend you / From seasons such as these?', which he then proceeded to put into words. It is rather that the thought forms in the process of articulating it. The evocative use of words, Leavis writes, allows poets to become more aware of their own feelings, so that language has an active relation to what they mean and feel rather than acting as a passive medium of it.

Poetry, Leavis argues, is at its finest when it is rooted in actual experience; but how literally this is to be taken is not always clear. As far as we know, Shakespeare never ran his sword through a tedious pedant lurking behind a curtain, but Polonius's death in *Hamlet* comes over authentically enough. Leavis, however, would seem to argue for a more intimate relation between the author and the work, a biographical emphasis rejected out of hand by Richards and dismissed for the most part by Eliot. He sees Swift's supposed hostility to humanity as the result of the 'channels of life' having become 'blocked and perverted' in him (CP, p. 86), and traces a similar disgust with life in Eliot's *Four Quartets* to some disordered inner state of the author. He also speaks of writers like Bunyan, Johnson and Lawrence as men whom one would be eager to meet. But this suggests too simplistic a link between life and art. For one thing, it is not at all certain that one would have enjoyed meeting the moody, humourless, hypercritical Lawrence, even if one regarded him as the greatest writer since Virgil. (Leavis rebukes a number of his fellow critics for overlooking Lawrence's wit and humour, but this is because one would need a particularly powerful microscope to see them.) When it comes to the relation between art and life, we would not necessarily be baffled to discover that Dante was a serial killer, or that Wordsworth had never clapped eyes on a mountain, and it might make no difference at all to our reading of their work.

Like Eliot, Leavis assigns a high value to the idea of impersonality. In fact, he considers that *The Waste Land* reveals too little of it

– that 'the symbolic Waste Land makes itself felt too much as Thomas Stearns Eliot's' (LA, p. 41). The writer's personal experience must be sculpted into a work which is more than just a piece of self-expression. The work of art is a social fact, not a scrap of autobiography. Yet Leavis also argues that Eliot's theory of impersonality involves too great a gulf between the work and its creator, leaving little space for the individual artist. Lawrence, whom he considered a finer literary critic even than Eliot, saw no such hiatus between the individual who experiences and the author who creates. The conservative Eliot largely disregarded the man or woman who produces the text, while Leavis, who had a liberal's regard for the individual, was uneasy with this indifference. (He actually voted Liberal, as well as supporting the party in other ways.) Eliot and Richards are both in flight from a nineteenth century which made too much of poetry as subjective self-expression. But whereas Richards sought to diminish the role of the individual author by turning to scientific materialism, Eliot moved in the opposite direction – to the Idealism of F.H. Bradley, for whom the self is a kind of fiction. Eliot's concept of tradition is another move against subjectivism, as individual authors are reduced to little more than the relay of a heritage far more precious than themselves. In the end, Leavis resolves the problem of how to preserve impersonality while still valuing subjectivity by drawing on the work of D.H. Lawrence, for whom the uniquely individual self has its roots in a depth which is as impersonal as the cosmos itself.[3] We utter what is not ourselves. At the core of the self lies that which is inconceivably other to it. What is closest to us is also what is most strange.

Leavis's ideal version of English is supremely exemplified by Shakespeare, whose creative-exploratory use of language is unparalleled. It can also be found in the 'rooted and racy Englishness' and native robustness of Ben Jonson (R, p. 17), as well as in the 'sinew and living nerve' of the poetry of John Donne (R, p. 12). It is with Donne, Leavis claims, that Shakespeare's language first enters non-dramatic poetry in England. Once the so-called dissociation of sensibility has set in, however, his critical judgements grow somewhat bleaker. Wordsworth is admired for his impersonality, as well as for the sanity, naturalness and 'normality' of his sensibility; but most of his sonnets are dismissed as lamentable claptrap, while the 'Intimations of Immortality' ode is accused of displaying an empty grandeur. It is hard to demur from either reproof. The very essence of Byron's manner 'is a contemptuous defiance of decorum and propriety' (R, p. 149), a phrase in which one can hear the voice of the son of the respectable shop-keeping classes. The highly esteemed Shelley betrays a weak grasp of the actual, a lack of critical intelligence and a failure to see things in their own right. Full of poetical vapidity and sentimental banalities, his verse is denounced in an astonishingly iconoclastic gesture as 'repetitive, vaporous, monotonously self-regarding and often emotionally cheap, and so, in no very long run, boring' (CP, p. 221). Rather than inhering in concrete situations, the emotion is pumped in from the outside. The stuff might seem intoxicating to a 15-year-old, Leavis remarks, but to more mature minds it is unreadable.

Tennyson 'doesn't offer, characteristically, any very interesting local life for inspection' (R, p. 5), though Christina Rossetti has 'her own thin and limited but very notable distinction' (R, p. 6), and Emily Brontë is highly praised. The same cannot be said for Dante Gabriel Rossetti, with his 'shamelessly cheap evocation of a romantic and bogus Platonism' (CP, p. 47). The impersonality of Walter Savage Landor's work 'is that of the stiff suit of style that stands up empty – impersonal because there's nothing inside' (CP, p. 285). George Meredith's poem *Modern Love*, considered by many critics at the time as a distinguished piece of Victorian verse, is 'the flashy product of unusual but vulgar cleverness working upon cheap emotion' (NB, p. 21). The finest Victorian poet is Gerard Manley Hopkins, whose performative language, sensuous precision, muscularity and living speech rhythms restore to the language something of the substance of which it has been stripped. His work demonstrates a unity of form and content (another idea Leavis inherits from Eliot), so that 'the technical triumph is a triumph of spirit' (NB, p. 182). Only a handful of Thomas Hardy's poems, by contrast, can be said to achieve true greatness, given the fact that their author writes 'with a gaucherie compounded of the literary, the colloquial, the baldly prosaic, the conventionally poetical, the pedantic and the rustic' (NB, p. 59). It is a familiar form of patronage of the man Henry James patted verbally on the head as 'the good little Thomas Hardy', and one with which we shall see Raymond Williams take issue.

As for the Georgian movement, it 'may fairly be considered as a "movement", since it can be considered as little else' (NB, p. 62). Rupert Brooke was afflicted by a prolonged bout of adolescence, though with his characteristic eye for quality Leavis singles out the then little-known Edward Thomas, whose originality, subtlety of technique and distinctively modern sensibility he holds in high regard. He also compliments the equally obscure war poet Isaac Rosenberg, whose technical dexterity he rates even more highly than Thomas's, and whom he deems superior to Wilfred Owen. Eliot's 'The Love Song of J. Alfred Prufrock' represents a definitive break with nineteenth-century aestheticism and sentimentalism, inaugurating a thoroughly modern form of consciousness. It represents a seismic shift or momentous turning-point in the history of sensibility. The poem articulates the modes of feeling of one fully alive to his age, which in Leavis's view is always an index of value, and its technique and experience are impossible to dissociate. Pound's *Cantos*, by contrast, are both vacuous and bullying – a bullying which consorts naturally with the author's fascism and anti-Semitism. The gradually maturing Yeats reveals an attractively 'spare, hard and sinewy and in tone sardonic' way of writing (NB, p. 42), but W.H. Auden is marked down for being cerebral, immature and overbred. He also became an American citizen, despite being 'English upper class, Public School and Oxford' (AK, p. 151), thereby rolling four mortal sins into one. The fact that he had been a Marxist in his youth does him no favours either.

The typical form of a critical judgement, Leavis claims, is 'This is so, isn't it?', which in a court of law would count as a leading question. It is neither the blank agnosticism of 'Is this so?' nor the dogmatism of 'This is so'. It solicits the assent, dissent or qualification of others, in what Leavis sees as the inherently collaborative process of critical approach. A literary judgement is one's own or it is nothing; yet it is never simply one's own, any more than a language is one's private property. Language is rather 'the upshot or precipitate of immemorial human living' (LP, p. 44), as it is for the Eliot by whom Leavis is so deeply influenced. 'A language *is* a life' (AK, p. 183), he insists. Like language, a literary work is the creation of a cooperative process rather than simply the product of an individual. It exists only in the convergence of minds on a printed page. You cannot point to a poem; rather, it exists in some virtual or intersubjective space, as the black marks on the page are recreated by a community of readers.

Literature for Leavis is cognitive, which we have seen is not the case for Richards and only equivocally so for Eliot. Literary works yield us social and personal knowledge, rather than simply impacting upon our visceral regions or redressing the balance of our impulses. In fact, in comparison with the social history provided by major novelists, the work of the professional historian strikes Leavis as empty and unilluminating. We are speaking, however, of a unique form of social knowledge, one which has no truck with statistics or measurable trends. Instead, the literary work inhabits what Leavis calls the 'third realm', situated somewhere between the brutely objective and the whimsically subjective. It is where all the most significant human activity takes place, and an alternative term for it would be 'culture', in the broad sense of the word. A literary work of art isn't an objective phenomenon like a pickled egg or a mobile phone, but neither is it purely subjective. It cannot be taken into the laboratory and dissected, but neither does it live simply in the mind of an individual reader. A critical judgement can be as mistaken as a miscalculation in arithmetic, but it is not mistaken in the same way. To describe the tone of a poem as sombre is more than a matter of subjective feeling; indeed, we pick up the concept of sombreness only by sharing in a language and form of life. Even so, the judgement cannot be scientifically demonstrated. Others, for example, may disagree, as there is no disagreement over the chemical composition of water. The locus of truth and meaning when it comes to literature is the endless conversation known as criticism. A meaning, Leavis observes, is where minds can meet – though he might have added that it is also where they can collide.

'The critic's aim', Leavis argues, 'is, first, to realise as sensitively and completely as possible this or that which claims his attention; and a certain valuing is implicit in the realising' (CP, p. 213). The critic must enter into possession of the work in its concrete fullness, 'feeling into it' rather than dealing in flat-footed generalities. Criticism must thus be distinguished from theory and philosophy: 'there may be an important function for an intelligence that, in its sensitive concern for the concrete, its perception of complexities, and its delicate responsiveness to actualities, is indifferent to theoretic rigour or completeness and does not mind incurring the charge of incapacity for strict thinking' (EU, p. 143). The criticism of Matthew Arnold, for example, a figure whom Leavis grossly over-rates, reveals 'the flexibility, the sensitiveness, the constant delicacy of touch, the intelligence that is inseparably at one with an alert and fine sense of value . . .' (MBC, p. 38). There have been quite a few literary types who reveal 'an incapacity for strict thinking', though not many of them rationalise the defect by making it part of their critical approach. If philosophy is a matter of precise thinking, criticism is a question of precise feeling, but feeling informed by a special, highly disciplined kind of intelligence. George Eliot, in a fine phrase, 'warms analysis into creation' (GT, p. 61). Leavis's wariness of theory, one might note, is also to some extent a nervousness of ideas. He has very little to say, for example, about the intellectual content of George Eliot's fiction or Joseph Conrad's vision of the world. His readings cling too tightly to the page for that.

By now, the reader should have gathered at least two things. First, that Leavis was a ferociously polemical critic. He once criticised a portrait of himself for looking too benign. It is a mode which does not endear him to those civilised souls for whom all polemic is ill-mannered. Secondly, it should be clear that he spoke a distinctive critical language, one largely of his own invention. A list of his favoured terms would include such words as mature, creative, concrete, vital, fine, serious, intelligent, right, subtle, delicate, complex, robust, intense, sensitive, realised, poised, refined, civilised, controlled, organised, organic, whole, precise, responsible and disciplined. In fact, his sentences sometimes seem to consist of a ritual reshuffling of these key words, as, for example, when he writes of Keats's 'Ode to a Nightingale' that 'the rich local concreteness is the local manifestation of an inclusive sureness of grasp of the whole. What the detail exhibits is not merely an extraordinary intensity of realisation, but also an extraordinary rightness and delicacy of touch; a sureness of touch that is the working of a fine organisation' (R, p. 245). The language could only be Leavis's, or that of an exceptionally fine parodist.

This list of terms, however, omits what is perhaps the most central of all Leavisite notions: 'Life'. Great literature, Leavis believed, allows us to feel more intensely alive, more supremely fulfilled in our creative capacities, than anything else. One might retort that if we feel at our most alive only when reading *Middlemarch* or *The Rainbow*, we must be in pretty poor shape. Literature is important, to be sure, but not *that* important. Much of the time, however, Leavis would endorse this judgement: great literary works are not only examples of fine living but manifest what is most life-enhancing in everyday existence, and how we might achieve it. It is in this sense that they are 'moral'.

Yet how are we to establish what 'makes for life' and what doesn't? Like the word 'human', 'life' hovers between a descriptive and a normative sense. It can mean how we actually live, or how we ought to. In its purely descriptive sense the term includes violence, greed, theft, torture and the like, which one assumes Leavis is not particularly keen to see literary works promoting. He is using the word in a normative sense, to mean those expressions of life we should esteem; but he gives us no way of discriminating between these and, say, genocide. Perhaps it is *creative* life which makes the difference, but genocide is creative in its own ghastly way. It involves being imaginative and resourceful, as well as bringing about a condition which did not exist before. The word 'imaginative' is by no means always affirmative, whatever the great majority of literary types seem to think. The same is true of the concept of empathy. Sadists need to be well supplied with it.

When invited to spell out what he means by life in more conceptual terms, Leavis declines to do so. This is because to define life would be to kill it dead, and would thus prove self-defeating. For Leavis as for Nietzsche, life is the enemy of definition. So it would seem that we are thrown back on intuition. Perhaps we simply feel in our bones what makes for life and what doesn't. But intuitionism is a form of dogmatism. There is no arguing over it. Either you feel it or you don't. Somebody might happen to feel that all Armenians are born with an innate desire to sponge off the state, and there's an end of it. Besides, such intuitionism really only works within a coterie of like-minded individuals, of the kind which (as we shall see later) Leavis gathered around himself. We don't need to argue over what counts as living well (the traditional moral question) if we share much the same situation, and are thus predisposed to agree in the first place. It is true that intuition plays a part in abstract thought, as when philosophers regard a proposition as counter-intuitive. It is just that one would be rash to rely on it alone. At the same time, one might argue that though Leavis does not *state* what he means by life, he *shows* us, and that this demonstration is the whole point of his criticism. Many of his accounts of literary texts are marvellously adept at drawing our attention to felicitous details, passionate intensities, enlivening ironies, vivid portrayals and so on. His principles are crystallised in his practice.

Does this mean, however, that all authentic literature must be life-affirming? Can everything worth reading from *Beowulf* to Saul Bellow be conscripted into a campaign for spiritual health? There are times when Leavis would appear to believe so. It is certainly a case advanced by his most venerated author, D.H. Lawrence, for whom life will inevitably triumph. If one individual proves incapable of being a transmitter of it, it will simply cast that person aside and find its embodiment elsewhere – in a snake or crocodile, for example, which in Lawrence's eyes can be quite as precious as a human being. The human for him has no inherent priority over other forms of animal life. Besides, Lawrence's insistence that the unfathomable forces of life will always prevail is not only a form of spiritual determinism but can smack of a crass triumphalism. Men and women in his eyes are essentially instruments of life, with little agency of their own. Spontaneity really means passivity. There is no genuine tragedy in his fiction, since to acknowledge human breakdown and defeat would be, in his own phrase, to 'do dirt on life'.

For his part, Leavis acknowledges the reality of tragedy, and by no means all the literary works he prizes, which include *Little Dorrit*, *Heart of Darkness*, *Nostromo* and *The Waste Land*, could be said to be in any very obvious sense life-enhancing. It is in their sensitive feel for the dire conditions they portray, their imaginative reach and verbal integrity, that they might be said to make for life. 'Life' here is more a question of treatment than content. Even so, one imagines that Leavis would be reluctant to concede that there can be a truly major literary artist (Samuel Beckett springs to mind) whose vision of humanity is implacably negative. It is true that he rated Beckett's compatriot Jonathan Swift as a great writer, despite his supposed disgust for humanity; but it is hard to see why, given that he also found him savage, insanely egoistic and by no means as intelligent as William Blake. The high value he places on Eliot's *Four Quartets* is severely qualified by what he rightly saw as its distaste for everyday life.

Leavis is sometimes described as a moralist, in a fruitful tradition of English moral thought from John Bunyan to George Orwell; but what this means needs to be specified. It does not mean that literature should teach us certain moral values; it means rather that literature *is* a form of morality, indeed the most resourceful form of it there is. In the course of the nineteenth century, there is a gradual shift away from a Kantian idea of morality as duty and obligation to a more generous, capacious sense of the term. By the time we arrive at Matthew Arnold, George Eliot and Henry James, the 'moral' refers to the qualities and values manifest in human behaviour. Its concern is with the closely woven texture of human lives; and since this is also the business of literature, and perhaps of the realist novel in particular, the literary and the moral become more or less synonymous. The term 'moral' began to shed its didactic sense, along with its suggestion of rules, codes and prohibitions, and became instead a question of how one evaluates lived experience. In an age when traditional moral orthodoxies were loosening their grip over men and women, the novel became the secular version of Scripture. Literary criticism was lent a new lease of life by the Death of God. The novel teaches us how to live, not by providing us with a list of regulations but by dramatising human situations. In granting us access to the interior lives of individuals, it allows us at the same time to see them in their social context, situate them in a specific history and pass judgements on their behaviour which take these conditions into account. Given the complexity of these factors, as well as its habit of imaginative sympathy, the realist novel tends to be alert to the difficulties of moral judgement, and the consequent need for balance, nuance and a sense of tolerance. It is, in other words, a liberal form, even if this is by no means true of all of its practitioners.

Leavis's study of the English novel, *The Great Tradition*, regards its subject as one of the most creative moral forces in English civilisation. His selection of a mere five novelists as indisputably great has provoked a good deal of ridicule and indignation; but he doesn't say that these are the only authors worth reading, and he praises a number of other writers en passant. Even so, the narrowness and excessive rigour of which he is so often accused is plainly a feature of the work. Walter Scott is demoted to a disparaging footnote, Dickens is dismissed as a mere entertainer, the gauche Thomas Hardy fails to make the grade, James Joyce lacks any genuine feel for life and there is no truly outstanding English fiction before Jane Austen. An exception is John Bunyan, who 'counts immeasurably in the English-speaking conscience' (GT, p. 11), but he, too, is relegated to a footnote. The Brontës are dealt with in a note appended to the main text. Trollope, Gaskell, Thackeray, Meredith and Virginia Woolf are all briskly shown the door. Samuel Richardson's *Clarissa* is 'really impressive', but as the longest piece of fiction in English it takes a prohibitive amount of time to read. Besides, 'the more [Richardson] tries to deal with ladies and gentlemen, the more immitigably vulgar he is' (GT, p. 13). One of the finest anti-novels of the literature, the eighteenth-century author Laurence Sterne's hilarious, proto-modernist *Tristram Shandy*, is not only irresponsible in its 'trifling' but positively nasty.

On the other hand, Leavis is surely right that Austen, Eliot, James and Lawrence stand head and shoulders above the Trollopes, Gaskells and Thackerays, though he overrates Conrad and has the usual inflated view of the second-rate novella *Heart of Darkness*. Generally speaking, he has a fine nose for quality, despite the fact that in *New Bearings in English Poetry* he lavishes praise on an obscure poet and former pupil of his called Ronald Bottrall, whom few people at the time had heard of and nobody has heard of since. Rigorous discrimination of this kind is not much in vogue in postmodern culture, which has little affection for 'hierarchies'. The truth, surely, is that though you can make a fetish of rankings and pecking orders, the act of discrimination is a regular feature of everyday social life, and it is hard to see why literature should be quarantined from it. It is those intellectuals who disown it in a surge of populist sentiment who are truly out of line with common practice. Why should we pass judgements on rock bands and football teams but not on poetry or chamber music?

Leavis certainly makes too much of league-tabling; but his drive to evaluate must be judged in the context of the literary milieu he berates, which at times seemed to feel that making value judgements was both presumptuous and discourteous. In an epigraph to *The Common Pursuit*, Leavis quotes a passage from Robert Graves's *Goodbye to All That* in which the author, while an English student at Oxford, is rebuked by a board of academics for having the audacity to prefer some authors to others. A gentleman would not tolerate inferior stuff in the literary canon any more than he would in his wine cellar. In a curious historical irony, this old-style hostility to sharp distinctions has been revived by postmodernism, which has been known to denounce preferring one thing to another as 'elitist'. But it is not elitist to rank Quentin Tarantino's work over *Mary Poppins.* Is it also unacceptable to value anti-racism more than racism, or to feed the hungry rather than letting them starve? And does not holding the view that value judgements are elitist unjustly exclude those who believe the opposite? Perhaps the shrewdest comment about literary evaluation was made by the Cambridge critic Graham Hough, who was taken captive by the Japanese during the Second World War, and who later remarked that when you find yourself in a prisoner of war camp with dysentery and a collection of Yeats's poetry, you find out which the great poems are.

We shall see later that Leavis's concern for quality was related to the vital social function he ascribed to the study of English. In the meanwhile, we should note what it is he found most worthwhile about the fiction he discusses. All five of his chosen novelists are supposedly 'distinguished by a vital capacity for experience, a kind of reverent openness before life, and a marked moral intensity' (GT, p. 17). Whether this is true of Conrad, who has a near-nihilistic streak inherited from Schopenhauer and Nietzsche, or whether these Lawrentian terms are really appropriate to Jane Austen, is surely a question worth raising, rather as 'reverent openness' would seem more typical of George Eliot than Jane Austen. Eliot, Leavis argues, brought to the novel from her Evangelical background a radically respectful attitude to life. Her moral standards are Puritan,

222

and like those of Leavis himself spring from a respectable petty-bourgeois upbringing. He fails to mention that this emancipated intellectual lived in a non-marital partnership with her lover. It may also be something of a strain to reconcile these puritanical values with a reverent openness to life, however that elusive notion is to be defined.

There is a clear class animus at work here. When Leavis speaks of George Eliot as 'admir[ing] truthfulness and chastity and industry and self-restraint', as well as 'disapproving of loose living and reck-lessness and deceit and self-indulgence' (GT, p. 23n), he is quoting the words of Lord David Cecil, aristocrat and Oxford literary academic, who was very much a Cavalier rather than a Roundhead. (Cecil, incidentally, seems not to recognise that the world is scarcely bursting at the seams with people who detest truthfulness and sing the praises of deceit, so that the force of his point is somewhat blunted.) In rightly taking Cecil's words as the condescension of the patrician to the petty bourgeois, Leavis insists that these values are among those he himself holds dear, and that 'the enlightenment or aestheticism or sophistication that feels an amused superiority to them leads, in my view, to triviality and boredom, and that out of triviality comes evil' (GT, p. 23n). In its moral depth and serious-ness, the great English novel is among other things a critique of upper-class frivolity, the aesthetes of Bloomsbury, social parasites, amateur-genteel critics and Oxford academicism. Jane Austen would no doubt have been surprised to hear it. Yet Austen herself is a satirist of the gentry, and Leavis's class instincts in this instance are surely sound.

Like Richards before him and Raymond Williams afterwards, Leavis is suspicious of the term 'aesthetic', which he takes to mean an attention to artistic form at the expense of moral content. This is to equate aesthetics with formalism or aestheticism, rather as some critics mistakenly see nothing in the subject but questions of beauty, value and the unique experience which art is supposed to afford. No such distinction between form and content, Leavis claims, can be made in the case of major English fiction. Jane Austen's interest in 'composition', the principles by which she organised her material, is inseparable from her moral values. 'Is there any great novelist', Leavis asks, 'whose preoccupation with "form" is not a matter of his responsibility towards a rich human interest, or complexity of interests, profoundly realised?' (GT, p. 40). The formal perfection of a work like *Emma* must be seen in terms of Austen's moral concerns and her engagement with 'life'. The later work of Henry James, by contrast, with its cobwebby style, excessive obliquity and fastidious discriminations, is not sufficiently informed by a feeling for moral value. As another critic put it, James chewed more than he could bite off. He was an author, Leavis declares, who 'did not live enough' (GT, p. 181), though one might add that he produced some magnificent literary art out of this very incapacity. *The Ambassadors* is dismissed as a piece of feeble word-spinning, while *The Wings of the Dove* is fussily vague and intolerably sentimental. In both cases, form overshadows content.

There is, Leavis declares, no such thing as 'literary values'. The merit of a literary work depends on its responsiveness to the values implicit in everyday living, and the depth and intricacy with which it explores them. Yet he also required that literary works should be fully 'organised', which sounds like a literary value of a kind. Conrad's *Nostromo* 'forms a rich and subtle but highly organised pattern' (GT, p. 211), though Leavis is sharp enough to perceive that there is something hollow at its heart. James's finest novels 'have the abundant, full-blooded life of well-nourished organisms' (GT, p. 179), which makes them sound more like farm animals than works of fiction. Every aspect of a work must contribute to the significance of the whole; there is no room for slack or redundancy. Joyce's *Ulysses* is reproved for its inorganic nature, its lack of any central organising principle. (In fact, its very title announces one.)

The demand that works of art must be tightly unified is at least as old as Aristotle; but it was being challenged in Leavis's own day by modernism, which saw no reason why a work should not be fragmented, dissonant or internally conflictive. Leavis, though he rarely uses the word 'modernism', is not entirely unsympathetic to such projects: hence his admiration for *The Waste Land* and a number of other experimental texts. Some of Lawrence's novels, not least *The Rainbow* and *Women in Love*, are in his view more boldly innovative in form than any other writing of the time. Even so, he remains for the most part firmly wedded to a realist poetics. Actual life and felt experience are the taproot of major fiction, and too much formal experiment risks losing touch with that foundation. The danger is exemplified above all by Gustave Flaubert, in whose work we find a sterile preoccupation with technique linked to a loathing of life. James Joyce is heading straight down the same cul-de-sac. Formalism is a particular pitfall for foreigners.

Leavis occasionally describes the novel as a 'dramatic poem', which is to say anything but a novel. He means by this that we must break with the old-fashioned analysis of character and storyline in order to appreciate the work as an organised pattern of themes and imagery. The novel is primarily a work of language rather than of character, psychology and situation. (William Empson, incidentally, was not of this view, maintaining that a discussion of character, however out of vogue at the time, was as relevant as ever.) Yet in discussing works of fiction Leavis often falls back on traditional talk of character, event, plot and narrative, overlooking the artistry of a text and treating it instead like a slice of real life. It is also true that that though he is as committed to so-called close reading as Richards and Empson, he frequently quotes large, sometimes page-long chunks of literary works without submitting them to a fine-grained verbal examination.

The novel, then, is the great Book of Life. In *The Great Tradition*, only one of Charles Dickens's works answers to this criterion: the schematic, grotesquely caricaturing *Hard Times*. This is partly because it is short enough to constitute an organic unity, unlike the 'loose inclusiveness' of the author's other works, and partly because it is the one novel by Dickens which is explicitly *about* 'life', in the sense of contrasting the mechanistic creed of Utilitarianism with the spontaneous vitality of a circus. Leavis speaks of 'the astonishing and irresistible richness of life that characterises the book everywhere' (GT, p. 257), and finds in one of the circus performers, Sissy Jupe, the prototype of a Lawrentian heroine, typifying 'the life that is lived freely and richly from the deep instinctive and emotional springs'

(GT, p. 254). It is not clear how clowns and trapeze artists are going to transform a heartless industrial capitalism, which provides the book's social context. They may offer an anarchic alternative to it, but that is another matter. In the figure of Gradgrind, Utilitarianism is reduced to a cold-hearted number-crunching, overlooking the fact that it was responsible for a number of enlightened reforms in Victorian society. Leavis is alert to some of the novel's flaws – its savage travesty of the trade union movement, for example, which was rather more of a positive social force in Victorian Britain than lion tamers. He also notes the mawkishness with which it treats its befuddled, Uncle Tom-like working-class hero, Stephen Blackpool. Yet these flaws are finally brushed aside. We are informed that 'in [Dickens's] ease and range there is surely no greater master of English except Shakespeare' (GT, p. 272), in which case it is odd that only one of his novels can be rescued from the junk heap of literary history.

That particular embarrassment, however, was later to be remedied. Patronised in *The Great Tradition* as no more than a great entertainer, Dickens was later to be rehabilitated in a full-length study co-authored with Queenie Leavis, *Dickens the Novelist*. We now learn that he 'was one of the greatest of creative writers' (DN, p. ix), and that to dismiss him as an entertainer would be utterly wrong-headed. Extraordinarily, however, there is no acknowledgement that this is exactly what Leavis himself had done 20 years earlier. The party line has changed, but if an air of infallible authority is to be maintained, the *volte face* must be quietly suppressed. As the Vatican official remarked of a possible reversal of the Catholic Church's ban on contraception, all it would mean is that the Church would have moved from one state of certainty to another state of certainty.

If Leavis was converted to a love of Dickens, no such road-to-Damascus epiphany was needed in the case of Lawrence. It is true that an early pamphlet of his on the writer has its reservations: it finds *The Rainbow* monotonous, and considers Eliot's charge that its author was spiritually sick to be not wholly without foundation. Leavis also lavishes praise on *Lady Chatterley's Lover*, a novel which (though he defended its publication in court) he came rightly to see as second-rate. By the time of *D.H. Lawrence: Novelist* 25 years later, however, scarcely a breath of criticism of 'our last great writer' (DHL, p. 9) is to be detected ('last' meaning not only 'latest', but that – modern civilisation being as bankrupt as it is – we are unlikely to see another of his stature). Adjectives like 'greatness', 'genius' and 'transcendence' tumble on each other's heels. It is curious to read this laudatory prose today, given that history has since rendered Lawrence almost unreadable for a good many students. All some of them know about him, apart perhaps from rumours of the *Lady Chatterley* trial, is that he was a racist, sexist, elitist, misogynistic, homophobic, anti-Semitic believer in 'blood hierarchies', which is not the strongest of incentives these days to take him from the library shelf. Hardly anything of these ugly opinions can be gleaned from Leavis's thoroughly sanitised account – not so much because he suppresses them as because he seems hardly aware of them. It is a drastically one-sided view of its subject.

Yet so is the prejudice that Lawrence is nothing but a case of monstrous political incorrectness. That he held a number of offensive views is beyond doubt; but he was also, however unevenly and sporadically, an outstandingly gifted artist, who produced some of the masterpieces of modern English fiction. It would be convenient if politically abhorrent art were always artistically shoddy stuff, but things are not quite so straightforward. Besides, even in political terms, Lawrence has much of value to offer. He may have been sexist and homophobic, but as the son of a miner he was also a ferocious critic of industrial capitalism. It is a system which involves what he called 'the base forcing of all human energy into a competition of mere acquisition'.[4] Possession, he comments, is an illness of the spirit. We do not even have possession over ourselves. As Lawrence observes of Tom Brangwen in *The Rainbow*, 'he knew that he did not belong to himself'. We are stewards of our selves rather than proprietors of them. We also confront each other as irreducibly 'other', and to seek to determine the being of another is a cardinal crime.

In Lawrence's eyes, humanity's dominion over Nature is a calamitous consequence of modern humanism. An overbearing will has cut the human species loose from its sensuous involvement with the creaturely world. Lawrence's aim was also to restore the flow and recoil of spontaneous-creative life between men and women, a flow deadened and disrupted by a puritanical morality and a mechanistic society; and the novel is his chief means of doing so. If *Lady Chatterley's Lover* is an audacious performance, it is not because of its talk of penises and vaginas. It is courageous because despite everything – exile, fury, isolation, near-despair – Lawrence refuses in the end to deny what he sees as the inexhaustible creativity of the human spirit. There is more to him than misogyny and anti-Semitism, as we shall see when we come to consider Raymond Williams's commentary on his work.

Leavis sometimes speaks of Lawrence's work as 'religious', meaning not that he is an orthodox believer but that the sense of belonging to a creative depth beyond oneself is typical of religious experience. Lawrence does not give this unsearchable abyss the name of God, but what he calls spontaneous-creative life is certainly a version of the Christian idea of grace. He is, in other words, a full-bloodedly metaphysical writer, as in his radically different way is Joseph Conrad; and this points to a rather curious aspect of the so-called great tradition of the English novel. The authors it includes may consort well together in terms of literary quality (though even that is arguable), but there is something incongruous about placing Conrad and Lawrence alongside Jane Austen and Henry James. The former two address the most fundamental of questions about humanity's place in the cosmos. They exemplify the kind of inquiry which Leavis formulates several times in his work as the question 'What for? What ultimately do we live by?'. Austen, Eliot and James, by contrast, are preoccupied less with the cosmos than with civilisation. They are maestros of manners and morals, not of Otherness and transcendence.

This contrast corresponds to two opposing aspects of Leavis himself. On the one hand, he is a champion of sociability, 'fine living', civilised intercourse and moral refinement. Henry James 'creates an ideal civilised sensibility; a humanity capable of communicating by the finest shades of inflexion and implication; a nuance may engage a whole complex moral economy' (GT, p. 26). Writing of

James's novella *Madame de Mauves*, Leavis saw the author as looking to a civilisation 'in which the manners belonging to a ripe art of social intercourse shall be the index of a moral refinement of the best American kind and a seriousness that shall entail a maturity of humane culture' (GT, p. 160). By contrast, one of James's compatriots, F. Scott Fitzgerald, lacks a 'sense of even the elementary decencies that one had thought of as making civilised intercourse possible'.[5] That Fitzgerald was an alcoholic is perhaps not irrelevant to this dyspeptic judgement. Manners and social intercourse are clearly no superficial affairs; rather, they reach down to the deepest sources of culture and morality. Ben Jonson, for example, combines his rooted and racy Englishness with a civilised refinement. If the seventeenth-century poet Andrew Marvell represents for Leavis the acme of English civilisation, it is because he is at once urbane and deep-thinking.

In the early eighteenth century, so-called Good Form was still morally significant. It belonged to a public sphere of common sense, sound judgement and polite, unspecialised discourse. The 'Augustan' virtues, Leavis writes in a finely perceptive sentence, include 'an easy sureness of diction and tone, a neat precision and poise of movement and gesture, an elegant constancy of point and an even decorum' (R, p. 148). The seventeenth-century poet Thomas Carew reveals a 'sophisticated gallantry' about which there is nothing 'rakish or raffish – nothing of the Wild Gallant; its urbane assurance has in it nothing of the Restoration insolence' (R, p. 16). In Leavis's view, there was a shift of sensibility from the dissolute climate of the late seventeenth-century Restoration to the mannered moral seriousness of the age of Addison and Pope. The word 'order' for Pope is no idle term but 'a rich concept imaginatively realised' (R, p. 92). Pope's verse is 'at once polite and profound' (R, p. 71), combining social grace with spiritual depth. Politeness, far from being superficial drawing-room stuff, is in the service of culture and civilisation. One might add that whatever his positive appraisal of civility, Leavis's own prose style is scarcely a model of it. One critic detects a certain strain of Puritan integrity, an aversion to show and suavity, in the way he writes.[6] He sacrifices good form and geniality to the unvarnished truth.

When Leavis is in civic mood, he is keen to reject any fundamental distinction between the individual and society – an opposition he regards rather dubiously as a specifically Romantic illusion. He even goes so far as to maintain that serious literature tends inevitably towards the sociological, even if it provides us with a type of social knowledge that nothing else can. The essential truth of the novel, he claims, is the social nature of the individual. It is a mildly surprising viewpoint for a liberal. Yet it is a social emphasis evident throughout Leavis's work. You cannot have a thriving drama, he insists, without a public theatre, and that in turn is impossible without a genuine community. Shakespeare's achievement would be inexplicable apart from the social context which shaped his means of expression, while the work of John Bunyan is the fruit of that collaborative achievement known as the English language. At the same time, Leavis is conscious of the danger of socialising both art and the individual out of existence, insisting instead that society exists only in the substance of individual lives. 'Without the distinguished individual', he warns, '. . . there is no art that matters' (AK, p. 179). It is as if the liberal in him is at war with the communitarian. Yet the two viewpoints can be reconciled: Samuel Johnson is a 'genius of robust and racy individuality' (CP, p. 104), yet he also values civility, sociability and social convention. He has a sense of society as a going concern in a way which means that he doesn't need to be conscious of it.

Leavis's interest in the early eighteenth century, then, sprang partly from his conviction that a flourishing literature requires a lively public sphere. It is this domain of informed judgement and civilised debate, animated by a spirit of free, disinterested intelligence, that he hoped to reconstruct for his own time. If Eliot was much less captivated by this historical period, it was largely because he was in search of a past which could be fruitful for his own literary art, which is to say an era of conflict and fragmentation, not of elegance and consolidation. Yet there is a thin line between a serious respect for social convention and a shallow one. 'The positive, concentrated, and confident civilisation we see registered in *The Tatler* and *The Spectator* is impressive', Leavis writes, 'but no profound analysis is necessary to elicit from those bland pages the weaknesses of a culture that makes the Gentleman *qua* Gentleman its criterion' (CP, pp. 103–4). You need to defend civility against the barbarians and Romantic individualists, but how do you do so without selling the pass to what Leavis scathingly calls the 'cocktail culture' of Bloomsbury? It is a milieu with which even Eliot, to Leavis's disgust, had thrown in his hand, exchanging avant-garde experiment for sophisticated chit-chat. He even grouses that the Bloomsbury set call Eliot Tom (everyone called him Tom), whereas it is hard to imagine Virginia Woolf calling Leavis 'Frank', or perhaps even allowing him across her threshold. The later Eliot, whose dislike of Lawrence Leavis finds offensive, has sold out to a coterie, which in Leavis's eyes is the opposite of an elite. An elite represents the most sensitive, pioneering conscience of an age, cultivating values without which civilisation will perish and safeguarding them from the philistine bankers and politicians; a coterie is a closed, self-admiring bunch of social layabouts whose primary function is to savour their own superiority.

There are other problems with the idea of civility. Leavis was a heretic who preferred for the most part to stand out against society, at least in its current shape, rather than conform to it. If he managed to sustain a social ideal, it is in the teeth of the social order to which he belonged. The word he uses of himself and his followers is 'outlaws'. Pope's 'adroit combination of animus and urbanity' (R, p. 93), another deft critical insight, suggests how you can be dissident and refined at once, but Leavis himself tips the balance rather too sharply towards the former. It was said of him as a person that he was the soul of courtesy, but also that he fostered a type of bohemianism. E.M. Forster, like Leavis a liberal devoted to the free play of critical intelligence, is a novelist of civilised personal relationships who nonetheless felt a radical dissatisfaction with civilisation; but Leavis, having sung Forster's praises in an early study, later turned vehemently against him, as he did with so many authors and colleagues. (This included the meek-mannered Richards, who on leaving a note for Leavis congratulating him on becoming a Companion of Honour received back a one-sentence reply which read 'We repudiate with contempt any approach from you'.) In the end, Forster's civility is not enough, though the note to Richards suggests that Leavis could have profited from it rather more than he did.

Henry James, an author who was more or less a permanent house guest of the English upper classes, may have been the epitome of social grace, indeed he appears at times almost absurdly overbred; but he also confessed in a private letter that 'I believe only in absolutely independent, individual and lonely virtue, and in the serenely unsociable (or if need be at a pinch sulky and sullen) practice of the same'. Leavis borrows this sentence for one of the epigraphs of *The Common Pursuit*, along with a comment about the Norwegian novelist Knut Hamsun: 'The Norwegian Society of Authors gave him a loving cup, but he asked them to scratch off the inscription and give it to somebody else'.

This – Companionship of Honour apart – has the authentic Leavisite ring. No public intellectual could have been less susceptible to the blandishments of the cultural establishment. The other problem with civility is that it doesn't cut deep enough. James may be in the first rank of writers, but he lacks the spiritual depth one finds in Lawrence. Leavis was a secularist who like many non-believers still hankered for transcendence. Like Eliot, he rejected Richards's wistful faith that literature might take the place of religion; but Lawrence's work, indeed, literature in general, served precisely that function in his thought. It is a haven of ultimate value in a godless world.

From 1932 to 1953, Leavis was editor-in-chief of *Scrutiny*, a critical journal based at Cambridge which had a global impact and transformed the face of literary studies. There has been no project in Britain to compare to it in the modern age, either in English studies or any other area of the humanities. Devoted as it was to rigorous judgement, its very name is faintly intimidating. It derives from a Latin term meaning to sort out rubbish, and sifting the literary gold from the dross was exactly the task which Leavis and his colleagues set out to accomplish. It was largely through *Scrutiny* that Leavis became such a formidable influence throughout the world, and this at a time when he was complaining that he had won little or no public recognition. (He meant, with typical provincialism, that Cambridge had not appointed him to a Chair.) What he did have, unlike the other figures discussed so far in this book, was a *school* – a sizeable band of international disciples whose role was to evangelise their colleagues and students by spreading the Leavisite word.

Scrutiny, in short, was not simply a journal but a militant campaign. It chalked up some notable achievements in the field of secondary as well as tertiary education, and there were a good many school students (myself included) who imbibed its values from an undercover, fifth-columnist Leavisite English teacher without being aware of the fact. By the late 1940s, there were Leavisites at every level of the national educational system, from professorial Chairs to secondary schools, adult education to teacher training colleges. Leavis and Denys Thompson's *Culture and Environment* was used in adult education courses, and there was a Leavisite journal run by schoolteachers of English. The heretical ideas of the 1930s were to become the literary orthodoxy of the following decade. By the end of the Second World War, *Scrutiny*'s ideas had become dominant in the teaching of English literature.

Since the Scrutineers formed a community of sorts, and since they also assumed an embattled stance towards modern civilisation at large, they could combine in their own persons the twin virtues of civilised conversation and cultural rebellion. Part vanguard, part elite, their aim was to create 'an intelligent, educated, morally responsible and politically enlightened public'.[7] It was hardly a modest proposal. After the 1944 Education Act, which admitted pupils from less well-heeled backgrounds to higher education, a new stratum of former working-class and lower-middle-class intellectuals, many like Leavis himself with provincial roots, found *Scrutiny*'s tough-minded rejection of Good Form, Good Taste and Polite Letters intuitively appealing. It was clear to them how deeply such values were interwoven with social privilege, so that, in a decisive shift of sensibility, power was wrested from the aesthetes, dilettantes and gentlemen scholars. In some conservative circles, *Scrutiny* was denounced for its narrowness, sectarianism, priggishness and quasi-religious zeal, as well as for its custom of verbally beating up its opponents; but Leavis himself became one of the most talked-about critics in the English-speaking world, and his gloomy diagnosis of contemporary culture was widely endorsed.

One of the most combative class warriors of the journal was Queenie Leavis, of whom her husband once remarked that there was enough energy in her to blow Europe to pieces. She was an outsider in Cambridge in terms of gender, class and ethnicity – a woman in a university where women were still thin on the ground, whose father was a lower-middle-class North London draper and who was brought up as an orthodox Jew. She was rejected by her family for marrying a Gentile, thus suffering a further form of exclusion. When Leavis found himself without any university teaching, it was Queenie who became the breadwinner. From her position on the periphery of academia, she could see more clearly than most insiders how closely its literary standards were bound up with its social assumptions. 'A life devoted to the humanities', she writes, 'means not following a vocation but taking up the genteelest profit-making pursuit, one which confers a high caste on its members; literary appreciation must obey the same laws as other expressions of social superiority. The Discipline of Letters is seen to be simply the rules of the academic English club'.[8] In a bitter invective against Virginia Woolf's *Three Guineas*, it is less Woolf's radical feminism which commands her attention than the fact that she belongs to a propertied cultural elite. Some commentary on Woolf today reveals the opposite blind spot. Q.D. Leavis was rather less enamoured of Woolf than of her father, the Victorian writer Leslie Stephen, whom she applauds for being a public intellectual rather than an academic. She also points out that the resistance to the early poetry of T.S. Eliot came from the same quarter as those who opposed the General Strike of 1926. It is interesting to note, incidentally, that she disliked Lawrence, which is rather like the wife of an Archbishop of Canterbury declaring herself a militant atheist.

What was *Scrutiny*'s diagnosis of modern civilisation? In a series of works produced by Leavis from early in his career to his later years, a consistent view of modern civilisation and its pre-history is proposed.[9] In *For Continuity*, he laments that 'the traditional ways of life have been destroyed by the machine, more and more does human life depart from the natural rhythms, the cultures have mingled, and the forms have dissolved into chaos, so that everywhere the serious litera-ture of the West betrays a sense of paralysing consciousness, of a lack of direction, of momentum, of dynamic axioms' (FC, p. 139). We were not, in short, in the best of shapes. In *Mass Civilisation and Minority Culture*, we are bizarrely informed that the motor car, symbol of the second industrial revolution, has broken up the family and disrupted social custom. Somewhat less strangely, we learn that society has been taken over by mass production, mechanised labour, the standardisation of individuals as well as commodities and a general emotional impoverishment. The cinema poses a potent threat to traditional working-class culture. Working-class men and women, Leavis complains, now carry around transistor radios, and the air reeks of the smell of their fish and chips. Standards have been subverted, authority has evaporated, tradition lies in ruins, language is in jeopardy from advertising and the popular press, and continuity with the culture of the past has been disastrously breached. The custodians of civilised values are now cut off from the powers that rule the world – powers which no longer represent an intellectual culture but which are wielded instead by a philistine middle class. As with artistic modernism, *Scrutiny* is for the most part the response of a disinherited sector of the intelligentsia to a mass society, one which threatens to undermine their own authority.

Modern civilisation, then, is mechanised, atomised, rootless, materialistic and utilitarian. Leavis will later capture the essence of this calamitous condition in the compound adjective 'technologico-Benthamite'. Jeremy Bentham, founder of Utilitarianism and a source of moral insight for both Richards and Empson, is now arraigned as the villain. Leavis seems not to be aware that Bentham, as we have seen already, was in many ways a progressive thinker: writing in the late eighteenth century, he opposed the criminalising of homosexuality, which is probably more than Leavis himself did. The term 'Benthamite' here is simply shorthand for a civilisation devoted to material means rather than spiritual ends. Even so, Leavis is right to recognise that Benthamism 'provided the sanction for the complacent selfishness and comfortable obtuseness of the prosperous classes in the great age of progress' (MBC, p. 34). He also notes its responsibility for the Victorian Poor Law.

In Leavis's view, one of the leading contemporary exponents of this creed was C.P. Snow, a vain, self-important Cambridge scientist and novelist who fancied himself as something of a sage, and who was the very epitome of an Establishment figure. Snow had deplored in a public lecture what he saw as the disabling gap between literary and scientific cultures, the unity between which was embodied in no less a personage than himself; and Leavis delivered a riposte to his argument in a now legendary public lecture entitled 'Two Cultures? The Significance of C.P. Snow'. It is an astonishing, immensely enjoyable performance, in which Leavis's scurrility is pressed to the point of barefaced libel. A request by the publishers of the piece to tone it down was adamantly refused.

Snow, Leavis remarks, adopts in his lecture 'a tone of which one can say that, while only genius could justify it, one cannot readily think of genius adopting it' (TC, p. 53). In fact, not only is Snow not a genius, but 'he is intellectually as undistinguished as it is possible to be' (TC, p. 54). He is, however, a portent, in that though negligible himself he has become a sage and mastermind for a vast, deluded public. His supposed insight into the modern age is characterised by 'blindness, unconsciousness and automatism. He doesn't know what he means, and doesn't know that he doesn't know' (TC, p. 55). To call his argument a process of thought is to flatter it. His lecture 'exhibits an utter lack of intellectual distinction and an embarrassing vulgarity of style' (TC, p. 56). As a novelist, 'he doesn't exist; he doesn't begin to exist. He can't be said to know what a novel is . . . I am trying to remember where I heard (can I have dreamed it?) that [his novels] are composed for him by an electronic brain called Charlie, into which the instructions are fed in the form of the chapter-headings' (TC, p. 57). Snow is utterly without a glimmer of what creative literature is, or why it matters.

One of Leavis's objections to Snow is that he labels anyone who challenges talk of productivity, material standards and technological progress as a Luddite, which is to say as one nostalgic for pre-industrial society; and prominent among the Luddites in Snow's judgement are literary intellectuals like Leavis himself. One of Snow's colleagues, the historian J.H. Plumb, complained that an antipathy to material progress ran through literary criticism like dry rot. Leavis is at pains to point out that he himself harbours no such prejudice, and has no hankering to return to the past – though he hands his critics a whole crateful of ammunition by inquiring rhetorically 'whether the average member of a modern society is more fully human, or more alive, than a Bushman, an Indian peasant, or a member of one of those poignantly surviving primitive peoples, with their marvellous arts and skills and vital intelligence?'

(TC, p. 72). It may be that some Indian peasants are less alive than citizens of the West in the sense of not getting enough to eat, though Leavis passes over the fact. In any case, almost every thinker who appeals to an idealised past ritually adds that there can be no returning to it.

Leavis's point, however, is that the felicity which Snow envisages 'cannot be regarded by a fully human mind as a matter for happy contemplation' (TC, p. 72). His adversary cannot see that along with 'the energy, the triumphant technology, the productivity, the high standard of living' (TC, p. 72) of modern times goes a moral vacancy and spiritual depletion. As a consequence of this carve-up of a figure lionised in the London clubs, Leavis was vilified by the Establishment, while Snow protested that the unwelcome publicity had deprived him of a Nobel Prize. The idea that this dismally undistinguished novelist would have ever been considered for a Nobel Prize is beyond absurdity. Some of Snow's supporters urged him to sue, but he opted instead for an air of injured innocence, while working hard behind the scenes to bring Leavis low.

Leavis was right to rebuke Snow for his crass faith in material progress and casual way with spiritual values. He was surely mistaken, however, to argue that science is simply a means to an end. This may well be true of technology, but large sectors of science are no more a means to an end than *The Brothers Karamazov*. Investigating the material world can be a project carried out for its own sake, and thus has more in common with the humanities than Leavis cares to acknowledge. It is hard to see how studying molluscs or black holes is going to benefit senior citizens. Besides, the overwhelming beauty which astrophysicists discern in so many features of the universe is an aesthetic matter closely linked to the pursuit of truth, rather as for Leavis the formal symmetry of a Jane Austen novel has an inner relation to its moral vision. Leavis tips his hat to science and technology, but in typical humanistic style is grudging and ill-informed about them both. He once scoffed that a colleague on a respirator was being 'kept alive by science'. With Richards, science was part of the solution; now it has become part of the problem. You can react to the frivolity of *belles lettres* either by being scientifically hard-nosed like Richards, mixing sound sense with analytic virtuosity like Empson or, like Leavis, by cutting beneath both scientific objectivism and literary subjectivism to certain abiding moral truths. As far as Leavis was concerned, Richards had chosen the wrong side in the dispute between science and the humanities, and his early friendship with him, as fellow *enfants terribles* in the Cambridge English Faculty, came to an end.

In *Scrutiny*'s view, things were not always as dire as they were now. In the early seventeenth century, so Leavis argues, there was a 'lusty', largely rural culture in which the relation between humanity and its environment seemed right and natural. There was no unbridgeable gap between 'high' and popular culture. A poet like Robert Herrick could be classical but at the same time in touch with the culture of the people. The Elizabethans and Jacobeans had a unified culture shared by all social classes, but by the late seventeenth century this common way of life had become rigidly stratified. The rural social order was further eroded by the growth of urbanism and industrialism, in the passage from field to factory. The monotony of industrial labour reduced culture to mere distraction or entertainment. By the modern age, the rhythms of the soil had been replaced by the inanities of jazz. The natural relations between humanity and the world had been disrupted, probably irreparably so. By the mid-nineteenth century, only a few vestiges of this age-old form of life survived. The spirit of the English language was formed while England was still mostly rural, characterised by a vital popular speech. It is this sturdy, muscular language which passed as a precious legacy to Shakespeare, Jonson and Bunyan, while the healthy, homogeneous community which produced it gradually withered away. The so-called organic society, then, migrated into the English language itself, or at least into those ways of using it that Leavis most admires.

By the early eighteenth century, with the growth of neo-classicism and the polite world of clubs and coffee houses, high culture was cut off from the culture of the people, which entered accordingly into a long decline. A homogeneous reading public, however, survived for some time. There was an educated minority audience for literature, nurtured not least by the great London periodicals from the eighteenth-century *Tatler* and *Spectator* to such Victorian organs as the *Westminster Review*. Leavis, in other words, combines his affection for the rural with a respect for the civilised. In the early nineteenth century, however, popular fiction was increasingly invaded by sentimentalism and sensationalism, while the end of the century witnessed the emergence of mass publishing and mass journalism to debase standards even further. All this had to be resisted by 'an armed and conscious minority', Queenie Leavis declared,[10] though one takes it she didn't have handing out machine guns in mind.

Thomas Hardy was perhaps the last author who could combine the serious and the popular. Before him, Charles Dickens had done so with incomparable verve and flair. In fact, we are told that speech at the time of Dickens was still a popular art rooted in a living culture, in which case it is hard to see how the organic society could have perished two centuries earlier. Leavis claims that polite culture was cut off from the culture of the people in the late seventeenth century, yet he was also particularly fond of a work by George Sturt, *The Wheelwright's Shop*, which appears to argue that at least some aspects of the organic society were alive and well at the end of the nineteenth century. For Richard Hoggart, author of the incomparable *The Uses of Literacy*, that community would seem to have survived in the form of working-class solidarity until the end of the Second World War. There are, then, a number of contending views on when the lapse from grace actually took place.

Even if an ideal rural order did pass away some time in the seventeenth century, the artist or intellectual was not entirely washed up by its demise. What took its place was a public sphere of polite letters and civilised intercourse, all the way down to the mid-nineteenth century. Literary types may have constituted a minority, but they could still trade on the presence of a responsive reading public. By the time of *Scrutiny*, however, even this was no longer the case. The general public had been hijacked by the media and mass publishing market, while the literary intelligentsia threw in their hand for the most part with cultural institutions (the BBC, the British Council, the so-called public schools, 'quality' newspapers and periodicals, metropolitan literary salons, the Royal Society of Literature, high-minded coteries such as Bloomsbury) for which *Scrutiny* had nothing but contempt. At one point, Leavis also throws in for good measure 'the publicisers, public relations men, heads of [Oxbridge] houses, academic ward-bosses, hobnobbers with Cabinet ministers and educational reformers' (LA, p. 25). Stranded between the masses and the mandarins, the journal found itself in the classic double-bind of the lower-middle class, disdainful of the populace below yet scornful of the social elite above. The Leavises disliked both the masses and the upper classes.

The organic society is of course a myth. 'At every moment of its history', writes the philosopher Jean-Luc Nancy, 'the Occident has given itself over to nostalgia for a more archaic community that has disappeared, and to deploring a loss of familiarity, fraternity and conviviality'.[11] In the first century BCE, Ovid was already lamenting the passing of the Golden Age in his *Metamorphoses*, though as usual with Ovid it is hard to know how serious he is intending to be. One of the most popular locations for the lost paradise is the medieval period, despite the fact that in the 1370s the poet William Langland can be found recording widespread social unrest among famished farm labourers. The Elizabethan poet Philip Sidney's pastoral romance *Arcadia* was written in a park which was created by enclosing a whole village and evicting the tenants. In the early seventeenth century, the English countryside was rife with disease, early death, appalling hardship and backbreaking labour. Land was for the most part exploited as capital, almost half the working population were wage-earners rather than peasants, and unemployment was high enough for public order to be recurrently endangered. 'There is plenty of evidence', writes C.B. Macpherson, 'that England approximated closely to a possessive market society in the seventeenth century'.[12] It is this that Leavis describes as 'the old fine order' (R, p. 34).

So there was no Fall from the happy garden into industrialism. It was not a question of one social order giving way to another, but of industrial capitalism gradually overtaking the agrarian capitalism with which it was interlocked. Capitalist social relations had colonised rural England some centuries before the industrial revolution. Besides, squalid and oppressive though the conditions of factory workers were, it is arguable that in the long run their material conditions improved in some respects in comparison with those of the traditional rural labourer. In this sense, if in few others, there is something to be said for Snow's case.

Some *Scrutiny* contributors warned against romanticising the wretchedly impoverished life of rural labourers. Queenie Leavis, among others, was conscious of the dangers of idealising Merrie England. As Robert J.C. Young remarks in a different context, 'Those who do not have access to modernity generally want it when they get the chance. Those who reject it on ideological grounds are often those who already have it'.[13] In any case, Leavis does not make as much of the old organic England as some commentators have suggested, and there is nothing necessarily amiss with nostalgia as such. In certain respects, the past was indeed preferable to the present, just as in other respects the present is an improvement on the past. There were no nuclear missiles in medieval England, but there was no anaesthesia either. The chimera of endless progress is just as one-sided as Leavis's view of history as decline. Karl Marx believed that the modern age was one of exhilarating emancipation, but saw it as one long nightmare as well. He also regarded these two narratives as being closely interwoven.

For a group so keen on fine judgement, the Scrutineers' view of contemporary civilisation was alarmingly indiscriminate. As far as popular culture went, Leavis would no doubt have seen no difference between John Wayne and John Coltrane, assuming that he was aware of either of them. From this Olympian height, the popular cultural landscape appeared uniformly barren. Modernity was almost unreservedly deplored as a spiritual waste land. There was no attempt to balance the pollution of rivers with advances in medicine and sanitation, to weigh the influence of the tabloid press against the growing power of women, or to offset the mass publication of so-called pulp fiction with the spread of literacy, democracy and civil rights. What was needed, given this soulless condition, was the cultivation of a civilised, educated reading public, of the kind once enjoyed by the eighteenth- and nineteenth-century periodicals; and *Scrutiny* would constitute the nucleus of this readership. Through a programme of social and cultural reform, it would concern itself not just with literature but with the destiny of modern civilisation as a whole. It would constitute a self-conscious elite, though, unlike Eliot's mixture of the landed gentry and conservative intellectuals, a thoroughly meritocratic one. Only in minorities, Leavis holds, is there life and hope. Dissociated from all partisan interests, the group would act as the custodian of creative values in a degenerate era. As such, it would represent that rare English phenomenon, an independent intelligentsia. Literary criticism was the best training ground for the development of a free, unspecialised, disinterested intelligence, which could be brought critically to bear on social existence as a whole. Literature itself was the prime depository of human values – indeed, of the inherited wisdom of the race. As one Scrutineer observed, 'English is not really a subject at all. It is a condition of existence'.[14] *Scrutiny*'s faith in the power of English studies was inflated beyond all reasonable proportion, yet this was partly because its dilettantish forebears had devalued the subject so drastically. The journal was reacting against the Quiller-Couches of this world by taking the discipline with intense, indeed excessive seriousness.

Literary criticism was a training in both intelligence and sensibility, and was naturally interdisciplinary. The ideal English school would thus involve economic, political, social and religious thought. We have seen already that Leavis himself had come over to English from History, while Queenie Leavis regarded herself as a cultural anthropologist. Nor would the school's literary preoccupations be confined to English writing. Leavis had a long-standing interest in American literature, despite his loathing of what he saw as the Americanisation (or 'cretinisation') of English society, and *Scrutiny* published commentaries on French, German and Italian authors. A transformed English school would act as a centre of humane value and judicious judgement within a larger forum of critique, the university itself. The university would become 'a centre of human consciousness: perception, knowledge, judgement and responsibility' (TC, p. 75). English schools would produce a stratum of authors, editors, journalists and other intellectuals who would exert a genuine influence on political power, while helping to generate the highly literate reading public of which society stood in sore need. An engagement in social and political affairs should be the business of those trained in the disciplined sensitivity which literary criticism could provide. English, in other words, would play the kind of role in producing cultivated administrators and civil servants which Classics had traditionally performed. A public sphere of a kind could be created from within the university – an irony, to be sure, since universities had in some ways replaced the original article. The worldly, debonair discourse of the eighteenth-century coffee houses, which congratulated itself on not being fustily academic, had finally retreated to the cloisters of Oxbridge.

The way to reform a degraded society, then, was through education. The main engine of education was the university; at the core of the universities lay the humanities; the queen of the humanities was literature, and the royal road to literature was literary criticism. If you believe in humanity, Leavis maintains, there is nothing more important than to keep alive the idea of the university. It is, in fact, hard to see how keeping the idea of the university alive is more vital to the fate of the species than the drugs trade or the prevention of sex trafficking. Besides, the universities in Britain were undergoing a drastic change for the worse in Leavis's eyes at roughly the time he was proposing them as an ideal. The expansion of higher education in the 1960s was not a change he looked upon benignly. He took an equally dim view of the wave of student militancy which swept across the globe shortly afterwards. Education on what he called an 'industrial' scale was the enemy of minority culture. Yet if he was defiantly elitist about this development, he was also one of the first public intellectuals to recognise that universities were destined to become service stations for the economy, as they are for the most part today; and it was in the teeth of this trend that he stressed the importance of higher education as the home of a free play of critical intelligence, one at odds with the priorities of industrial capitalism.

In this sense, *Scrutiny* was in general on the political left. It is likely that had he lived to see it, Leavis would have heartily approved of the Green movement. In his early years, he even considered the possibility of some form of economic communism, while rejecting Marxism for what he saw as its denial of the autonomy of the human spirit. In any case, Marxism was not radical enough: it was just another version of the soulless industrial order which was corroding the sources of creative life. It was, Leavis argued, 'a characteristic product of our "capitalist" civilisation', placing the word 'capitalism' in scare quotes in order not to seem complicit with the very form of critique he was dismissing.[15] He also remarked that he detested collectivist ideologies. Even so, he read Leon Trotsky's *Literature and Revolution* with interest, and offered to lend a hand when some upper-class louts threatened to break up a protest against the West's invasion of the Suez Canal in 1956, remarking that he was good in a rough-house. Whether or not this was true physically (he had been gassed in the First World War and regarded himself as disabled), it was certainly true metaphorically.[16]

Yet if *Scrutiny* had something of the left's social conscience and scorn for privilege, it could also reproduce a few of its less palatable features. There were times when those who ran the journal behaved like the most ferociously sectarian of Trotskyist groups, ostracising those members who deviated from the party line, detecting malignant enemies behind every mild demurral, and spending rather less time mauling the opposition than scrapping with each other. These conflicts owed a good deal to the embattled temperaments of the Leavises, but they also reflected the strains and contradictions inherent in the enterprise itself. English studies were at the heart of that project, yet *Scrutiny* looked askance on much that was done in their name. The home of English studies was the universities, yet the universities were increasingly in thrall to a philistine rationality. The humane values which English stood for formed the essence of civilisation, but actual civilisation was sterile and mechanistic. Only at Cambridge, Leavis insists, could the idea of *Scrutiny* have taken shape; yet the actual Cambridge had pushed him and his partner to the margins and refused to award lectureships to some of their most ardent acolytes. Hence Leavis's celebrated declaration that 'We were, and knew we were, Cambridge – the essential Cambridge in spite of Cambridge' (TC, p. 76). As with a set of Chinese boxes, the vital centre of civilisation was the universities, the living heart of the university was English studies, the exemplary university was Cambridge and the essence of Cambridge was *Scrutiny*. Yet at every stage, the ideal ran counter to the reality. It was under these pressures that the Leavisites could be venomous in the cause of creative life and stridently partisan about the idea of impartiality.

It is perhaps not surprising, then, that Leavis's final years were dogged by a sour sense of defeat. He had closed down *Scrutiny*, he remarked, because he had failed, but also because no intelligent review could survive in the modern age. As far as failure went, he was thinking of the fact that he had proved incapable of shaking up Cambridge, which was not entirely true. There was a Leavisite presence in the Cambridge English Faculty for some years after the journal folded, and a large number of students were influenced by this trend, all the way down to imitating the Master's distinctive accent and gestures. His own published work was for the most part more generously received than his grousing about reviewers would suggest. And beyond Cambridge lay an international academic community which had been indelibly stamped by his spirit.

All the same, his mood darkened in his final years. *Nor Shall My Sword* fulminates against 'our desperate sickness' (NSS, p. 180), which includes sexual permissiveness, student unrest, drugs and absenteeism. If one has to state the alternative to all this, there is little to be said beyond 'creativity'. The book also decries workers who demand higher wages, the destruction of the grammar schools and those bleeding-heart liberals who wish to atone for the British Empire. The British did an immense amount of creative work in India, Leavis maintains, and he is proud to call himself a Little Englander. The assumption that there can be democracy in India or 'black Africa' is ludicrous. His wrath is unleashed upon migrants, student militancy, enlightened liberals who preach social compassion, 'multiracialism', Jimi Hendrix and those who don't see that elites are a permanent fixture of existence. He had always been suspicious of feminism, big-heartedly pointing out in *The Great Tradition* that George Eliot had 'an extremely vigorous and distinguished mind, and one in no respect disabled by being a woman's' (GT, p. 96n). Henry James's young heroine Daisy Miller 'is utterly uneducated, and no intelligent man could stand her for long since there could be no possible exchange of speech with her: she has nothing to recommend her but looks, money, confidence, and clothes' (GT, p. 159). There is a reference to the 'spinsterly limitations' of Jane Austen (R, p. 125). Leavis's preference for sinewy, muscular language itself betrays a masculinist bias. The radical who declared that 'the academic is the enemy' (TC, pp. 75–6) had begun to sound like a purple-faced colonel firing off letters from his club to the *Daily Telegraph*.

By and large, this is how Leavis has been remembered, in so far as he is remembered at all. It is the elitism, narrowness, sectarianism and later illiberalism which have lingered in the cultural memory. What is less often recalled is that in an age of genteel amateurs and aesthetic poseurs, who regarded literary appreciation as a superior form of wine-tasting, he played a pivotal role in establishing English as a serious moral and intellectual discipline. Raymond Williams, a student in Leavis's Cambridge, writes that it was 'the range of Leavis's attacks on academicism, on Bloomsbury, on metropolitan literary culture, on the commercial press, on advertising, that first took me'.[17] Leavis's passion for education, he adds, was an additional attraction. If he was disputatious, not to say downright abusive, it was partly because there was so much at stake for him in transforming English studies, not least issues which resonated far beyond the walls of academia. No doubt he and his colleagues overrated the importance of the subject. When one reacts, one generally overreacts. In the early 1960s, a fist fight broke out between two of Leavis's most ardent camp-followers, one of them now an eminent novelist. The cause of the scuffle turned out to be a disagreement over the supremacy of George Eliot.

In order to retrieve English from those who had trivialised it, Leavis was prepared to take on the whole of the cultural and academic Establishment. With impressive courage, he was never afraid to infuriate in the name of his principles those who might have helped him off the bread line in his early years. He was a man of exceptional integrity who stuck to his guns whatever the cost in personal advancement. He warned prophetically of the dangers of universities falling victim to a bone-headed utilitarianism which measured outcomes in the manner of a biscuit factory. He was also a superb teacher, deeply devoted to his students, whom he advised to cultivate intellectual promiscuity rather than settle for tunnel vision. His conception of literary studies was unusually generous for the time, shading into history, religion, economics, sociology and anthropology. His powers of discrimination may have failed when it came to popular culture, but he was surely right to protest that ordinary men and women deserved better than the kitsch with which they were being served up by whole sectors of the popular press, popular fiction, advertising and television. He had a keen sense of responsibility not just to literary studies but to the quality of life of society as a whole. He was also a critical pioneer, championing writers like Hopkins, Eliot, Pound, Yeats, Edward Thomas, Isaac Rosenberg and others before their reputations were well established.

As a critic, Leavis could be excessively rigorous in his judgements, but most of them turned out to be sound enough. He scandalised the Shakespearian scholars by describing Othello's nobility as 'the disguise of an obtuse and brutal egoism. Self-pity becomes stupidity, ferocious stupidity, an insane and self-deceiving passion' (CP, pp. 146–7). It is a devastatingly accurate assessment, one which refuses to judge the character by his own inflated self-image. The actor Laurence Olivier put the interpretation to the test with excellent results in a stage production of the play. Leavis could be a magnificent analyst of literary works, and introduced a new language into literary studies. He was capable of some strikingly apt formulations: Thackeray's 'clubman's wisdom', Matthew Arnold's 'thin, sweet, meditative melancholy', the occasionally 'unctuous cadences' of Yeats's early prose, Pound's 'rhythmic suppleness', the 'rich disorganisation' of *The Waste Land*, the 'hypnoidal vaguenesses' of the Celtic Twilight. For all his egregious faults, those who regard him simply as a crusty old elitist whose favourite novelist was nothing but a misogynistic homophobe would do well to think again.

5

RAYMOND WILLIAMS

'Queenie did it all in the Thirties' was F.R. Leavis's comment on the work of Raymond Williams.[1] He presumably had in mind Q.D. Leavis's critique of popular culture in her *Fiction and the Reading Public*; but though the book is indeed a pioneering study, it can hardly be weighed in the scales against the work of the greatest socialist thinker of post-war Britain. It is true, however, that among its other achievements *Scrutiny* was a source of what would later become known as cultural studies. If its treatment of popular culture was emphatically negative, it also acknowledged its growing influence. Yet as Williams himself points out, there was a more important factor at work here. The critical analysis of newspapers, cinema, advertisements and the mass media first got under way in the adult education movement in the 1950s, in the period when Williams himself, along with the labour historian E.P. Thompson and the literary and cultural critic Richard Hoggart, were working in this field.[2]

Williams was born in 1921 in a small Welsh village not far from the border with England, and metaphorically speaking he lived in border country all his life. He was caught between England and Wales, city and country, middle class and working class, intellectual and popular culture, the experience of mobility and a love of the place where he grew up. One might add to these polarities the division between mental and manual labour: he did some hedging and ditching in the countryside and had a remarkably quick feel for material processes, along with a practical understanding of how things worked untypical of an intellectual. His materialism, in a word, was not just a cerebral affair.

The son of a railway signalman and the descendant of generations of farm labourers, Williams read English at Cambridge, but had to break off his course of studies to fight in the Second World War. As a lieutenant in an anti-tank regiment at the age of 22, he was engaged in military action in Continental Europe, and regarded the Allies' campaign as a form of solidarity with the Red Army. Some years later, he was deprived of his military commission for refusing to fight in the Korean War, but managed to avoid imprisonment for this offence. After returning to Cambridge to complete his degree, he took a political decision to teach in the adult education movement and the Workers' Educational Association, a career which he later described as a vocation rather than a profession. It was work of rare value – though as Williams once wryly remarked to me, it could sometimes be a matter of teaching doctors' daughters rather than (as at the male-dominated universities of the day) doctors' sons. In the late 1950s he was involved with the early New Left and the Campaign for Nuclear Disarmament, and on the strength of his path-breaking study *Culture and Society 1780–1950* was appointed to a lectureship at Cambridge and later to a Chair. He died in 1988.[3]

Williams's Chair was in drama, a subject which concerned him practically as well as theoretically. He wrote two plays for television, along with some theatre scripts. There is a mutedly theatrical, powerfully emotive strain in much of his non-fictional work, suggestive of an artist writing as a critic. There are also snatches of rather portentous rhetoric. In his mature work, drama is exemplary of what he calls cultural materialism, meaning the study of culture as a set of material practices; but his early writing on the subject is very far from such an approach. *Drama from Ibsen to Eliot* (1952) and *Drama in Performance* (1954), published at a time when Williams was still much under the influence of Leavis, are pieces of conventional literary criticism which have almost nothing to say about the social conditions of production of the drama with which they deal. Instead, the plays are treated simply as a set of texts to be examined, a method that the later Williams would decisively reject.

Even so, to apply the close reading of the Cambridge school to drama was a relatively original move. Williams's experiment, as he calls it, is to apply the techniques of literary criticism to the stage, whereas the later Williams will turn his back on criticism altogether, in a culture which he came to see as 'rotten with [it]' (PL, p. 240).[4] At this early point, he had not yet found his distinctive voice, or discovered a way of uniting his politics with his intellectual interests. In fact, in *Reading and Criticism* (1950), another Leavis-influenced study, he manages to discuss Joseph Conrad's novella

Heart of Darkness without mentioning imperialism. It is also remarkable that in *Drama from Ibsen to Eliot* he should claim that moral issues do not fall within the boundaries of literary criticism, and that to question the values implicit in T.S. Eliot's drama would be to transgress the proper borders of the discipline. Readers at the time would no doubt have been astonished to learn that the author of these studies considered himself a communist. As Williams was to remark later, he was a 'relatively sound academic' before he was an actual member of academia, meaning while he was still working in adult education, but became much less orthodox and acceptable when he was a university teacher (PL, pp. 211–12).

All the same, these early offerings, along with *Preface to Film* (1954, co-authored with Michael Orrom), have strengths which prefigure the innovative, revolutionary Williams of the 1970s and 1980s. He was already preoccupied by what one might call the politics of form – of how a whole way of seeing or feeling, one with powerful political implications, is inherent in the structures and conventions of a work of art, not simply in its extractable content. *Drama from Ibsen to Eliot* is a critique of one such form, dramatic naturalism, which aims for verisimilitude – which is to say, creating the illusion of reality by representing a familiar world on stage. In his later work, Williams would come to acknowledge the radical nature of naturalism in the late nineteenth century: its militantly secular rejection of the supernatural, its attention to the poor and disregarded, its exposure of sordid realities which polite society would prefer to suppress, its materialist vision of humanity as the product of its environment, its close affinities with the socialist movement and with the enlightened world view of science.

Naturalism as verisimilitude in art, however, is a different matter. In *Drama from Ibsen to Eliot*, Williams is conscious of the limits of naturalism, or indeed of any representational form of art. There are deeper realities, as well as inner ones, which a portrayal of the everyday world is unable to reveal. Putting a factory on stage, Bertolt Brecht remarked, will tell you nothing about capitalism. So this theatrical form has political effects. Naturalistic theatre is also marked in Williams's view by an impoverishment of language, which he relates in Leavisite style to the tarnished, threadbare speech of modern industrial society. The emotional paucity of George Bernard Shaw's dramatic prose is a case in point. The dramatic representation of everyday speech, Williams claims, is less satisfying in modern conditions than it was in Shakespeare's day. An exception can be found in the pre-industrial Ireland of J.M. Synge, an author once described as the only man who could write in English and Irish simultaneously.

Serious drama, Williams maintains, requires a rich common language; it also demands a community of sensibility between artist and audience which cannot flourish in a 'mechanised' social order. Synge, by contrast, discovered in the west of Ireland a community of expression, which may be a more charitable way of saying that all his characters sound much the same. It is true, Williams concedes, that his extravagantly poetic dialogue, which at times can be no more than a verbal 'flavouring', falls short of Shakespearian stature, and is pressed to an extreme in his compatriot Sean O'Casey's 'adjectival drunkenness' (DIE, p. 117). Even so, the burnished splendour of Synge's language is based in Williams's view on an organic form of life, whereas O'Casey's dialogue, adjectival drunkenness apart, reflects the

261

drab, bleached speech of the city. (He fails to note that Dublin, the city in question, also gave birth to one of the most verbally opulent of all modern literary works, James Joyce's *Ulysses*.)

Williams once remarked that the two deepest formative influences on him in Cambridge were Leavis and Marxism, and it would seem that the former has the upper hand here. Yet his critique of naturalism is itself an implicit form of politics. Naturalist authors like Ibsen, Zola and Strindberg, Williams would argue later, belong to a dissident fraction of the middle class, hostile to its values yet unable to break decisively with its outlook. One might see in this an allegory of Williams's own situation in a politically becalmed post-war Britain, as a socialist who felt the lack of any credible force for social change. But there is another political implication as well. Naturalism presents its audience with an instantly recognisable, meticulously lifelike world, usually that of a living room; but this very sturdiness may suggest that the form of life we are witnessing is immune to change. The political message implicit in the play's form ('this situation is here to stay') may then be in conflict with its content, which might clamour for social transformation.

The image of the naturalistic room crops up again and again in Williams's writing, as characters are trapped in an enclosed space in which their destinies are being determined by external powers over which they have little or no control. The work of Chekhov is a case in point. A whole way of viewing humanity, with strong political implications, is crystallised in a specific artistic form. Men and women are no longer authors of their own history. They cannot grasp the nature of the forces which fashion them. Because the naturalist frame forbids bringing these forces directly on stage, we can observe nothing but the characters' passive reaction to them, as one might 'stare from a window at where one's life is being decided' (DIB, p. 335). What cannot be shown directly can only be alluded to obliquely, mainly by the use of symbolism: the seagull, the cherry orchard, the tower, the wild duck, the mountain peaks, the white horses and so on.

Williams was finally to break out of his own isolated room, one in which he wrote his celebrated *Culture and Society 1780–1950*, into new forms of political activity. European drama had made the break with the work of the later Ibsen, Strindberg and others, who eventually abandoned naturalism for Expressionism. If the theatre was to reveal the anguished subjectivity of modern life, shaped as it is by the pressures of the unconscious, it would need to ditch the sofa and sideboard and draw instead on the resources of dream, fantasy and unconscious desire. The result is a world in which characters split and merge, the past blends with the present and there is no longer any firm frontier between self and others, inner and outer, image and reality, conscious and unconscious. Alternatively, you can fight your way out of the private room into the public sphere of a Bertolt Brecht, creating a form of theatre which can put social realities directly on stage. There is no living room in *Mother Courage and her Children*. These dramatic techniques found their equivalents in cinema and later in television, so that there is a logical progression from Williams the critic of drama to Williams the theorist of popular culture.

Generally speaking, Williams preferred modernist experiment in drama and realism in the novel. In *The Long Revolution*, he calls for a new realism, meaning 'the kind of novel which creates and judges the quality of a whole way of life in terms of the qualities of persons' (LR, p. 278). The formula is derived from the work of the Hungarian Marxist critic Georg Lukács. Genuine realism rejects the kind of fiction which reduces the world to the consciousness of a solitary individual, but also refuses to treat individuals as mere functions of their environments. Instead, characters remain what Williams calls absolute ends in themselves, while society, rather than behaving simply as 'background', represents the living substance of their actions and relationships. As he puts it in his study of the English novel, 'a unique life, in a place and a time, speaks from its own uniqueness and yet speaks a common experience' (EN, p. 192).

In this sense, realism is the form which corresponds most closely to Williams's socialist humanism. He opposed a society which severs the links between individual lives, but also one which reduces men and women to mere effects of the social totality. Realism, so to speak, is an antidote to both capitalism and Stalinism. Where he differs from Lukács is in the latter's conviction that realism must involve verisimilitude, presenting a familiar world in recognisable ways. It is this which underlies the Hungarian critic's stiff-necked hostility to modernist experiment. Williams, by contrast, had lived through a Cambridge in which Joyce, Eisenstein and Surrealism were revered in student socialist circles, so that realism for him was open to a variety of formal techniques. It is a way of seeing, not a matter of trying to write like Stendhal or Tolstoy. All the same, his commitment to realism in the novel is implicitly prescriptive: a particular way of viewing the world, whatever literary form it assumes, is privileged above all others. By and large, Williams disliked an art which he saw as abstract, distancing, bloodless and analytic, all of which can be taken as shorthand for modernism. If he could admire literary works which hold the world at arm's length in their crystalline concern with purity of form and psychological depth, it was against the grain of his deeper inclinations.

Over a decade after the appearance of *Drama from Ibsen to Eliot*, Williams was to publish a far more embattled study of theatre, *Modern Tragedy* (1966). Convinced that he had encountered various forms of tragedy in his own life, he found himself being informed by traditionally minded literary scholars that this could not possibly be so. Tragedy concerned the death of princes and the downfall of the mighty, not the misfortunes of ordinary men and women. It involved a belief in gods, heroes, myth, fate, blood sacrifice, cosmic order, the nobility of suffering and the exaltation of the human spirit. Since none of this had survived in the prosaic world of modern democracy, tragedy had perished along with it. In this sense, the very title of Williams's work is a gesture of defiance. Tragedy, it would appear, did not die with Jean Racine, at least not for this thinker. The book thus represents a courageous political intervention, defending tragedy in the everyday sense of the term against the patrician disdain of the academics. There is a cold, sardonic anger about the work which is very far from Williams's earlier writings. It is a tone which we shall hear repeatedly in the studies that follow.

'War, revolution, poverty, hunger; men reduced to objects and killed from lists; persecution and torture; the many kinds of contemporary martyrdom; however close and insistent the facts, we are not to be moved, in a context of tragedy. Tragedy, we know, is about something else' (MT, p. 62). For the conservative scholars whom Williams has in his sights, Aeschylus is tragic but Auschwitz is not. Some of these scholars point to the Nazi concentration camps as testimony to the malevolence of human nature, evidence of an evil at the heart of the human condition which no political change could cure. For the humanistic Williams, however, this meant falsely generalising a historically specific fact to a demeaning view of humanity as a whole. He was one of the few writers to make the point that 'while men created the camps, other men died, at conscious risk, to destroy them' (MT, p. 59). Indeed, he himself had risked death for the sake of others. Throughout his career, Williams spoke up for hope while keenly aware of human cruelty and corruption. He was also conscious of how incorrigibly naive the virtue of hope is bound to seem in a world characterised by what he calls 'a widespread loss of the future' (PM, p. 96).

In fact, tragedy and hope are not in his view mutually exclusive. Not all stage tragedies end in death and breakdown. On the contrary, the emergence of new life, however frail and precarious, is an integral part of the classical tragic action. In an imaginative move, Williams linked this fact to the nature of modern political revolution. Revolution, he believed, is needed in any society which cannot incorporate all of its members in their full humanity. It is thus an essential project 'in all societies in which there are, for example, subordinate racial groups, landless landworkers, hired hands, the unemployed, and suppressed or discriminate [*sic*] minorities of any kind' (MT, p. 77). This is not how most academics were speaking in the mid-1960s, though by the turbulent end of that decade a size-able minority of them had come to adopt such views. *Modern Tragedy* was written in a period of anti-colonial insurrections across the globe, a series of events which taken as a whole represent the most successful political revolution of the late-modern era. Williams saw these scattered seizures of power as constituting a complete action, one which he regarded as 'the inevitable working through of a deep and tragic disorder' (MT, p. 75). The action is tragic not because it ends in failure, but because of the fearfully steep price it is forced to pay for justice and freedom. If life is to flourish, it must pass through the possibility of death. The need for emancipation cannot be denied, but neither can the affliction it brings in its wake. The two are linked in a single tragic condition. Tragedy, then, did not end with Euripides, Corneille or Ibsen. On the contrary, it is the keynote of the world in which Williams is writing.

It was *Culture and Society 1780–1950* (1958) which first brought Williams widespread acclaim. As with many an influential work, its impact was a matter of the spirit of the times as well as of its inherent value. In a world of relative post-war affluence, dissident novelists, playwrights and film-makers, the emergence of cultural studies, the politics of the New Left and the Campaign for Nuclear Disarmament, the Cold War, the imperialist debacle of Suez and the crisis of the Communist parties with the Hungarian revolt of 1956, Williams's book spoke urgently to the condition of Britain in the late 1950s. Faced with a Stalinised form of Marxism on the one hand and a deeply compromised Labourism on the other, he had few political resources to hand. Accordingly, he reached back into English social thought in order to construct a radical tradition of his own. It is this remarkable project that *Culture and Society* represents.

The heritage in question is a moral and cultural critique of industrial capitalism. It is an attempt to base social thought on the idea of a general humanity, rather than on the specialised language of politics, sociology and economics. Because so many thinkers in these fields had been co-opted by the conventional wisdom, it had been left largely to artists, cultural thinkers and free-floating intellectuals to challenge the social order, from William Blake and Samuel Taylor Coleridge to George Orwell and F.R. Leavis. Edmund Burke stands at the source of this current, with his insistence that 'the state ought not to be considered nothing better than a partnership agreement in a trade of pepper and coffee, calico or tobacco . . . it [is] a partnership not only between those who are living, but between those who are living, those who are dead, and those who are to be born' (quoted in CS, pp. 21–2). In his assault on a crass utilitarianism, Burke 'prepared a position', Williams comments, 'from which the march of industrialism and liberalism was to be continually attacked' (CS, p. 23). A contemporary of his, William Cobbett, may have idealised the Middle Ages but showed 'an attachment by instinct and experience to the labouring poor' (CS, p. 32).

There is also the heritage of the radical Romantic artist, who Wordsworth sees as 'carrying everywhere with him relationship and love' (CS, p. 63). Such individuals find in art 'certain human values, capacities, energies, which the development of society towards an industrial civilisation was felt to be threatening or even destroying'

(CS, p. 56). So the Romantic poet is less a lonely visionary than the bearer of a common humanity, resisting a view of human beings as mere extractors of profit or instruments of production. The creative imagination is a political as well as poetic force, directed against mechanical production, the cult of utility and a coercive politics. 'The arts', Williams writes, 'defined a quality of living which it was the whole purpose of political change to make possible' (CS, p. 211). From Schiller and Coleridge to Marx and Matthew Arnold, culture in the sense of the harmonious development of human faculties is pitted against the stunting of human potential by industrialism. 'Mechanism', comments Thomas Carlyle, 'has now struck its roots down into man's most intimate, primary sources of conviction; and is thence sending up, over his whole life and activity, innumerable stems – fruit-bearing and poison-bearing' (quoted in CS, p. 104). At the same time, cash payment has become the sole nexus between individuals.

For Victorian sages like John Ruskin, the art of a period is a measure of the quality of life which produced it. 'The art of any country', Ruskin writes, 'is the exponent of its social and political virtues' (quoted in CS, p. 184). Two concepts of culture – as art and as a whole way of life – are yoked fruitfully together. Culture involves wholeness of being and creative self-realisation, both of which are hard to come by among the cotton mills of Lancashire. As Ruskin protests in *Stones of Venice*:

> The great cry that rises from all our manufacturing cities, louder than their furnace blast, is all in very deed for this – that

we manufacture everything there except men; we blanch cotton, and strengthen steel, and refine sugar, and shape pottery; but to brighten, to strengthen, to refine or to form a single living spirit, never enters into our estimate of advantages. (quoted in CS, p. 190)

In the life and work of William Morris, Romantic artist and Marxist activist, these values are harnessed for the first time to a specific political force, the working-class movement. 'It is the province of art', Morris observes, 'to set the true ideal of a full and reasonable life before [humanity]' (quoted in CS, p. 202). It is not a question of using art as an instrument for moral or political ends, but of finding in it an image of self-fulfilment with political implications.

One of the most eminent twentieth-century inheritors of the 'Culture and Society' legacy is D.H. Lawrence, the child of a working-class home close to the countryside, with whom Williams strongly identifies. The communitarian impulse in himself, Lawrence remarked, was stronger than the sexual one. True freedom consists in belonging to a living homeland, not in straying and breaking away. Democracy is a condition in which 'each man shall be spontaneously himself – each man himself, each woman herself, without any question of equality or inequality entering in at all; and that no man shall try to determine the being of any other man, or any other woman' (quoted in CS, p. 276). What Lawrence felt in the presence of another human being was neither equality nor inequality but (in his own term) Otherness, and few English writers have conveyed so finely a sense of the 'thisness' or uniqueness of persons, animals and objects. He has a remarkable sense of what the philosopher Martin Heidegger calls *Gelassenheit* – the capacity to be open and responsive to the pure givenness of another being, without any attempt to bend them to one's will. We cannot possess one another, and only on this understanding can there be genuine intimacy between us.

A number of the figures whom Williams examines are nostalgic for an organic society, one which flourished before the calamitous Fall into possessive individualism, mechanistic habits of thought and the replacement of 'natural' bonds between individuals with commercial or contractual ones. Williams himself repudiates this homesickness, sardonically remarking that the only sure thing about the organic society is that it has always gone. It is a judgement which represents a decisive break with Leavisism. The dream of such an ideal order, he points out, can be found however far back we look. There were thinkers in antiquity who mourned the decline of parental authority and the neglect of the gods. Williams knows enough of the history of the countryside to be aware of the ignorance, frustrated intelligence, deprivation, petty tyranny, disease, mortality and backbreaking labour which have disfigured it. This is one way in which one might describe him in his early years as a Left Leavisite, sharing many of Leavis's values yet opposed to his cultural elitism, and determined to demolish the myth that the modern industrial age represents a steep decline from the creative to the cretinous. Instead, in a style reminiscent of Marx, he highlights the benefits as well as the barbarisms which modern life has bestowed on humanity. In this respect, he belongs to the camp of Richards and Empson rather than that of Eliot and Leavis – though his belief in the possibility of human advancement is rooted in his socialist trust in human capabilities, not in some arid rationalism.

All the same, *Culture and Society* is rather too indulgent to the reactionary viewpoint of most of the authors it considers. If it does not overlook such beliefs, it certainly plays them down. In this respect, the book delivers a thoroughly sanitised narrative. Edmund Burke was an advocate of colonialism, an enemy of revolution and a doughty defender of private property, while Coleridge ended up as a High Anglican Tory hostile to popular democracy. Thomas Carlyle was an unbridled racist and imperialist who venerated the strong, recommended the planned emigration of 'surplus' workers, revealed a savage contempt for the common people and supported authoritarian rule. Matthew Arnold may have ranked among the leading liberals of the Victorian era, but this did not prevent him from calling for state violence to suppress working-class protest. John Henry Newman advocated the harmonious development of human faculties, but his was a mind aloof from the most pressing social issues of his day, and usually on the wrong side of such questions when it deigned to consider them. John Ruskin was an old-school Tory paternalist who placed his faith in a hierarchical social order and hymned the virtues of order, obedience, authority and subordination. We have already noted the unsavoury politics of D.H. Lawrence. The same goes for T.S. Eliot, to whom Williams devotes a chapter.

It is true that most of these writers were critical of laissez-faire, liberal individualism, rampant commercialism, the dereliction of

duty by the ruling caste and the semi-destitute conditions of some
of those they governed. They spoke up instead for community, the
creative imagination, positive bonds between individuals, mutual
responsibility and spiritual self-fulfilment. Yet though most of them
were adversaries of industrialism, few of them were critics of industrial capitalism. Only William Morris was a revolutionary socialist,
who recognised that it was this system, not simply industrialism,
which held the key to contemporary social ills. In this sense, most
of the figures the book admires supported a form of life at odds with
the values they wished to see flourish. T.S. Eliot, as Williams points
out, believed in a corporate social order rather than an individualist
one, but lent his support in practice to a capitalist set-up which
threatened to undermine his own ideal. What Williams traces, then,
in the absence of a widespread, deep-seated socialist tradition, is a
radicalism of the right. The anarchy of the free market is opposed
not by socialist democracy but by order, authority, hierarchy and
paternalism. It is a remarkably copious, fertile inheritance, one
which was to reach its peak in modernism; but for the book to make
light of some of its more discreditable features is a serious flaw, as
Williams himself came to acknowledge.

Culture and Society ends with a Conclusion remarkable for its
wisdom and authority. It is an outstanding document in a politically
barren era. Williams argues for what he calls a common culture, by
which he means not a uniform way of life, nor (as with Eliot) a single
culture shared at different levels, but a society in which the channels of
participation are open to everyone; which is thus commonly made as
well as commonly shared; and which would accordingly involve a

good deal more diversity than we enjoy at present. We are speaking of what Williams several times calls 'an educated and participating democracy'. Such a form of life could not be conscious of itself as a whole (indeed, much of it would be profoundly unconscious), or be available as a whole to its members. It would form a series of specialised, highly complex developments rather than some simple totality. In any case, since it would be perpetually in the making, it could never be fixed and bounded. Inequalities in skill and knowledge would coexist with what Williams calls equality of being, in the mutual respect of members of the culture for each other's contributions.

We need to provide the means of life and the means of community, by which one takes it Williams means socialist institutions; but what will be lived by those means cannot be prescribed in advance. We must thus remain open to every offered value and meaning, since we can never predict which of them might prove fruitful. A culture is essentially unplannable. The very word, transplanted like Williams himself from the country to the city, means the active tending of natural growth; and though the tending is conscious and organised, the growth itself is spontaneous. There is a minority who would impose their own selfish priorities on this common form of life, and who must therefore be opposed. This is why the symbol of the working-class movement must remain a clenched fist. Yet the clenching, Williams insists, should never be such that the hand cannot open and the fingers extend, to give shape to a new reality.

If a common culture is not to be some idle utopia, it is because in Williams's view the nucleus of such a future exists in the present. It can be found in the values of the working-class movement, with its belief in solidarity rather than individualism, cooperation rather than competition, mutual responsibility rather than individual self-interest. For this political ethic, society is viewed 'neither as neutral nor as protective, but as the positive means for all kinds of development, including individual development' (CS, p. 427). Solidarity, Williams concedes, can have negative, even noxious implications; but there are constructive versions of it as well, as his own personal experience would confirm. In an essay entitled 'Culture is Ordinary', produced at the same time as *Culture and Society*, he claims that the working-class way of life he once knew himself, 'with its emphases of neighbourhood, mutual obligation, and common betterment, as expressed in the great working-class political and industrial institutions, is in fact the best basis for any future English society' (RH, p. 8). If Williams looked back to his childhood home, it was not in Romantic nostalgia but to find a way forward.

Socialism, then, involves the extension of certain existing values into society as a whole, though Williams is clear that no value is ever disseminated on such a scale without being transformed in the process. Working-class culture is not primarily a question of works of art – in fact, most of what goes by the name of such culture is produced for the people, not by them. It is rather a question of institutions such as the trade unions, the cooperative movement, socialist organisations and the like, all of which Williams rightly regarded as remarkable cultural achievements in their own right. It is this above all that the class from which Williams himself came has bequeathed to civilisation, as vital in its own way as Romantic poetry or the realist novel.

It was in the 1950s that the political left first identified the media as a major problem. *Culture and Society* was published around the time that the concept of mass communications began to emerge. Williams rejects the term on two grounds. First, because to describe others as a 'mass' is itself a symptom of alienation on the part of the observer. There are, in fact, no masses, simply ways of seeing people as masses. Masses are other people. We do not generally consider our families or ourselves as part of the masses, so why should we not extend this respect to others? Secondly, the notion of mass communication is hard to disentangle from the reality of manipulation. Any genuine theory of communication, Williams insists, must be a theory of community – of how we should speak to one another, of the sharing of life and experience as an end in itself, whereas the whole concept of mass communications depends on a minority exploiting a majority. The so-called masses form a faceless public to be cajoled, persuaded, diverted and instructed, and the chief motive behind this process is the accumulation of profit. At the same time, the public is fed with political views, if only by the silent exclusion of certain convictions, which buttress the status quo, including the power and financial resources of the press and media themselves. A small clutch of billionaires are able to mould public opinion to promote their own interests, and this in a supposed democracy. It is striking that for all we learn of the state of popular culture from Richards and Leavis, George Orwell and Richard Hoggart, it is not until the work of Williams that this cheapening of everyday existence is set in the context of a capitalism which preys on the ignorance or cultural inexperience of millions of men and women in order to reap a lucrative gain from it. For Richards or the Leavises to have broached such questions would have meant overstepping the limits of their liberalism. In their view, the solution to the problem lay in education, which is more of a defensive strategy than a transformative one.

Williams is rather less long-term. When asked his opinion of entrepreneurs like the media baron Rupert Murdoch in the set of interviews entitled *Politics and Letters*, he replies with disarming bluntness that such men must be driven out. He also produced a brief but original study, *Communications*, which instead of simply bewailing the flashiness of advertising or the sensationalism of the tabloid press, advances concrete proposals for transforming the ownership and management of the press and media, removing them from the distortions of the marketplace without succumbing to the dangers of state control. Even so, he rejects the pessimistic view of Eliot and the Leavises that there has been a catastrophic decline in cultural standards. Empson, as we have seen, took a similar view to Williams, while Richards believed in cultural degeneration but also in the possibility of renewal. Williams is similarly judicious: there is indeed a good deal of shoddy art, journalism and entertainment around, but there is also some superb popular culture, as well as a notable increase in the audiences for ballet, opera, museums, art exhibitions and classical music. 'You can find kitsch in a national theatre', he remarks, 'and an intensely original play in a [TV] police series' (RWCS, p. 163). He might also have pointed to film – a cultural form which fascinated him as a student, which he was among the first to teach at Cambridge, and which has produced one masterpiece after another while remaining enormously popular.

Williams does not idealise the working class, as some of his fiction bears witness. His portrayal of working people in these novels is for the most part clear-eyed and undeceived, and he has an unerring ear for the speech of Welsh working-class men and women in what was once his home. What he proposes as a source of value is less working-class life in general than the ethic of cooperation and common responsibility which informs its political institutions. He would have encountered this ethic as a child in the activities of his father, who took part in the General Strike of 1926 and was secretary of his local Labour Party branch. Middle-class intellectuals who romanticise working people do not generally picture them as engaged in strikes, pickets, lock-outs and demonstrations, actions which can pose a threat to their own interests.

Yet the fact that Williams's father was a political activist also makes him untypical of working people in general, as well as making it easier for Williams to rebut the case that ordinary men and women are materialistically minded, politically apathetic and more enthused by Bingo than Bolshevism. Williams was fortunate enough to experience the class into which he was born at its finest; and though this lends his work much that is precious, it also breeds in him a trust in the capacities of ordinary people, as well as of humanity in general, which is occasionally too credulous. He is reluctant to acknowledge just how monstrously human beings can behave – partly because he believes that this would be to concede too much to the conservative notion of an innately corrupt human nature, and partly because it runs counter to his own formative experience. There are times in his writing where he uses the word 'human' as a positive term, as though torture and genocide were not human as well. He writes, for example, of those 'who answer death and suffering with a human voice' (MT, p. 204), but if Nelson Mandela spoke with a human voice, so did Hermann Göering.

Part of what Williams learnt from the close-knit community in which he grew up was the inseparability of the individual and society. If he held to this as a social and literary doctrine, it was one based on actual experience. Indeed, he points out in *The Long Revolution* that the word 'individual' originally meant 'indivisible', or inseparable from the whole. Unlike most critics, he was not bred to a culture of liberal individualism, and thus could identify its limits more easily than those who have gradually to learn them. In this sense, his social background is not simply a biographical fact about him. It is the reason why he approached social orthodoxy at an angle which makes it seem more questionable than it is for others. Simply because he was conscious of an alternative form of life, he was more likely to sense the social bias or historical relativity of certain assumptions. The same can be said of many post-colonial critics today.

He also brought from his background a trust in the creativity of the common life which is untypical of modern criticism. For a good deal of Formalism and modernism, everyday life is alienated and inauthentic, and only by being fractured or estranged can it be made to reveal some merit. The only worthwhile art is one which breaks with common conventions in innovative, experimental style. Drawing on his own more positive experience of the everyday, Williams questioned this aesthetic. The artist's task is as much to affirm and consolidate common meanings as it is to disrupt them. This, too, is an implicit rebuke of modernism. It also stands opposed to a postmodernism for which value can be found only in what deviates from the common life, transgressing its norms and flouting its conventions.

Looking back at *Culture and Society* from the standpoint of Williams's later work, one is struck by the emollience of its tone. If it is one of the key documents of the modern political left, it is far from an abrasive one. Its style is reasonable, circumspect and respectful. This is surely one reason for its remarkable success, as well as for the admiring reviews it received from members of the academic Establishment. They were to be far less enthusiastic about the study which followed it up, *The Long Revolution*. A good many readers, not wholly without justification, took *Culture and Society* to be the work of a liberal rather than a socialist, a misinterpretation which ironically might be said to have launched Williams's public career. For it was largely on the basis of this study that he was offered a Cambridge Fellowship, only for the academic world to discover that they had invited a barbarian into their citadel. The later Williams observed that he no longer knew the person who wrote his 'breakthrough' work, describing it dismissively as 'first-stage radicalism' (PL, p. 107). The authors discussed in it, he comments, put the right questions but gave the wrong answers. It is hard to think of a more succinct way of summarising the book. If he speaks dismissively about the study, it is because it was taken to define who and what he was at just the point when he was moving beyond it.

One of Williams's abiding interests was the novel, a form of which he himself was a practitioner; and his reflections on the subject are at their most searching in *The English Novel from Dickens to Lawrence* (1970). In the 1840s, when the English became the first predominantly urban people in history, the novel 'brought in new feelings, people, relationships; rhythms newly known, discovered, articulated; defining the society, rather than merely reflecting it' (EN, p. 11). There were deep changes in 'inward feelings, experiences, self-definitions' (EN, p. 12). The fiction of the Brontës, Dickens, Elizabeth Gaskell and others does not simply portray a rapidly changing social order; instead, it catches up and helps to define its rhythms and habits of feeling, its modes of perception and forms of consciousness. Far from being a mere reflection of history, it reveals aspects of it which would not otherwise be knowable. It shows society not as a static backdrop to its characters but 'as a process that entered lives, to shape or to deform' (EN, p. 13). History, then, is present in the very forms and styles of realism. As society is transformed, so is human subjectivity; and the novel, while registering this crisis of feeling and identity, also lends it some of the terms in which it can be formulated.

An example of this can be found in Williams's remarks about Dickens. Dickens is the first great novelist of urban England, but the city does not enter his writing simply as setting and social background. It is also to be felt in his way of delineating his characters, who are presented often enough by way of some single fixed feature: a trick of speech, an eccentric walk, a peculiar facial feature and so on. This, Williams claims, is 'a way of seeing men and woman that belongs to the street' (EN, p. 32). It is the kind of rapid, partial perception we have of pedestrians we bump into at some busy crossroads and never see again. Figures emerge for a moment from the crowd and are instantly swallowed up by it. We do not view them in the round, as we do with George Eliot's rural figures, since in the anonymous space of the city the lives of others are inaccessible. It is though they exist simply as vivid appearances, shorn of any history or complex hinterland. Individuals in Dickens often enough collide rather than relate, bounce off each other, speak past or at each other rather than engage in meaningful dialogue. In this great web of coincidences and random encounters, people live in the interstices of each other's lives. They are strangers to one another, even if the plots of the novels sometimes bring to light concealed relations between them. And all this, while a symptom of some grievous alienation and disconnection, is also exhilarating in its constant novelty and mutability, so that Dickens's own style, rather than being 'the controlled language of analysis and comprehension' (EN, p. 31) we associate with Jane Austen or George Eliot, is one of rhetoric, display, theatricality, emotional empathy, public exhortation. It is in this way that history can be found secreted in the very forms of his work, not simply in its portraits of workhouses and debtors' prisons.

To grasp this idea more completely, we need to understand something of Williams's key concept of a 'structure of feeling'. The phrase is almost an oxymoron, since 'structure' suggests something fairly solid, while 'feeling' is more elusive and impalpable. As Williams observes, 'it is as firm and definite as "structure" suggests, yet it operates in the most delicate and least tangible parts of our activity' (LR, p. 48). It thus reflects something of the dual character of literary criticism, which deals in feelings but in an analytical way. Or one might regard it as a bridge between criticism and sociology, since the latter deals largely with structures and the former takes more account of lived experience. Williams works for the most part at the point where the two converge. It is this stress on lived experience – 'this felt sense of the quality of life at a particular place and time' (LR, p. 47) – that the arts can contribute to a more sociological study of human cultures, without which it is bound to be incomplete. The influence of Leavis lingers on in Williams's description of the concept. 'Structure of feeling' also suggests that feelings are shared and social rather than merely subjective. A structure of feeling is a precise historical pattern of feeling which can be typical of a whole age, but also of a group, an artistic current or an individual work of art. In this sense, the concept can be used as a link between a broad span of history and more specific phenomena. There can also be conflicting structures of feeling within the same artwork or social condition.

It is a novel concept for a Marxist to employ. As Michael Moriarty points out, almost no other writer in the Marxist tradition has seen the human response to history as mediated not essentially through discourses or beliefs but through feelings.[5] One advantage of the concept is that it allows Williams to avoid the term 'ideology', which he associates with clear-cut doctrines and abstract ideas. (There are, in fact, less intellectualist versions of the notion.) Ideology and structure of feeling are not synonymous; but the latter is one of the ways in which a dominant power seeks to legitimate itself, and 'ideology' is the traditional name given to this process at the level of ideas. There are also, however, resistant or oppositional structures of feeling, as well as artistic works or stretches of social life where dominant and resistant lock horns. For Williams, then, power is a question of affect and experience, not simply of creeds.

One of the disadvantages of the idea, however, is that it invests rather too deeply in the notion of experience, a more slippery, ambiguous phenomenon than Williams would seem to acknowledge. Marx points out that the underlying mechanisms of capitalism do not show up in our regular experience, rather as for Freud the unconscious can be glimpsed in it only indirectly. Besides, your experience of a situation may be at odds with mine, and the same experience may lead us to different conclusions. Williams's political views, as we have seen, arose partly from his upbringing, but you could live through much the same childhood and adolescence and arrive at a very different political stance. Plenty of people have. Perhaps the traditional term for Williams's coinage is 'sensibility', which can also be used both of a specific work and of a whole period or society. We can speak of the sensibility of Thackeray's *Vanity Fair*, but also of the sensibility of the late Victorian age. Williams might have felt that 'structure' was a more precise, analytic concept than the rather fuzzy idea of sensibility; but he did not carry through such structural analysis in any extended form.

Williams sometimes saw a structure of feeling as an emotional pattern which is still emergent, and has yet to crystallise into a definitive shape. It is, so to speak, feeling still in solution or suspension. All societies, he argues, are made up of a complex interaction between values and meanings which are dominant, those which are inherited from the past but remain active in the present (the residual), and those which are gradually coming to birth (the emergent). There are always feelings which can't as yet be fully articulated – embryonic 'elements of impulse, restraint, and tone; specifically affective elements of consciousness and relationship' (ML, p. 132) – which have yet to be formalised into an ideology or world view, and which may be first detected by the sensitive antennae of art. Williams was especially attracted to Antonio Gramsci's idea of hegemony, which he took to mean how the culture of a dominant class saturates the whole process of social living – not just with ideas, but with certain forms of lived experience.[6] Hegemony is in Williams's view a more vital conception than either culture or ideology – partly because it raises the question of power, which is not necessarily true of the notion of culture, and partly because its roots sink deeper than ideas, which is not always the case with the concept of ideology. If it is more politically pointed than culture, it is also more complex and inward than ideology. Even so, he wants to insist against certain pessimistic brands of Marxism that no ruling order can exhaust all human energy and meaning, and that what one might call practical consciousness is often in conflict with 'official' beliefs.[7]

In his study of the English novel, Williams writes of the world of the Brontës as one of 'desire and hunger, of rebellion and pallid convention: the terms of desire and fulfilment and the terms of oppression and deprivation profoundly connected in a single dimension of experience' (EN, p. 60). One could take this as an account of English society at the time, when the hunger could be quite literal (the 1840s are sometimes known as the Hungry Forties), and when the devastating impact of early industrial capitalism involved both rebellion and deprivation. But it is also an account of the structure of feeling of the Brontës' fiction, in which the hunger in question is metaphorical (though just as real), desire clashes with convention and characters like Heathcliff and Jane Eyre stage a smouldering revolt against authority. History invades the Brontës' writing, but obliquely, spontaneously, through certain recurrent patterns of feeling. 'When there is real dislocation', Williams writes, 'it does not have to appear in a strike or in machine-breaking' (EN, p. 65).

Another mediation between art and society is convention, which in Williams's view is at root a matter of social relationships. Consider, for example, the convention of the omniscient narrator in the realist novel, with its implications of authoritative judgement, a capacious vision and the ability to steer a unified narrative through a prodigal host of characters and conditions. It is not hard to relate the self-assurance of this project to the historical heyday of the middle class, which can rank the realist novel as among its most magnificent cultural achievements. One might then contrast this with the shattered world of so much modernist fiction, in which there may no longer be any unquestionable truth, solid foundation or commanding viewpoint, simply a set of clashing perspectives and unsettling ambiguities. A crisis of literary form springs from a deeper upheaval, as middle-class society enters into the turbulent period around the First World War. In Williams's view, cultural forms and conventions have a historical foundation.

The English Novel from Dickens to Lawrence challenges a good deal of standard critical opinion. It is a critical commonplace that Jane

Austen ignores the momentous historical events of her time, such as the Napoleonic wars; but Williams points out that few historical realities were more significant at the time than the fortunes of the landed families with which she deals. Austen sets her fiction not in some timeless, tranquil countryside but in a world of complex interactions between inheritance, landed property, fortunes reaped from commerce and colonial exploitation, marriages into estates and a number of other sources of wealth. For all its elegance and decorum, this is an openly acquisitive society, as landed, trading and colonial capital increasingly interlock. Despite the conflicts and instabilities which all this generates, Austen manages in Williams's view to achieve a remarkable unity of tone – a moral poise and assured judgement which reflect the confidence and maturity of her social class. She measures the traditional genteel order, as well as the social climbers trying to scramble into it, by certain absolute standards of moral conduct, and can pass some tart comments on how dismally so many of her characters fall short of them. It is hard to imagine the liberal-minded George Eliot or Henry James remarking of the death of one of their characters, as Austen does, that it was a stroke of good fortune for his parents. But she is also a thoroughly materialist author, with a quick eye for the value of a country residence or the revenue yielded by a piece of land. As Williams points out, it is these things she sees when she looks at a field, not anyone actually working there. Farm labourers are largely invisible. The countryside becomes real only in relation to the houses of the gentry; otherwise it is mostly a place to walk in.

Williams's personal familiarity with rural society also allows him to demolish a number of myths about Thomas Hardy. Hardy's fiction does not deal with the peasantry, for the good reason that they hardly existed in the England in which he wrote. The class had been more or less driven from the land by the late eighteenth-century enclosures. In its place we have a world of capitalist landowners, tenant farmers, farm labourers, dealers and craftsmen. Grace Melbury of *The Woodlanders* is no simple country lass but the daughter of a successful timber merchant. Tess Durbeyfield speaks the West Country dialect at home but Standard English when she is away from it. She is seduced not by a wicked aristocrat but by the son of a retired manufacturer. She, too, is no benighted rustic, but as the daughter of a life-holder and small dealer has been reasonably well educated at a national school. Williams points out that Hardy himself, like George Eliot and D.H. Lawrence, has been patronisingly described as an 'autodidact' or self-taught individual, even though all three of these authors received a better education than the great majority of their fellow citizens. 'Autodidact' in this context can be translated as 'didn't go to public school or Oxbridge'.

Tragedy in Hardy springs from circumstance, not fate. Nor, Williams insists, is it the result of a timeless rural way of life being invaded and undermined by urban influences. There is no major clash between the rural and the urban, not least because in English society the capitalist relations typical of the city first took hold in the countryside. If Hardy's Wessex is a precarious place in which to live, it is largely because of disruptive forces which are internal to it: poverty, the hazards of tenancy and small-capital farming, the leasing and renting of land, the gradual dwindling of the class of craftsmen, dealers, small tradesmen, cottagers and the like. What is also unstable in the novels is Hardy's own relation to this social landscape, as the son of a small-time rural builder who knows it from the inside, yet who is also an educated observer, with one eye on the place itself and the other on the metropolitan readership for whom he is writing.

This ambiguity, Williams argues, is built into Hardy's use of language. If Tess alternates between the Wessex dialect and a more 'correct' form of speech, Hardy himself is caught between a direct form of description of rural society in the easy idiom of the insider, and a more elaborate, self-conscious, 'literary' style of writing, one which aims to be acceptable to a middle-class metropolitan audience, for many of whom the countryside is a realm of rural idiocy. He calls these two modes of speech 'customary' and 'educated', and argues that neither will finally serve Hardy's purpose: as Williams puts it, 'the educated dumb in intensity and limited in humanity, the customary thwarted by ignorance and complacent in habit' (EN, p. 107). Form, once again, is social and historical: a stylistic disturbance is symptomatic of a deeper social crisis. A similar tension between the articulate and inarticulate, belonging and not belonging, the need for rootedness and freedom of spirit, is traced by Williams in the work of D.H. Lawrence, in his view the most gifted English novelist of his time.

If Williams is illuminating on Austen, the Brontës, Dickens, George Eliot and Hardy, he is distinctly less impressive on Joseph Conrad, Henry James, James Joyce and Virginia Woolf. One cannot really discuss Conrad without some reference to his metaphysical or philosophical vision, but Williams, like Leavis, is weak on philosophy and puts this aspect of his work aside. The same is true of his treatment of D.H. Lawrence, whose metaphysical notions are vital to an understanding of his fiction. As for Henry James, one of the finest of all English-language novelists, Williams appears strangely uneasy about him. As with Austen, he stresses how thoroughly materialist James is beneath the mannered surface. His fiction is all about wealth, possession and exploitation, yet Williams inexplicably regards him as excluding history from his art. He also sees him as a modernist rather than a major realist, one for whom the novel becomes its own subject matter. 'Consciousness in James', he writes, '. . . is the almost exclusive object and subject of consciousness' (EN, p. 135). This may be true of the late James, though even that is arguable, but it is a travesty of his work as a whole. So is the suggestion that Joyce's Dublin in *Ulysses* is less a real city or 'knowable community' than a symbolic abstraction. A knowable community is exactly what *Ulysses* depicts; indeed, it is true to some extent of this small post-colonial capital today, where everyone seems to have been at school or college with everyone else. The city is said to have wonderful acoustics. Joyce's novel is still acclaimed as a great work of art, but the most astonishingly avant-garde literary work in English, the same author's *Finnegans Wake*, is dismissed in a couple of sentences. D.H. Lawrence's *Women in Love*, one of its author's most adventurous imaginative experiments, is paid due (if rather perfunctory) homage; but in the end Williams opts for the more realist *Lady Chatterley's Lover*, with its feel for the common life, over the 'abstract symbolic language' of the former work. It is a spectacularly wrong-headed judgement.

Williams's view of these modern writers is skewed by his hostility to modernism, and nowhere more obviously so than in his aversion to Virginia Woolf. He sees her fiction as a world in which the common reality he values has been stripped away, leaving only an isolated, disembodied consciousness. In *The Waves*, 'all the furniture, even the physical bodies, have gone out of the window, and we are left with feelings and voices, voices in the air' (LR, p. 279). But why should one expect Woolf to write like Balzac or Turgenev? Williams delivered this judgement before Woolf became a feminist icon, and there is no distaste for feminism implicit in his critique of her art. In fact, the work in which he writes these words, *The Long Revolution*, lists what he calls 'the complex of relationships based on the generation and nurture of life' (LR, p. 114) alongside politics, economics and culture as the main sectors of any society. A social order which regards the birth and care of human beings not as a primary concern but as a way of being supplied with potential workers is to be resisted. The growth of love and the capacity for loving, Williams comments, are fundamental to the development of a society. In 1961, the year of publication of *The Long Revolution*, these were far from received positions, on the political left or anywhere else.

Williams remarks elsewhere that 'it is scarcely possible to doubt the absolute centrality of human reproduction and nurture and the unquestioned physicality of it' (PL, p. 340), and notes how sexuality is among the subjects which have traditionally been excluded by Marxism. He has, in fact, little directly to say of it himself; in fact, there is a certain puritanical evasion of the issue in his work, as there is a similar prudish streak in the writings of Leavis. Yet he also approaches the now rather modish issue of the human body from a revealing new angle, insisting on the 'very deep material bond between language and the body' (PL, p. 340). As early as *The Long Revolution*, he was interested in the effects of poetic rhythm 'on the blood, on the breathing, on the physical patterns of the brain' (LR, p. 24). There is a parallel here to Eliot's concern with poetry's effect on the visceral regions. Unlike postmodern culturalism, for which biology is largely an embarrassment, Williams retained a materialist grip on the idea of human beings as physical organisms. Whatever nobility of spirit we may attain, we remain in the first place lumps of material stuff.

Williams's account of English rural society is developed on a larger scale in *The Country and the City* (1973). It is a work which he found harder to write than any of his other books, perhaps because it touches on matters so central to his own identity. Among other things, the study considers the country house tradition in English poetry from the standpoint of the exploited farm labourers who were Williams's own ancestors, seeing such mansions as 'commanding statement[s] in stone' (CC, p. 106). 'Very few titles to property', he writes, 'could bear humane investigation, in the long process of conquest, theft, political intrigue, courtiership, extortion and the power of money' (CC, p. 50). These are not the terms in which literary criticism has traditionally discussed such poetic masterpieces as Ben Jonson's 'To Penshurst' or Thomas Carew's 'To Saxham', and the book met with a frosty reception from a number of reviewers. Yet it is worth noting that one of the earliest examples of pastoral verse that we have, Virgil's *Bucolics*, combines its idealisation of rustic life with a cry of outrage at the plight of those smallholders evicted by the Roman regime under which the author lived.

The Country and the City delivers an unflinchingly materialist account of the history of struggle, deprivation and outright robbery which underlies the picture-postcard image of a timeless rural England. It is remarkable that there is hardly any discussion of Empson's *Some Versions of Pastoral*, apart from a couple of curtly dismissive sentences. Perhaps this is partly because Williams found the book as baffling as most other readers did. In any case, he came to dislike close textual criticism, seeing it as a way of avoiding more general issues. He certainly seems to have no sense of how political Empson's book is. On the subject of the city, which receives significantly less attention than the countryside, the study is less enlightening. Williams was not fond of urban life, despite his rather dubious claim of 'needing' to visit foreign cities. He never lived in a city larger than Cambridge, and was no more of a metropolitan figure than Leavis, let alone a cosmopolitan one. Like all socialists, however, he was an internationalist, with a belief in the global solidarity of working men and women.

From *Culture and Society* onwards, it is hard to give a name to Williams's intellectual project. As critic, sociologist, novelist, cultural theorist and political commentator, he is a bookseller's nightmare, given that there is no obvious slot on the shelves to house his works. He is also something of a sage or moralist in the tradition he records in *Culture and Society* – the latest character, so to speak, in his own drama. He himself comments on the first page of *The Long Revolution* that 'there is no academic subject within which the questions I am interested in can be followed through' (LR, pp. ix–x). In the end, he himself helped to bring such a subject to birth, namely cultural studies. Because the idea of culture concerns the quality of a way of life, it is suitable that a study of it should spring chiefly from literary criticism, which is similarly devoted to questions of value and qualities of experience. Literary criticism is also a subject with such ill-defined boundaries, encompassing everything from death to dactyls, that it can open up to other fields of inquiry more easily than most disciplines. Indeed, in Williams's case it opens up so much that, as we shall see later, it virtually disappears.

The term he was finally to use to define his project was cultural materialism, the beginnings of which can be found in *The Long Revolution*. The book includes studies of the growth of the popular press and the reading public, the evolution of Standard English, the social history of English writers and of dramatic forms. Only three years had intervened since the appearance of *Culture and Society*, but the tone is notably more abrasive. Whereas the earlier work uses terms like 'a common culture', 'mutual responsibility' and 'the means of community' almost as euphemisms for socialism, the later one speaks openly of class and capitalism. All the same, the revolution referred to in the title is not of the kind that leaves the streets running with blood. It signifies rather a process already well under way: the gradual extension of democracy, industry, literacy, education and new forms of communication. The revolution, in short, is gradual and threefold: political, economic and cultural.

This, one might note, would not count as a revolution in classical Marxist terms, which consists in the transfer of power from one social class to another and which usually involves violent confrontation; but Williams's relation to Marxism was always a complex, ambiguous affair. He is commonly described as a Marxist; but though he was a member of the Communist Party for 18 months when he was a student, he explicitly distances himself from the creed in *Culture and Society*. *The Long Revolution* is certainly anti-capitalist, but its concept of revolution, as we have just seen, is not one of decisive political rupture; and though *Modern Tragedy* speaks of armed revolution, it is mostly of an anti-colonialist rather than anti-capitalist kind. Some years later, when Williams developed his theory of cultural materialism, he spoke of it somewhat cautiously as 'compatible' with Marxism rather than as an aspect of it.

The issue is complicated by the fact that what counts as being a Marxist is far from self-evident. There are thinkers who have laid claim to the title while rejecting one or several key doctrines of Marx himself; and a number of ideas which are sometimes thought to be Marxist were already well known when he came to write. They include communism, revolution, alienation, social class, class struggle and the class nature of the state. The concepts of use-value and exchange-value, though not the terms themselves, can be found in the work of Aristotle. Both Adam Smith and Jean-Jacques Rousseau believed in the primacy of material production in social affairs, and so in a sense did Sigmund Freud. One of the few theses which is arguably peculiar to Marx is the contradiction between the forces and relations of production, which is also one of the most controversial of his claims. Williams makes scarcely any comment on this supposedly indispensable feature of Marxist thought.

Even so, there is no doubt that by the time of *Marxism and Literature* (1977), Williams's position had shifted decisively to the revolutionary left. In this sense, his career challenges the dreary cliché of the street-fighting young firebrand who matures into a placid middle age. The development of his views coincides with the period from the late 1960s to the mid-1970s in which the political left was briefly in the ascendant. Williams was even to speak positively at this time of the brutal Chinese Cultural Revolution.[8] It was also a time which witnessed the influx into Britain of various neo-Marxist theories, in most of which culture, language, art, consciousness and communication were granted a more pivotal role than the Marxism of Williams's student days had ever allotted them. As work by Lukács, Gramsci, Goldmann, Sartre, Brecht, Bakhtin, Benjamin and Adorno grew increasingly influential on the British left, it was as though Marxism had caught up with Williams rather than the other way round. There was now a humanistic, non-doctrinaire version of the theory with which he could readily affiliate, and which seemed to meet what had been his primary objection to Marxism all along: the fact that it assigned culture and communication secondary rather than primary status. They belonged to the so-called superstructure rather than to the material base, and this was a case which Williams could never accept.

His rejection of it is evident as early as *The Long Revolution*. In a chapter entitled 'The Creative Mind', he argues that communication is never secondary to reality; on the contrary, it is only through language and interpretation that reality is constituted. Art is traditionally regarded as creative, in contrast to everyday consciousness; but in Williams's view the distinction is false, since the whole of our routine activity depends on learning, description, communication and interpretation. Perception itself is creative, and art is simply a specialised case of it, with no particularly privileged status. In an interaction of subject and object, consciousness continually reorganises reality and is reorganised by it in its turn. Some of Williams's later work then turns this case against the orthodox Marxist claim that culture and communication have only a secondary, derivative place in social existence. To believe so, he argues, is to dematerialise these activities, so that the trouble with orthodox Marxism is that it is not materialist enough. It fails to grasp culture as a set of practices quite as material as coal mining or cotton spinning. This is true, but risks missing the point. What most Marxists have held is that culture and communication are material practices, but not ones which are finally *determinant*. They are not the main motors of historical change.

It is this demotion of culture, as Williams sees it, that cultural materialism can rectify. Culture, he insists, is a mode of production in its own right, involving certain specific social relations and historical conditions, and it is the analysis of this which should take over from literary criticism as classically conceived. Means of communication are also means of production, both in the sense that they give rise to a product (speech, news, art, information), and in the sense that they are an integral part of material production as a whole. Language, similarly, is not just a 'medium' but is actively productive of meaning. It is constitutive of social activity, and forms an indispensable part of the social process. It is not a reflection of reality but a reality in its own right; and it is less a closed system than a process of production.

Williams tackles the topic of language directly in *Keywords*, a strikingly original study in historical semantics. The book explores the tangled, conflictive, sometimes discontinuous history of a range of terms (class, democracy, elite, realism, tradition, literature, intellectual and the like) which make up a vocabulary of culture and society. It shows the way in which meanings are produced by innovation, interaction, transfer, transformation, overlap and extension, and how the history of language acts as the material body of the history of thought. Somewhere behind the book, as somewhere behind the linguistic work of I.A. Richards, lies Coleridge's belief in his *Biographia Literaria* in words as living growths or organs of the human soul, along with his recording of what he calls language's periods of natural growth and accidental modifications. Given a difference of idiom, this is not far from the project of *Keywords*.

The work might also be described as Williams's equivalent to *The Structure of Complex Words* – though Empson, misreading the book as claiming that language exerts a deterministic power over thought and action, gave it a rather negative review. (What Williams actually claims is that an understanding of terms like 'class' contributes very little to the resolution of actual class struggles. This contrasts with the liberal-rationalist case, exemplified by I.A. Richards and perhaps shared by Empson, that conflicts may be resolved by dispelling misapprehensions.) Even so, Williams and Empson are at one in rejecting Richards's contention that meaning can be wholly dissolved into context. Contexts are vital, but terms for Williams have 'their own internal developments and structures' (K, p. xxxiv) which cannot be reduced to their verbal surroundings. For him as for

Empson, they are mini-texts which weave a whole series of complex historical strands into their compact space. *Keywords* unpacks over 130 words into their diverse historical components, reversing, so to speak, the tapestry of the language in order to reveal the sprawl of untidy stitching which went into its making.

It is worth adding that Williams has his own keywords, in the sense of terms which crop up constantly in his work: complex, difficult, diverse, variable, specific, active, changing, connecting, extending, growth, form, relationship, negotiate, meanings and values, feeling, experience. One or two of these words – 'active', for example – are repeated so often that they end up almost entirely void of meaning. 'Complex' and 'difficult' are meant among other things to guard against the oversimplifications of vulgar Marxism; 'growth', 'changing' and 'variable' belong to the questionable belief that mutability is generally positive, while 'diverse' is partly a strike at Stalinist uniformity. In postmodern culture, diversity and plurality have become something of a mantra, and are not easily reconciled with conviction and commitment. One of the remarkable strengths of Williams's work, by contrast, is that diversity and commitment are in his view not in the least incompatible. In fact, he can be found using the word 'diversity' almost from the outset. He has no doubt that a genuinely socialist society, given that it would extend active participation to a far greater number of citizens, would inevitably be more complex and heterogeneous than the social order we have at present, where meanings and values are largely determined by a minority.

Culture on this view is a signifying system through which a society is experienced and communicated, and is intrinsic to any social, political or economic formation. This has implications for literary studies. As long as Marxism provides us with just another way of interpreting literary texts, it remains trapped within the same paradigm as the criticism it opposes. Nor is it in Williams's view a question of relating two fixed, knowable entities called art and society, since both of these are abstractions from the total social process. What is needed rather is a decisive shift to new ground, in which 'writing' (not simply the recent historical invention known as literature) will be studied as a material, historical practice. Such an approach will acknowledge that 'we cannot separate art and literature from other kinds of social practice, in such a way as to make them subject to quite special and distinct laws' (PMC, p. 44).

In a period in which culture and communication have burgeoned into massive corporations, Williams's rejection of a distinction between the primary (material production) and the secondary (art, culture) makes obvious sense. If cultural materialism is not an approach confined to advanced capitalism, it is certainly borne out by it. It also has implications for political action, as when Williams writes that 'the task of a successful socialist movement will be one of feeling and imagination quite as much as one of fact and organisation' (RH, p. 76). Yet the fact that farms and concert halls are both material does not necessarily mean that they weigh equally in shaping the course of history. We could do without concert halls at a pinch, but not without food. Human beings need shelter, but they do not need strip joints. Williams overlooks this aspect of Marxist theory for a while, before finally coming to acknowledge it in *Politics and Letters*. He also recognises more fully than he did before that for

Marxism, areas like law, art, politics, religion and so on are superstructural not because they are less material than sweatshops, but because among other more admirable things they help to legitimate the kind of society in which sweatshops are possible.

Cultural materialism, then, is the study of the conditions of production of art by real human agents in changing historical circumstances. It involves 'an analysis of the specific relationships through which works are made and move' (PM, p. 173), and treats literature as one form of language and signification among many. In his brief study *Culture*, Williams is no longer looking at individual works of art but at questions of markets, patrons and sponsors, along with such formations as guilds, schools, movements, fractions and avant gardes. Literary works are to be considered less as objects than as 'notations', to be variably interpreted according to specific conventions; and these conventions have deep roots in social relationships as a whole. The reception of art, in other words, must be examined alongside its production. Without this historical context, we are left only with 'naked reader before naked text' (WS, p. 189).

With the development of a market for literary products, literature becomes a commodity like any other, and what one might call the literary mode of production merges with material production in general. This provokes a reaction from artists who find themselves confronted with an audience which has become anonymous, and whose work seems degraded to the level of shirts and saucepans. The creative imagination is now subject to the very mechanising processes to which it deems itself superior. One name for this reaction is Romanticism, which generally fails to reckon with the benefits of mass production in the form of a vastly increased readership. In pre-modern times, however, there were more varied forms of literary production: tribal bards who recited their poetry in public, monastic scribes, hawkers of ballads and chapbooks, authors of court masques in the pay of the monarch, theatres patronised by the state, manuscripts passed by hand among a courtly coterie, literary journalists whose writing was intended for clubs and coffee houses, poetry dedicated to aristocratic patrons, fiction serialised in 'high' journals. Even when literature is driven primarily by market forces, alternative practices and social relations emerge: the small press, worker writers' associations, radio and TV drama, book clubs, literary festivals, amateur theatrical companies, public poetry readings and so on. To attend to all this is not simply to inspect the sociological outworks of culture, since it helps to shape the form and technique of literary works themselves. W.B. Yeats, for example, has behind him an Irish tradition of public, political poetry, so that much of his verse is composed in ways which lend it to being declaimed, as T.S. Eliot's do not.

Cultural materialism is among other things a riposte to structuralism and post-structuralism, which were popular at the time but which in Williams's view are damagingly formalist and unhistorical. In fact, his reaction to the growing influence of these theories probably helped to move him further to the left, and this at a time when a number of erstwhile Marxists were scrambling in the opposite direction. He has a rather British distrust of theory, which strikes him as too remote from lived experience. As a radical historicist, he is also hostile to what he sees as closed, static, absolute systems.

Instead, he prefers the changing, diverse and open-ended. This inclination needs to be questioned. Change is not valuable in itself. Nor is a diversity of fascist parties to be applauded. There is no virtue in being variable in one's degree of generosity. A guarantee that you will not be buried alive should not be open-ended. The static and immutable may be deeply desirable: one hopes that women having the vote won't ever mutate into women being deprived of the vote. System is not to be rejected in itself: to think through the interconnections between things in a rigorous spirit may be emancipating rather than imprisoning. It is partly in reaction to Stalinism that Williams, along with his New Left colleagues E.P. Thompson and Stuart Hall, is so wary of systematic thought. Neither is there anything wrong with absolutes. In traditional moral thought, 'absolute' simply means that there is no set of circumstances one could think up which would justify a certain action: roasting infants over fires, for example.

It is not clear how cultural materialism differs from a traditional sociology of culture, which also investigates such matters as reading publics and artistic formations; and there would seem to be no ready answer to this, beyond the fact that Williams's brand of cultural sociology is more Marxist than most. Yet if culture is to be studied not so much in itself but in terms of its conditions of production and reception, isn't one in danger of overlooking the role it can play as social critique? And what becomes of the pleasure of the text – of its utopian aspect, along with its capacity to yield its readers insight and enjoyment? Are these to be set aside for an account of the social provenance of authors or the changing nature of theatrical forms? Williams also overlooks the fact that historical or sociological inquiries into art are by no means always radical. From Edmund Burke onward, historicising has been at least as typical of the political right as of the left. Besides, you do not produce a subversive reading of *Tom Jones* simply by setting it in historical context, even in a context of conflict, or by investigating its means of production. Despite all this, there are important political implications in this turn from texts to institutions. As we have seen already, it allows Williams to advance concrete proposals for the transformation of the culture industry in a way that Richards or *Scrutiny* never did.

One might claim that Williams starts out by overrating the importance of literary criticism, a mistake he inherits from Leavis, and ends up by underestimating it. As we have seen, *Drama from Ibsen to Eliot* approaches its subject primarily as a set of isolated texts rather than as a matter of the theatre as institution, whereas Williams's later work, despite his insistence that 'the varieties of close readings . . . seem to me certain to be indispensable' (WS, p. 215), bends the stick in the opposite direction. One wonders how far this is partly because close textual analysis, particularly of poetry, was never among his strengths. Like Leavis's *The Great Tradition*, *The English Novel from Dickens to Lawrence* quotes lengthy passages from novels without scrutinising them in any detail, while *The Country and the City* treats literature purely as social documentation. At one point the book quotes some verse by the minor nineteenth-century writer James Thomson without mentioning the most obvious fact about it, namely how atrocious it is. In fact, Williams grew steadily more hostile to literary evaluation, which he associated with the conventional criticism he wanted to abandon. Like Leavis, he was suspicious of the idea of the aesthetic, rejecting it as an abstract category but conceding that there are specific, variable experiences which have been grouped under this heading. These experiences, he believed, represent a range of values which the dominant social order has sought to suppress. They also protest against the reduction of human life to sheer utility. So if there are times when Williams dismisses the concept of the aesthetic as too abstract and universalist, there are other occasions when he rather grudgingly recognises its force. Like many modern critics, both Williams and Leavis tend to narrow the concept of the aesthetic to the idea of a special, insulated form of experience, as well as to the question of beauty, which then makes it easier to write off. But classical aesthetics is much broader than this.

A distrust of abstract ideas is part of Williams's Leavisite legacy. But 'class', 'culture' and 'equality' are abstract ideas, and are not to be sent packing on this account. It is the concrete and historically specific which continually engage his attention; yet he discusses them in a style so cocooned in abstraction that it is often hard to decipher. Take this paragraph about *Wuthering Heights* from *The English Novel from Dickens to Lawrence*:

> Between the given and the willed, between the necessary and that plausible world which can appear to be separable, the action drives to its conclusion. A necessary experience of what it is to be human – of that life-desire, that relationship which is

given – is frustrated, displaced, lost in these specific difficulties; but is then in a profoundly convincing way – just because it is necessary – echoed, reflected back, from where it now exists only in spirit; the image of the necessary, seen moving beyond that composed, that rearranged life; the reality of need, of the human need, haunting, appearing to, a limited scaled-down world. (EN, p. 68)

The passage is slightly more intelligible in context, but only just. There are far more lucid stretches of prose in Williams, but there are some even more opaque ones as well. Generally speaking, his writing is stilted, ponderous and convoluted. His mind was strong, deep and steady, but it had nothing of the nimble, mercurial quality of an Empson. It is typical of his style, as the above quotation suggests, that it manages to invest the abstract with the emotional, or abstract from the emotional without dispelling it altogether. What is in one sense a private, idiosyncratic language is cast into a resonantly public, authoritative form of speech, sometimes in too self-consciously sage-like a way. His voice is so weightily authoritative that he hardly ever bothers to cite a source or quote a fellow critic. There is, so the sociologist Michael Walzer tells us, 'a saying in the Talmud that when a scholar acknowledges *all* his sources, he brings the day of redemption a little closer', in which case Williams has managed to postpone the Messiah's arrival indefinitely.[9] Not that he always had that many sources to quote. There were many significant thinkers whom he never read; and while this reflects something of his originality and independence of mind, the way he draws so deeply on his own resources, it also betrays a certain pride and aloofness, a refusal to be beholden to his fellow intellectuals, which is not easy to square with his politics. It is the style of a man who is continually speaking up on behalf of others – of his own people, of working people in general, even of humanity as such – yet who is also curiously detached and self-isolating. Some of those who were close to him detected these qualities in his personal life, curiously combined with a warmth and geniality not always conspicuously on show in Cambridge Senior Combination Rooms.

One of the most striking features of Williams's work is the depth of its humanity. In a period which witnessed some of the most fundamental changes ever to take place in the forms and technologies of cultural production, he was the primary spokesperson in that realm for working people, and the advocate of a social order which would grant them full respect. 'By my educational history', he writes, 'I belong with the literate and the literary. But by inheritance and still by affiliation I belong with an illiterate and relatively illiterate majority' (WS, p. 212). Yet if Williams was much concerned with culture, it was not at the expense of Nature. Like his favourite poet William Wordsworth, he grew up among farms and mountains. It was from him that I first learnt the meaning of the word 'ecology', which he himself had picked up from his son's biology homework. He was an ecologist long before the word was in general currency. The ominous final words of *Culture and Society* pre-date an awareness of ecological catastrophe, and have weapons of mass destruction in mind instead; but it is not hard to read them as prophetic of the global calamity that now confronts us: 'There are ideas, and ways of thinking, with the seeds of life in them, and there are others, perhaps deep in our minds, with the seeds of a general death. Our measure of success in recognising these kinds, and in naming them making possible their general recognition, may be literally the measure of our future' (CS, p. 442).

NOTES

INTRODUCTION

1. I.A. Richards, 'Our lost leaders', in *I.A. Richards: Collected Shorter Writings 1919–1938*, ed. John Constable (London: Routledge, 2001), p. 337.
2. Raymond Williams, 'Realism and non-naturalism', in Jim McGuigan (ed.), *Raymond Williams on Culture and Society* (London: Sage, 2014), p. 200.
3. I have been unable to explore these critics' creative writing in this book, which would have made it at least twice as long. In any case, Eliot has been analysed to death, Richards's poetry is best passed over in charitable silence and Williams's fiction does not seem to me the most valuable part of his work. Empson's superb poetry would certainly repay further study, though not, alas, here, and a competition could be held in which candidates would submit a version of the kind of novel that Leavis might have written.

1 T.S. ELIOT

1. The works by Eliot quoted in this chapter, along with the abbreviations used for them after quotations, are as follows: *The Sacred Wood* (London: Faber & Faber, 1920, reprinted London: Faber & Faber,

1997), SW; *For Lancelot Andrewes* (London: Faber & Gwyer, 1928, reprinted London: Faber & Faber, 1970), FLA; *Selected Essays* (London: Faber & Faber, 1932, reprinted London: Faber & Faber, 1963), SE; *The Use of Poetry and the Use of Criticism* (London: Faber & Faber, 1933, reprinted London: Faber & Faber, 1964), UPUC; *After Strange Gods* (London: Faber & Faber, 1934), ASG; *Essays Ancient and Modern* (London: Faber & Faber, 1936), EAM; *The Idea of a Christian Society* (London: Faber & Faber, 1939), ICS; *Notes Towards a Definition of Culture* (London: Faber & Faber, 1948), NDC; *On Poetry and Poets* (London: Faber & Faber, 1957, reprinted New York: Farrar, Straus & Giroux, 2009), OPP; *To Criticize the Critic* (London: Faber & Faber, 1965, reprinted London: Faber & Faber 1978), TCC.

2. For an excellent account of the journal, see Jason Harding, *The 'Criterion': Cultural Politics and Periodical Networks in Interwar Britain* (Oxford: Oxford University Press, 2002).

3. Quoted by Stefan Collini, *Absent Minds* (Oxford: Oxford University Press, 2006), p. 314.

4. For this cultural heritage, see Francis Mulhern, *Culture-MetaCulture* (London: Routledge, 2000).

5. Raymond Williams, *Culture and Society 1780–1950* (London: Chatto & Windus, 1958, reprinted London: Vintage Classics, 2017), p. 334.

6. Raymond Williams, *The Long Revolution* (London: Chatto & Windus, 1961), p. 52.

7. Graham Martin, 'Introduction', in Graham Martin (ed.), *Eliot in Perspective* (London: Macmillan, 1970), p. 22.

8. Lachlan Mackinnon, 'Aesthetic certainty', *Times Literary Supplement* (31 January 2020), p. 30.

9. Stefan Collini, *The Nostalgic Imagination* (Oxford: Oxford University Press, 2019), p. 186.

10. Quoted in Collini, *The Nostalgic Imagination*, p. 187.

11. I.A. Richards, 'Nineteen hundred and now', in *Collected Shorter Writings 1919–1938*, ed. John Constable (London: Routledge, 2001), p. 178.

12. Barry Cullen, 'The impersonal objective', in Ian MacKillop and Richard Storer (eds), *F.R. Leavis: Essays and Documents* (London: Continuum, 2005), p. 161.

2 I.A. RICHARDS

1. In this chapter I have made use of *I.A. Richards: Selected Works 1919–1938*, superbly edited by John Constable, which comprises the following volumes, all published by Routledge in 2001: vol. 1, co-authored with C.K. Ogden and James Wood, *The Foundations of Aesthetics* (1922), FA; vol. 2, co-authored with C.K. Ogden, *The Meaning of Meaning* (1923); vol. 3, *Principles of Literary Criticism* (1924), PLC; vol. 4, *Practical Criticism*, PC; vol. 5, *Mencius on the Mind* (1932), MM; vol. 6, *Coleridge on Imagination* (1934), CI; vol. 7, *The Philosophy of Rhetoric* (1936), PR; vol. 8, *Interpretation in Teaching* (1938), IT; vol. 9, *Collected Shorter Writings 1919–1938*, CSW; vol. 10, *I.A. Richards and his Critics*, RC. I have also used I.A. Richards, *Speculative Instruments* (London: Routledge & Kegan Paul, 1955), SI. The abbreviations given after some of these titles are those used in the text after quotations. The most exhaustive study of Richards is John Paul Russo (ed.), *I.A. Richards: His Life and Work* (Baltimore: Johns Hopkins University Press, 1989). Among the more illuminating of the many critical studies available is W.H.N. Hotopf, *Language, Thought and Comprehension: A Case Study of the Writings of I.A. Richards* (London: Routledge & Kegan Paul, 1965).

2. Quoted by Stefan Collini, *Absent Minds: Intellectuals in Britain* (Oxford: Oxford University Press, 2006), p. 303.

3. Emile Durkheim, *The Division of Labour in Society* (London: Palgrave Macmillan, 2013), p. 43.

4. See Basil Willey, 'I.A. Richards and Coleridge', in Reuben Brower, Helen Vendler and John Hollander (eds), *I.A. Richards: Essays in his Honor* (New York: Oxford University Press, 1973), p. 232.

5. See Justus Buchler (ed.), *Philosophical Writings of Peirce* (New York: Dover Publications, 1955), p. 99.

6. Ken Hirschkop, *Linguistic Turns 1890–1950* (Oxford: Oxford University Press, 2019), p. 167.

7. Joseph North, *Literary Criticism: A Concise Political History* (Cambridge, MA: Harvard University Press, 2017), p. 51.

8. Geoffrey Hartman, 'The dream of communication', in Brower et al., *I.A. Richards*, p. 167.

9. Michael Moriarty, 'The longest cultural journey', in Christopher Prendergast (ed.), *Cultural Materialism: On Raymond Williams* (Minneapolis: University of Minnesota Press, 1995), p. 100.

10. I am reporting here on Richards's own views of Mencius and the Chinese language in general, without the competence to assess the validity of his judgements.

11. I.A. Richards, 'Semantic frontiersman', in Roma Gill (ed.), *William Empson: The Man and His Work* (London: Routledge, 1974), p. 100.

3 WILLIAM EMPSON

1. Quoted in John Paul Russo (ed.), *I.A. Richards: His Life and Work* (Baltimore: Johns Hopkins University Press, 1989), p. 526. The works by Empson quoted in this chapter, along with the abbreviations used for them after quotations, are as follows: *Seven Types of Ambiguity* (London: Chatto & Windus, 1930, reprinted London: Penguin, 1961), STA; *Some Versions of Pastoral* (London: Chatto & Windus, 1935, reprinted London: Penguin, 1966), SVP; *The Structure of Complex Words* (London: Chatto & Windus, 1951, reprinted London: Penguin, 1985), SCW; *Milton's God* (London: Chatto & Windus, 1961), MG; *Using Biography* (Cambridge, MA: Harvard University Press, 1984), UB; *Argufying: Essays on Literature and Culture*, ed. John Haffenden (London: Hogarth Press, 1988), A.

2. See Haffenden, 'Introduction' to *Argufying*, p. 60.

3. William Empson, *The Face of the Buddha*, ed. Rupert Arrowsmith (Oxford: Oxford University Press, 2016).

4. Paul Fry, 'Empson's Satan: an ambiguous character of the seventh type', in Christopher Norris and Nigel Mapp (eds), *William Empson: The Critical Achievement* (Cambridge: Cambridge University Press, 1993), p. 156.

5. Norris and Mapp, *William Empson*, 'Introduction'.

6. John Haffenden, *William Empson: vol. 1, Among the Mandarins* (Oxford: Oxford University Press, 2005), p. 215.

7. Haffenden, *William Empson: vol. 1*, p. 204.

8. Michael Wood, *On Empson* (Princeton: Princeton University Press, 2017), p. 94.

9. Haffenden, *William Empson: vol. 1*, p. 4.

10. See Helen Thaventhiran and Stefan Collini (eds), 'Introduction' to William Empson, *The Structure of Complex Words* (Oxford: Oxford University Press, 2020).

11. Quoted by Wood, *On Empson*, p. 145.
12. F.R. Leavis, *Revaluation: Tradition and Development in English Poetry* (London: Chatto & Windus, 1936), p. 80.
13. What I hope is a rather less crude account of sacrifice can be found in Terry Eagleton, *Radical Sacrifice* (New Haven and London: Yale University Press, 2018).
14. See, for example, Stefan Collini, *The Nostalgic Imagination* (Oxford: Oxford University Press, 2019), pp. 111–13.
15. See Thaventhiran and Collini, 'Introduction'.
16. Christopher Norris, *William Empson and the Philosophy of Literary Criticism* (London: Bloomsbury, 2013), p. 86.
17. The comment is by Frank Kermode, on the dust jacket of Empson's *Using Biography* (London: Chatto & Windus, 1984).

4 F.R. LEAVIS

1. Quoted by Ian MacKillop, *F.R. Leavis: A Life in Criticism* (London: Penguin, 1997), p. 207.
2. The works by Leavis quoted in this chapter, along with the abbreviations used for them after quotations, are as follows: *New Bearings in English Poetry* (London: Chatto & Windus, 1932, reprinted London: Chatto & Windus, 1961), NB; *For Continuity* (Cambridge: Minority Press, 1933), FC; *Revaluation: Tradition and Development in English Poetry* (London: Chatto & Windus, 1936, reprinted London: Chatto & Windus, 1969), R; *Education and the University* (London: Chatto & Windus, 1943), EU; *The Great Tradition* (London: Chatto & Windus, 1948, reprinted Harmondsworth: Penguin, 1962), GT; (ed.), *Mill on Bentham and Coleridge* (London: Chatto & Windus, 1950, reprinted Cambridge: Cambridge University Press, 1980), MBC; *The Common Pursuit* (London: Chatto & Windus, 1952, reprinted London: Faber & Faber, 2008), CP; *D.H. Lawrence: Novelist* (London Chatto & Windus, 1955, reprinted Harmondsworth: Penguin, 1978), DHL; *'Anna Karenina' and Other Essays* (London: Chatto & Windus, 1967), AK; with Q.D. Leavis, *Lectures in America* (London: Chatto & Windus, 1969, reprinted in *Nor Shall My Sword*), LA; with Q.D. Leavis, *Dickens the Novelist* (London: Chatto & Windus, 1970), DN; *Nor Shall My Sword* (London: Chatto & Windus, 1972), NSS; *The Living Principle* (London: Chatto &

Windus, 1975), LP; *Two Cultures? The Significance of C.P. Snow* (Cambridge: Cambridge University Press, 2013), TC.

3. For an excellent account of this and other theoretical topics in Leavis's work, see Barry Cullen, 'The impersonal objective', in Ian MacKillop and Richard Storer (eds), *F.R. Leavis: Essays and Documents* (London: Continuum, 2005).

4. Quoted in Raymond Williams, *Culture and Society 1780–1950* (London: Vintage Classics, 2017), p. 265.

5. Quoted in MacKillop, *F.R. Leavis*, p. 169.

6. See Michael Bell, *F.R. Leavis* (London: Routledge, 1988), p. 72.

7. The words are from Leavis's collaborator Denys Thompson, quoted by Francis Mulhern, *The Moment of 'Scrutiny'* (London: New Left Books, 1979), p. 128.

8. Quoted by Mulhern, pp. 24–5.

9. The works in question include *Mass Civilisation and Minority Culture* (Cambridge: Minority Press, 1930), with Denys Thompson, *Culture and Environment* (London: Chatto & Windus, 1933), *For Continuity* (1933), *Education and the University* (1943) and *English Literature in Our Time and the University* (London: Chatto & Windus, 1969). Q.D. Leavis's *Fiction and the Reading Public* (London: Chatto & Windus, 1932) is another key work in this area.

10. Q.D. Leavis, *Fiction and the Reading Public*, p. 270.

11. Jean-Luc Nancy, *The Inoperative Community* (Minneapolis: University of Minnesota Press, 1991), p. 10.

12. C.B. Macpherson, *The Political Theory of Possessive Individualism* (Oxford: Oxford University Press, 2011), p. 61.

13. Robert J.C. Young, *Postcolonialism: An Historical Introduction* (Oxford: Wiley-Blackwell, 2001), p. 109.

14. Denys Thompson, quoted in Mulhern, *The Moment of 'Scrutiny'*, p. 102.

15. 'Scrutiny: a retrospect', *Scrutiny*, vol. 20 (Cambridge: Cambridge University Press, 1963), p. 4.

16. It might be thought an example of vulgar Freudianism to see in some of Leavis's key critical terms – vital, sane, robust, vigorous, muscular and so on – an unconscious compensation for his disability. There might also be some truth in it.

17. Raymond Williams, *Politics and Letters* (London: New Left Books, 1979), p. 66.

5 RAYMOND WILLIAMS

1. Reported to me by Williams himself.
2. The term used nowadays is 'continuing education', since regular students are adults as well.
3. See Dai Smith, *Raymond Williams: A Warrior's Tale* (Cardigan: Parthian, 2008), a biography of Williams's career up to 1961.
4. The works by Williams quoted in this chapter, along with the abbreviations used for them after quotations, are as follows: *Drama from Ibsen to Eliot* (London: Chatto & Windus, 1952, reprinted London: Chatto & Windus, 1961), DIE; *Culture and Society 1780–1950* (London: Chatto & Windus, 1958, reprinted London: Vintage Classics, 2017), CS; *The Long Revolution* (London: Chatto & Windus, 1961), LR; *Modern Tragedy* (London: Chatto & Windus, 1966), MT; *Drama from Ibsen to Brecht* (London: Chatto & Windus, 1968, reprinted London: Hogarth Press, 1996), DIB; *The English Novel from Dickens to Lawrence* (London: Chatto & Windus, 1970), EN; *The Country and the City* (London: Chatto & Windus, 1973), CC; *Keywords* (Oxford: Oxford University Press, 1976, reprinted Oxford: Oxford University Press, 2015), K; *Marxism and Literature* (Oxford: Oxford University Press, 1977), ML; *Politics and Letters* (London: New Left Books, 1979), PL; *Problems in Materialism and Culture* (London: New Left Books, 1980), PMC; *Writing in Society* (London: Verso, 1983), WS; *Resources of Hope*, ed. Robin Gable (London: Verso, 1989), RH; *The Politics of Modernism* (London: Verso, 1989), PM; *Raymond Williams on Culture and Society*, ed. Jim McGuigan (London: Sage, 2014), RWCS.
5. Michael Moriarty, 'The longest cultural journey', in Christopher Prendergast (ed.), *Cultural Materialism: On Raymond Williams* (Minneapolis: University of Minnesota Press, 1995), p. 92.
6. In most Marxist thought, hegemony refers to all the ways in which a ruling class secures the consent of the rest of society to be governed, which might include such strategies as uses of the tax system or the granting of civil rights. Ideology is one part of hegemony, concerned with how consent is secured through the diffusion of values, sentiments and beliefs. On this view, there would be no point in replacing ideology with hegemony, as Williams does, because it already includes it.
7. Williams chiefly has in mind here the work of the Marxist philosopher Louis Althusser, for whom ideology is pervasive throughout social existence and always will be. Williams mistakenly takes this to

mean that all individuals are imprisoned by false or distorted social ideas, and that there is no possibility of this ever changing. But by ideology Althusser means, in effect, lived experience. This may not be much use as a definition, but it does not suggest that false consciousness is universal, and is here to stay.

8. See Terry Eagleton and Brian Wicker (eds), *From Culture to Revolution* (London: Sheed & Ward, 1968), p. 298.

9. See Michael Walzer, *Spheres of Justice* (New York: Basic Books, 1983), p. xvii. On the question of 'voice' in Williams's writing, see David Simpson, 'Raymond Williams: feeling for structures, voicing "history"', in Prendergast (ed.), *Cultural Materialism.*

INDEX

317

INDEX

INDEX

INDEX

modern literary criticism, 86–7; on grammar, 89; influence of Coleridge, 87, 109, 115, 120, 127; influence of Utilitarianism, 91; influence on education, 83–5; influence on Empson, 142; and intentionality, 113; internationalism, 82–4, 131–2; on language, 87–90, 116–19; liberalism, 85–6, 90, 99, 102–4; materialism, 91–2, 121–2; and meaning, 111–16, 127–9; member of the Heretics Club, 85; on metaphor, 119–21; moral ideals, 96; mountaineering, 81; on myth, 123–4; and nominalism, 111–12; physiology of poetry, 71; poetic language, 107; poetry as salvation, 123; practical criticism, 3, 86, 134–6; pragmatism, 92, 111; and pseudo-statements, 105–11; and psychology, 93–5; and role of the reader, 125–7; on science as myth, 107–8, 122; and semantic instability, 115–16; as speaker of verse, 117; supporter of League of Nations, 131; T.S. Eliot on, 80; on tone in poetry, 129–30; visits to China, 82–3, 125, 130–1; visits to Japan, 82, 83; writing style, 10

Writings: *The Foundations of Aesthetics*, 96; *How to Read a Page*, 115; *Interpretation in Teaching*, 113; *The Meaning of Meaning*, 88–9; *Mencius on the Mind*, 130–4; 'Our Lost Leaders', 94; *The Philosophy of Rhetoric*, 113; *Practical Criticism* (1929), 82, 92, 125, 134–7; *The Principles of Literary Criticism* (1924), 82, 95; *Speculative Instruments*, 89

Richardson, Samuel, 220
Riding, Laura, 170
Rockefeller Foundation, 85
Romanticism, 44–5, 198, 268–9, 302
Rosenberg, Isaac, 212, 256

Rossetti, Christina, 203, 210–11
Rossetti, Dante Gabriel, 211
Rousseau, Jean-Jacques, 295
Ruskin, John, 269–70, 272
Russell, Bertrand, 155, 191

Saintsbury, George, 24
Sappho, 60
Saussure, Ferdinand de, 112
Scott, Walter, 220
Scrutiny (journal), 235–9, 243–53, 257
semiotics, 112, 125
Shakespeare, William: Empson on, 153, 159–60, 168–9, 187; F.R. Leavis on, 207–8, 210, 256; T.S. Eliot on, 41, 42, 50; *Antony and Cleopatra*, 172
Shaw, George Bernard, 261
Shelley, Percy Bysshe, 75, 170, 199, 210
Sidney, Philip, 246–7
Smith, Adam, 295
Snow, C.P., 240–2
Spender, Stephen, 143
Spenser, Edmund, 159, 198
Spinoza, Baruch, 44
St Louis, Missouri, 13
Stephen, Leslie, 238
Sterne, Laurence, 220–1
Stevens, Wallace, 75–6
Strindberg, August, 262, 263
structuralism, 302
Surrealism, 104
Swift, Jonathan, 186, 198, 208, 218
Swinburne, Algernon Charles, 205
Symbolist Movement, 74
Synge, J.M., 261

Tennyson, Alfred, Lord, 68, 102, 205, 210
Thackeray, William Makepeace, 220, 256, 284
Thomas, Dylan, 55, 143
Thomas, Edward, 212, 256
Thompson, Denys, 236

322

INDEX